British Official Films in the Second World War

British Official Films in the Second World War

a descriptive catalogue

FRANCES THORPE &
NICHOLAS PRONAY
with
CLIVE COULTASS

Sponsored by the Imperial War Museum, the InterUniversity History Film Consortium and the University of Leeds

CLIO PRESS
Oxford, England · Santa Barbara, California

British Library Cataloguing in Publication Data

Thorpe, Frances
British official films in the Second World War
1. World War, 1939-1945 – Propaganda
2. Moving-pictures in propaganda
3. Moving-pictures – Great Britain – Catalogs
I. Title
016.94054'886'41 D810.P7G7

ISBN 0 903450-27-5

Clio Press, Ltd.
Woodside House, Hinksey Hill
Oxford OX1 5BE, England.

Typeset by Gem Graphic Services.
Printed in Great Britain
by Cotswold Press Ltd., Oxford.

Contents

Preface

During the period of the Second World War 1,887 films were officially 'presented' to people in Britain and overseas by propaganda agencies of the British government. In addition, there were some 3,200 newsreels and some 380 feature films which had to be approved, sometimes in detail, by the Ministry of Information before they could be made or shown in Britain. In terms of range, sophistication, and, as far as comparative figures can be ascertained, numbers, this was one of the most extensive uses of the medium of film for propaganda purposes.

The intention of the present volume is to provide, as far as possible, a comprehensive record of the 1,887 films through which the British government directly sought to influence British people of all ages – not only in cinemas, but also in factory canteens, church halls, and schoolrooms – and through which the image of Britain was projected abroad. This volume contains a descriptive catalogue of every film for which there is evidence that it was officially produced or distributed by an accredited agency of the British government, with the addition of as much information as possible concerning the authorship and the sponsoring and distributing agencies of the films.

The preparation of the catalogue, including the establishing and checking of the data relating to the films, was the work of Frances Thorpe and the staff of the Slade Film History Register, with the cooperation of Clive Coultass and the staff of the Department of Film, Imperial War Museum,

The arrangement, classification system and introduction were the work of Nicholas Pronay.

Acknowledgements

The publication of the catalogue was jointly sponsored by the Imperial War Museum, the InterUniversity History Film Consortium and the University of Leeds. A grant from the British Academy assisted in the collation of source materials. The work of preparing the catalogue was carried out by the Slade Film History Register with assistance from the Department of Film of the Imperial War Museum. Personal acknowledgements for editorial assistance are due to: Sue Keen, Lira Fernandes and Jeannette Harkin, formerly of the Slade Film History Register, and to Anne Fleming, Christopher Dowling and Roger Smither of the Imperial War Museum. The following persons have kindly assisted in finding and identifying films: Mrs. J. Robinson of the Central Office of Information; Elaine Burroughs and Roger Holman of the National Film Archive; Brenda Davies of the British Film Institute; Michael Barrett, formerly of the British Council; Joel Doerfler of Brandeis University; James Ballantine of the British Universities Film Council; Eileen Bowser of the Museum of Modern Art, New York; William T. Murphy of the US National Archives and Records Service; Patrick J. Sheehan of the Library of Congress; and Jana Vosikovska of the Public Archives of Canada.

In the preparation of the introduction, I am much in debt to my research students; Timothy Hollins in respect of Conservative film propaganda, Trevor Ryan concerning the relationship between Labour and film, Paul Swann in respect of the documentary movement, and Dr. P.M. Taylor in respect of the Foreign Office and the British Council.

A particular indebtedness to Professor J.A.S. Grenville must be recorded: he has encouraged and supported this project from its inception to its publication.

It is remarkable how many films have survived from the Second World War into an age when historical interest has finally become focused on the struggle for hearts and minds. As historians we owe a considerable debt to the dedicated and often unacknowledged work of the small group of film archivists who resisted pressure from many quarters to 'junk' wartime propaganda films during years when there was little historical interest in their preservation. It is a pleasure to acknowledge it here.

Introduction

The Ministry of Information and propaganda policy

The decade of the 1930s was a period of foreboding in Britain. The tremendous loss of life and the horrors of trench warfare suffered during the Great War were still fresh in the memory. Yet the means for international settlement of disputes, created in the decade following the war, were already disintegrating by the time the Disarmament Conference broke up in failure in 1934. As the possibility of another world war grew into a probability, so did the realisation that the next war could involve even greater loss of life and even greater danger to the whole fabric of Britain. Developments in aerial warfare appeared to favour the attacker and caused fear that the horrors suffered by the soldiers in the Great War would be extended to wives and children, bringing the front line from 'off the premises so to speak to just outside of the front door' as Sir John Anderson warned the public through the newsreels in the spring of 1939.

Once the Disarmament Conference had failed and Hitler established control of Germany, the need to prepare for the possibility of a war came to be accepted by a deeply reluctant British Cabinet. The Cabinet began the preparation of contingency plans for the next war in 1934, but with a particularly heavy heart. It was realised, if anything too firmly, that the options open to the planners amounted to little more than anticipating, and as far as possible mitigating, catastrophes at home and of preparing retaliatory catastrophes for the peoples of the enemy.[1] Instead of planning bloody perhaps but exhilarating military and naval campaigns, as in the past, the Chiefs of Staff and the Committee of Imperial Defence had to spend much of their time considering plans for the mass evacuation of British cities, the protection of women and children from mustard gas, the provision of vast numbers of psychiatric beds for civilians driven out of their minds, and for the burial of hundreds of thousands of non-combatant casualties of incendiary and high-explosive bombs. The overall strategy was based on the assumption that fighting on land would soon become a stalemate in front of the Maginot line and that thereafter the war would develop into a relentless exchange of aerial bombing, with total defeat going to the side whose civilians' morale broke first.

It was in this atmosphere and with these possibilities in mind that the Ministry of Information was being planned.[2] The importance attached to maintaining civilian morale under aerial bombardment, the fear of parachuted enemy agents, of enemy radio broadcasts interfering with the normal channels of communication, and of disaffection amongst the working classes led to the planning of a very large Ministry of Information, with an initial establishment of over a thousand officials. At the same time the planners' awareness of how little was actually known about 'morale' or the means of affecting it, and the difficulty of finding civil servants conversant with the technology and organisation of the new world of mass communications led to a slow and intermittent development of the plans and contributed to their still incomplete state in September 1939. There was also a measure of complacency as a result of Britain's essay into propaganda warfare during the First World War.

Between 1915 and 1918 Britain had pioneered modern propaganda warfare, as she had pioneered armoured warfare and developed advanced ideas concerning strategic bombing. This was to prove a mixed blessing for the planners of what became the second Ministry of Information. On the one hand, the experience they had gained in the conducting of war propaganda eventually enabled British propagandists in the Second World War to evolve new and, in the long run, effective policies; these put Britian once again a jump ahead of the Germans, who repeated many of the mistakes of Britain's first Ministry of Information. On the other hand, their experience encouraged the mistaken belief that, in the case of those departments which already existed in 1918, including films, little was needed beyond a more centralised structure, some streamlining and the extension of earlier procedures. In the short run, this view led to a near-disastrous beginning to the propaganda war in 1939. The chief causes of this mistaken approach were first the overready acceptance of the view that the work of the First World War Ministry of Information had been an unqualified success, and second the failure to maintain a peacetime propaganda organisation after the end of the Great War, except the News Department of the Foreign Office.

Of the wartime ministries, Information was the first to be wound up, by 16 December 1918, despite the powerful arguments presented by Lord Beaverbrook for the necessity of continuing propaganda operations at least for the duration of the Peace Conference, and by Lord Northcliffe about the need to launch a campaign for the political reeducation of the German people.[3] Thus the Ministry had the good fortune to be dissolved during the first flush of the euphoria which followed the Armistice. Within Parliament, in the short and formal debate upon the termination of the Ministry, both Houses paid generous compliments to its work and leaders. Outside Parliament, the press was virtually unanimous in praising the leaders of the Ministry and in magnifying rather than criticising its achievements. The fact that Beaverbrook, Northcliffe and Rothermere were the leaders of the propaganda efforts, loosely controlled by the Ministry, and that their senior assistants in the Ministry included many editors and leading writers, no doubt helped in producing such an unusual consensus of praise in the British press. On 31 October 1919 *The Times* – owned by Northcliffe, then in his most imperious period of ownership – summed up the views generally accepted at the time: 'Good propaganda probably saved a year of war, and this meant the saving of thousands of millions of money and probably of at least a million lives'. It was only after the Second World War that doubts about this view were widely expressed.

The Ministry of Information also escaped the reappraisals which the gradual publication of the volumes of the *Official history* during the interwar years engendered in the case of many other aspects of the conduct of the war. It was a nice paradox that, of all the wartime ministries, it was only the Ministry of Information which did not endeavour to produce an official history of its own achievements. The Carnegie Trust's series of departmental histories, which often, though not always, took a more critical line than *Official history*, also omitted to cover the Ministry of Information. Instead, a racily written account by Sir Campbell Stuart, Lord Northcliffe's second-in-command in the Department of Enemy Propaganda, entitled *Secrets of Crewe House: the story of a famous campaign* – something of a bestseller – provided further additions to the paeans of uncritical praise.

From countries where British propaganda had been active came further apparent evidence of its great effect and efficient organisation. Soon after the end of the war a storm of protest broke out in the United States over what was claimed to have been a plot brilliantly executed from Wellington House, the headquarters of British propaganda aimed at the United States. It was claimed that the British succeeded, by infiltrating the American press, in conducting a very effective but secret propaganda campaign which tricked America into war. This accusation provided sensational material for the newspaper world for some years, was taken up by popular histories of the war, and then resulted in a steady output of scholarly American appraisals, all of which credited British propaganda with great successes. This literature appeared regularly up to and even into the Second World War, and while such 'revelations' were sometimes embarrassing to the government, they nevertheless reinforced the belief that the First World War Ministry of Information and British propaganda in general had been effective and could therefore be readily relied on as a pattern for future wars.[4]

The portrayal of British propaganda by its other major recipients, Germany and her allies, had a similar effect. All over the territories formerly comprising the Central Powers, British propaganda was depicted as one of the chief causes of the collapse of morale in 1918, and so was credited with directly contributing to the defeat of Germany and Austria. General Ludendorff, Chief of the German General Staff, published his memoirs very soon after the end of the war, and claimed that the collapse of 1918 was primarily due to Allied propaganda. He was followed by other members of the German High Command, and his book set the tone for this apparently authentic view from the side of those at the receiving end of the work of the Enemy Propaganda Department at Crewe House.[5] Ludendorff was also the father of the dangerous belief that the Germans were a people particularly susceptible to propaganda. Adolf Hitler, who began his postwar career serving in one of the Wehrmacht's hastily established counter-propaganda units, fully accepted and reinforced Ludendorff's views. In *Mein Kampf*, which is not a book characterised by its author's readiness to pay generous tributes in acknowledgement of intellectual debts, Hitler went out of his way to pay fulsome compliments to the genius of the British in propaganda and he explicitly exhorted his readers to learn from them. He was particularly impressed with the British use of atrocity and hate stories.[6] In the face of these fulsome statements from Germany concerning what Hitler called 'the brilliant work' of Crewe House, it was only partially realised in Britain that both Ludendorff and Hitler were anxious to argue a special case. Extolling the effectiveness of British propaganda fitted only too well with their 'stab in the back' theory of the cause of German defeat. In Ludendorff's case, there was the additional attraction that it helped provide him with an excuse for his own failures as Chief of Staff. For Hitler, it provided justification for his cynical views about the gullibility of the German masses and the means required to persuade them to follow the Nazi party and himself.

These testimonials by foes and friends to the value of British propaganda, though on the one hand suspect,[7] were nevertheless reassuring to those responsible for planning the new Ministry of Information. They concluded that they could rely largely on the operational formulae of the last war. They were overworked civil servants and were only too glad to accept what, on the face of it, were good reasons for not planning entirely afresh. There was, in any case, a good deal of continuity of personnel and in some areas, notably in the control of the news agencies and covert propaganda, there was a measure of institutional continuity as well. But there was another element in all this which the planners, even in these circumstances, should have more fully realised, for it was a corollary of the praise and attention attracted by the work of the British Ministry of Information. The element of surprise, especially important in propaganda, had been lost: the British government was now expected to produce sophisticated propaganda devices and everyone at home and abroad would be on the lookout for them.

Another factor which affected the planning of the Ministry of Information originated from the domestic aftermath of British propaganda in the First World War. The discovery that many of the stories circulated during the war concerning German atrocities had been fabrications shocked Englishmen of widely different backgrounds, including many who were to play a part in the planning of the next Ministry of Information. Although it was clear that some of the more virulent and memorable stories had originated from private enterprise propagandists and not from the official machine, and that they had gained currency before the development of effective central control of propaganda, nevertheless, the general responsibility of the government for a not-too-scrupulous approach to propaganda could not be altogether explained away. Wellington House (the original centre for overseas propaganda), Crewe House (the headquarters of Enemy Propaganda), the Press (Censorship) Bureau and the Cinema Propaganda Department were all undoubtedly official establishments led by men who belonged to the inner circle of the government, such as C.F.G. Masterman, Lord Beaverbrook, or F.E. Smith (Lord Birkenhead). Many people came to feel that, by commission or omission, these organisations had played a large role in the dissemination of either fabricated or grossly exaggerated atrocity stories. By the 1930s there was little doubt in the minds of many that the government had employed, or knowingly permitted to be employed, untruths as weapons of war, on a large scale and both at home and abroad. An influential expression of these views appeared as early as 1925, in Sir Arthur Ponsonby's *Falsehood in wartime*.[8]

The demagoguery and hysteria which hate propaganda could cause at home and the deleterious effect that this could have on the political fabric of Britain were additional factors in the postwar thinking which lay behind the planning of the propaganda policy for the next war. Horatio Bottomley had fed on the hysteria produced by hate propaganda and the spectacle of mob orators coming to power in various parts of Europe kept that lesson alive throughout the period.

As thought-provoking and perhaps as important was the bitterness felt by reputable and influential scholars when they realised that they had lent the authority of their names to propaganda compilations based on false information supplied to them. A. J. Toynbee, for example, the author of *The German terror in France* (1917) and of several other such 'authentic' accounts,[9] was – through his association with the Royal Institute of International Affairs – an influence during the interwar period on Foreign Office thinking about propaganda and its influence on foreign policy. Another, though related, aspect of war propaganda also affected the views of the Foreign Office. It became firmly convinced that a policy of handing out unrealistic or contradictory promises through the propaganda machine, in order to attract allies and divide enemies, would be counter-productive in the long run. Such tactics may indeed be the stuff of diplomacy in a tight corner, but as long as it is kept between diplomats there is no real harm done. The propaganda machine, however, obliterated the delicate conditional clauses and bypassed expert readers. This policy, pursued with vigour in the latter stages of the war by Crewe House – especially in relation to the subject races of Austria-Hungary – proved in the postwar years to be manifestly detrimental to the winning of the peace, whatever its effect might have been on the course of the war.

Atrocity stories and contradictory promises were, however, age-old staple techniques of war propaganda – why should there have been so much concern over them? The reason was the gradual understanding, by many able-minded people who had been brought into close contact with propaganda in Britain during the war, of the effect on propaganda of the fundamental changes in communication technology. Both atrocity stories and conflicting promises had, in the past, depended on two conditions: the slowness with which information travelled, and the ability of governments to control its channels, at least to a substantial degree. These old techniques amounted to 'reporting' something untrue from one place to another place, or to promising one man in one place something different from what was promised to another man in another place, by utilising the superior network of communications available to all governments, but especially to those with a commanding navy. In both cases success depended on the slowness of lateral communication to delay the discovery of the truth until it was too late to affect the outcome.

By the 1930s the development of telecommunications called for a fundamental revision of these classical, and classically simple, techniques of propaganda. Indeed, the speed with which the damaging disclosures about First World War propaganda came out after the war indicated that it was the last war in which these methods could still be used effectively. The introduction of radio was the final overturning of the old world of propaganda techniques. Radio waves could transmit information instantly from one hemisphere to the other; claims and promises could now be instantly compared. The trumpcard of the Wellington House propagandists, the cutting of the cables linking Germany with America on 5 August 1914 by the Admiralty, could never again be played. The diffusion of efficient radio receivers among the population and the impossibility of effectively jamming foreign broadcasts fundamentally changed the conditions within which home and foreign propagandists would have to operate.

It was fortunate for Britain that John Reith (Lord Reith), a man with a remarkably original mind, was in charge of the development of British broadcasting. It was equally fortunate that Reith could conclusively demonstrate to the political leadership the power and utility of radio during the General Strike.[10] He was thus accepted as the government's principal adviser on propaganda matters, even though he alternately accepted and rejected offers to take charge of the planning of the whole of the wartime propaganda work.[11] The immediate consequence was that the BBC came to be accepted from the outset as the keystone of the information and propaganda structure planned for the next war. The administrative headquarters of the propaganda planning organisation was located within the walls of Broadcasting House. This, however, also had the undesirable effect of causing far too much of the available time, energy and thought to be devoted to working out the wartime operational plans and organisation of the BBC at the expense of planning the structure of the Ministry of Information. In the long run, the impeccable work of the broadcasters, both for home and overseas services, and the remarkably well thought out and intelligent approach to the use of accurate information for propaganda purposes – the hall-mark of British propaganda in the Second World War – more than compensated for the unbalanced approach to planning the Ministry of Information. It was at the BBC (and substantially the contribution of Reith himself) that the concept of 'propaganda with truth' – actually, propaganda with facts – with 'news as the shock-troops of propaganda' was evolved and the complexities of the concept thought out. In the event, it proved to be the answer to the problems posed by the new world-wide, interconnected, unstoppable and unjammable news communications system, in which the old games of propaganda could no longer be played. The acceptance of this approach as the basic policy for the Ministry of Information, and the unwavering stress on its paramount importance by Reith and his disciples at the BBC, led to the gradual evolution of the sophisticated network of functionally differentiated organisations which characterised British propaganda work during the later stages of the Second World War and during its immediate aftermath.

The basic idea behind this network of organisations was the realisation that in the new conditions of telecommunications it was vital to draw a careful distinction between overt and covert propaganda. Thus, as the plans gradually evolved, the original quadruple function of the Ministry, derived from the First World War – the control of propaganda at home, in neutral, allied, and enemy territories – was revised and delineated. In overt propaganda, i.e. that put out attributably by any agency of the British Government, it was 'news' which was to become, as Reith wrote, 'the shocktroops of propaganda'. Here the essential element was comprehensive and central control of all outlets, because 'propaganda with the truth' is a sophisticated exercise which calls for editorial expertise and depends on quick central direction. So the first priority given to the planners was the construction of an effective censorship machinery for the control of 'news'.

Censorship, of course, was intended to prevent the publication of any information of use to the enemy, a category which had increased manifold with the arrival of aerial warfare; but that was no longer to be its only function. Its job would also be to ensure that what was put out would be believed. It was therefore important that the public should receive approved information in as many different forms, and through as many different channels, as possible. Moreover, since the British public had long been accustomed to a pluralistic press, it was important to try to avoid as far as possible apparent deviation from the peacetime variety of journalistic styles and editorial selection policies. It was therefore decided to reject proposals for adopting a system, like one used in France during the war, which would have consisted of censoring newspapers coupled with the provision of lengthy official communiqués that all newspapers would be expected to print. Instead, the idea was adopted of censoring news at the source. Domestic British news was therefore to be censored at the terminal point of the privately owned internal cable network which feeds the British press as well as the BBC and which is located in the Press Association building in central London. Foreign news was similarly censored at source, at the terminal point of the international cable network which carried foreign news to Britain and British news overseas. The telegrams, traditionally known to the press as the 'ticker-tape', having been censored before they went out, could be safely left for each individual newspaper to select from in accordance with their particular style of journalism – which is what they had long been accustomed to doing anyway. Any information not received through 'the tape' the editor was expected to clear with the censors, but they could go ahead and do what they wanted with the bulk of their news material, as in times of peace.

By ensuring that departmental and especially the Services' press officers were obtaining and releasing a good quantity of information and that its own officials sought out and put out as much 'newsy' material as possible, the Ministry of Information would be able to feed a large volume of newsworthy material into the network. This, in turn, meant that newspaper editors would be content and the public would be supplied with its accustomed volume and variety of 'news'. The public would be further reassured by the consistency of the information content at the core of the greatly varied news stories. They would first hear 'it' on the 'Nine O'Clock News', then read 'it' in as many forms as they cared in their morning newspapers the following day, and finally they could also see 'it', with their own eyes (and hear 'it' again on the soundtrack) a few days later in their cinemas on the newsreels. The public would be unaware that the information came, in the first place, to the BBC and the newspapers through the same central point: the Press Association in whose building the censors were housed. Newsfilm, of course, was provided through the Ministry's own 'rota' to all the reels alike. This system also provided for simultaneous control over both incoming and outgoing news and thus there were no 'embarrassing' differences between what Reuters, known to be government-controlled, put out abroad and what foreign correspondents in Britain could read in British newspapers. The fact that Reuters occupied the other half of the same building as the Press Association made this system unobtrusive as well as enabling it to work with speed and efficiency. Backed by a peerless monitoring service covering broadcasts all over the world, run by the BBC, this system could give both the requisite speed of response and the possibility of harmonising the content of all forms of news presentation. In addition, the Ministry was to be provided with wide-ranging powers of censorship including suppression, in case they were needed. If the system worked, however, it would hardly ever be necessary to use them, since the Minstry would have complete control over the news media's common sources of information. There were also other reasons why not much use of the inevitably clumsey and double-edged censorship powers would ever be necessary. The BBC, at the centre of the system, always preempted and predetermined news presentation by the mere fact that its broadcasts reached the public before the newspapers did: the whole point of the 'Nine O'Clock News' was that, normally, by that time the next day's newspaper stories had already broken.

It was a system which was both novel and sophisticated.[12] It took Sir John Reith himself, as Minister of Information, to make it work; but from the period of his relatively brief tenure in the early months of 1940, the system made a remarkably successful reality of the policy of 'propaganda with the truth'.

Different principles and priorities, however, applied to propaganda aimed at fomenting disaffection among the enemy's peoples or those under the enemy's control. As a corollary of developing a sophisticated new policy for home, as well as for allied and neutral countries, based on 'news', a clearer definition of this other area became necessary. Of course broadcasting 'news' of the same kind would play a part in enemy propaganda, but as the plans developed it was realised that this was an essentially different kind of propaganda work also calling for specialist skills. These skills were related more to intelligence work than to editorial work. Here again, the rapid development of technology, the aeroplane, the parachute and portable radio transmitters in a material sense, and the development of Freudian psychology in a more imaginary sense, transformed the old game of subversion, the stirring up of the subjects of the enemy.

As a result of rethinking this ancient form of warfare in the light of new developments, Enemy Propaganda was restructured. The clandestine propaganda sections of Political Intelligence (known as Electra House) and of Military Intelligence (known as Section 'D'), under the control of the Foreign Office and the War Office respectively, came to be integrated with the embryo Enemy Propaganda Department of the Ministry of Information. Together they formed a newly conceived organisation dealing with covert, or 'black' propaganda, dignified with the new name of political warfare.

Political warfare was a component part of a new central organisation designed to use subversion to fight the war – the Special Operations Executive. It was initially known as SOE 1, while the cloak-and-dagger section was SOE 2. The SOE itself was a component of the Ministry of Economic Warfare which linked it together with economic sabotage and blockade into a single command, dubbed by Winston Churchill 'the Department of Ungentlemanly Warfare'. Its first ministerial head was Hugh Dalton. Within this essentially new organisation, responding to the new technological conditions for fighting the enemy within his own territory, subversive propaganda could develop as a specialist skill. In 1943, SOE 1 was renamed the Political Warfare Executive and was given the position of a semi-autonomous specialist unit, under the joint control of the Foreign Office, the military and the Minister of Information, who was by then Brendan Bracken, a personal confidante of the Prime Minister. This structure enabled the Foreign Office to ensure that the mistakes of First World War Enemy Propaganda were not repeated and that the PWE would not cause embarrassment after the war.[13]

The separation of Enemy Propaganda from the Ministry of Information was of great importance. For, although close liaison between covert and overt propaganda at the top level was necessary – and here a crucial factor was that Brendan Bracken was especially in Churchill's confidence and that Eden was content to follow Churchill without asserting the traditional independence of Foreign Secretaries – the ethos and *modus operandi* of the two departments were so different that organisational separation was desirable for maximum efficiency in both. The overt propagandist in the age of modern mass communications must ensure the maximum flow of information as accurate as the needs of the moment permit, but with his thoughts firmly fixed on the goal of the long-term credibility of the government of which he is a part and a representative. His motto must be, as Sir Ivone Kirkpatrick, Director-General of the Ministry of Information put it, 'the truth, nothing but the truth and as near as possible the whole truth'. The political warfare officer, on the other hand, must deal in the rumours, ruses and subversions needed at the moment, with his thoughts firmly fixed on the goal of ensuring that his handiwork cannot be traced back to his government.

The credit for first realising the essential separateness of Enemy Propaganda from the new Ministry of Information, firmly committed to the Reithian policy of 'propaganda with the truth', belongs to Sir Reginald (Rex) Leeper. He withdrew from the planning body of the Ministry of Information at the beginning of 1938 and began to build up a political warfare organisation within the Foreign Office at Electra House. After September 1938, Sir Campbell Stuart, the First World War deputy director of Enemy Propaganda, was brought back and he continued the development at Woburn Abbey. The relationship between Woburn Abbey and Electra House in the early stages is not clear, but neither formed part of the Ministry of Information. In 1940, an attempt by the leaders of the Ministry to reincorporate Enemy Propaganda was rebuffed at Cabinet level. The separation of overt propaganda, the job of the Ministry of Information, from covert propaganda, the job of the Political Warfare Executive, made a fundamental contribution to the success of both.

Potentially overlapping functions were not so well thought out in other areas. The Ministry's position in respect of the Empire and Commonwealth was left as a somewhat grey area. The Colonial Office and the British Council had both been in the field already and remained in it. The British Council was also engaged in its own 'cultural' branch of overt propaganda in neutral and allied countries, and of course the Foreign Office was also. It took a good deal of time to reduce the considerable duplication of effort and 'Whitehall warfare' to an acceptable level. Much of the credit for the improved cooperation, such as it was, which emerged towards 1941 must go to the civil servants, for they were given an entirely unresolved situation by the planners of the Ministry.

Equally difficult was the position of the Ministry of Information in respect of the 'publicity' work of other ministries on the home front. It was one of the lessons of the First World War that these 'publicity' efforts by the multitude of wartime ministries must be centrally controlled.[14] Conflicting propaganda at home had proved self-defeating and it could easily deteriorate again into do-it-yourself amateurism, damaging the precious credibility of the whole of the government's propaganda. Accordingly, the new Ministry of Information was given the task of supervising and coordinating the 'publicity' output of all the other ministries and government agencies. The sheer size of this task and the demands it would make on personnel were not sufficiently foreseen, nor the power needed to overcome the opposition which taking over the publicity of any ministry was likely to provoke. Endless arguments, duplication and confusion ensued when the war broke out and in the end the Ministry never fully realised its role as the central producer of publicity. The Ministry of Food was, however, the only ministry which went wholly its own way – and successfully so, largely due to the exceptional flair for propaganda of its minister, Lord Woolton. Many allied areas were left as unresolved points of conflict, recurring over and over as the war progressed, such as the perennial question of who should control the Citizens' Advisory Bureau.

At the outbreak of war there were thus both weaknesses and strengths in the preparations which had been made for war on the front of morale. Too little was accomplished in the planning of the administrative structure and position of the new ministry, too little in training personnel, and far too little in explaining to the service departments and to the other ministries that the policy of 'propaganda with the truth' depended on an ample flow of accurate information. In these respects Germany was much better prepared at the outset of war and able to score heavily in 1939-40. On the other hand, a good deal of fundamental thinking had taken place concerning the role and techniques of propaganda. The lessons provided by Britain's pioneering essay into propaganda during the First World War were gradually digested, and new ideas evolved. There was a pool of very able men in the BBC, the Foreign Office and elsewhere, who had thought through the implications for propaganda of the communications revolution in the context of a pluralistic political system at war with a totalitarian state. In this sense Britain was potentially much better prepared, especially for a long war, than the Germans were. Their ideas were essentially still the same as those which Lord Northcliffe's Crew House employed against them in 1918, short-term shock tactics without regard for long-term credibility. In one sense, of course, this was not necessarily a disadvantage, for it matched German strategy based on a short *Blitzkrieg*. Once British propaganda had survived the initial chaos caused by inadequate administrative preparations, it was able to mobilise a pool of able men with new ideas. It took only a short time to make the administrative structure serviceable and to overtake the Germans, particularly in 'overt' propaganda directed at neutral and allied countries.

By the time the first important test came, in the months following the fall of France and during the German bombing offensive, the system was able to play its part properly and it confirmed its worth during the second desperate period of defeats before Alamein. By the summer of 1943 the

British could take a professional pride in observing Dr. Goebbels adopting their policy of 'propaganda with the truth' for preparing Germany for a long and bitter war. By the following year 'V' signs all over Europe and many other kinds of evidence showed that British propaganda had achieved great penetration and also credibility, one of the highest attainments in this branch of warfare.

It would be premature to attempt to assess the contribution made by the propagandists to winning the war. Much work has yet to be done, and much of what has been done has not yet been published. Their contribution, if any, to the fact that British morale did not crack under aerial bombardment will certainly remain an area of conjecture for a long time, and no final answer may ever emerge. Their role in the maintenance of a remarkably harmonious and undismayed public mood in the face of the desperate situation facing Britain during 1940-42 is also, as yet, unclear. Likewise, it is still uncertain what part propaganda played in the equally remarkable equanimity and absence of vindictiveness or hysteria displayed when victory at last became only a matter of time – so markedly different from the performance in 1918. Some credit surely must go to them for both, however.

As far as subversive propaganda, or political warfare is concerned, the central fact for the historian is that German morale did not collapse as it did in 1918. Thus, the ultimate propaganda achievement in the offensive sense was certainly not attained; the war had to be won by military means at the cost of slaughter to the very centre of Berlin. Compared with the very material contribution which German subversive propaganda made towards their victories over Norway, Belgium and, particularly, France, a contribution which might have been crucial, the contribution of British subversive propaganda to Allied victories seems of a much smaller order. Even if one were to accept that the resistance movements of Western Europe largely resulted from the work of the agencies under or associated with political warfare, their contribution to the success of the reconquest of France was, again, of a minor order. It is only when we compare the years following victory in 1918 with those following victory in 1945 that there seem to be good reasons to argue that something very important was achieved by the propagandists, overt and covert. In the First World War British military, naval and economic power had played the decisive role in the victory. In the Second World War this was not the case. Yet, Britain enjoyed a much greater fund of prestige, respect and even affection everywhere in Europe and even in the USA after 1945 than in 1918. British institutions, and the admirable aspects of the traditions of her system of government and culture, had never before been so well known and so much admired. In contrast to 1918, when British power was a reality, it was after 1945 that Europe looked to Britain as a political example and leader. The propagandists can certainly claim a major and particular share in the creation of the fund of goodwill and prestige which proved so important during the bad years following the Second World War, and which was so sadly wasted as Britain could not decide between her imperial past and European future.

The Films Division

Film was one of the communications media which had been pioneered both for information and propaganda purposes during the First World War.[15] Under the overall direction of Sir William Jury as Director of the Cinema Propaganda Department, the Ministry of Information and its variously named predecessors used film successfully to reach ordinary folk. The young and working class men and women were at this time regular cinema-goers, even if they were far from being regular readers of newspapers – despite the claims made by historians of the British press.[16]

The aim of the system evolved during the First World War was to engage the talents and resources of the existing commercial cinema industry, both for the production and the distribution of 'official' films. Very little production was undertaken directly by the Cinema Department, and even these films were produced by established commercial producers and directors employed by the Department. As far as newsfilm from the front was concerned, the system operated on the basis of accredited 'War Office cinematographers'. They were nominated from among the camera-men of the main newsfilm companies by a coordinating committee, which was started by the trade and which gradually acquired official status and official membership. Its first 'official' chairman was Sir Max Aitken – Lord Beaverbrook – but its moving spirit was Sir William Jury, who owned a newsfilm company as well as other cinema interests. In addition, a more or less official newsreel was created, the *War Office Topical News*, by acquiring the stock of the Topical Budget film company. The responsibility for the newsreel was eventually transferred, following Lord Beaverbrook and the committee, to the Ministry of Information in 1918. The production of the official newsreel was carried out by the trade, and it was initially distributed by Sir William Jury's company. Profits were largely given over to wartime charities.

With minor exceptions the Cinema Propaganda Department of the first Ministry of Information operated a flexible and personal system of either commissioning productions, or purchasing material produced independently. On occasion the Ministry offered a subsidy and entered into a partnership with the production company. All this was done in closest co-operation with the commercial cinema industry. The result was a mobilisation of the resources and varied talents of the existing industry rather than the creation of some new organisation or a new genre of propaganda film. Those whose business had been the production of brief melodramas with fiendish villains and innocent heroines came to serve the war effort by putting the villains in German uniforms, and they had the additional attraction of being able to add more *risqué* scenes of rape and violence than before: the censor was prepared for more realism when the film depicted a Hun. Studios which had specialised in 'true story' and travelogue films took up the production of 'accounts' of German atrocities, Austrian oppression, Serbian heroism and Empire pluck. Very little detailed control of either the scripts or film techniques was exercised by the Ministry, which had not felt the need to build up its own personnel of scriptwriters and producers. Negative control, preventing unsuitable films from reaching the public, was also left largely to the trade through its own essentially private British Board of Film Censors (BBFC). This body, however, maintained close liaison with the War Office, the Home Office and finally, after February 1918, with the Ministry of Information Cinema Department. The drawback of this system was that the talents of the cinema industry were too varied. Most of the leading producers and distributors of the time had started with nickelodeons and peep machines, and while they certainly did not lack vigour and the common touch, blood curdling came more naturally to them than other forms of public persuasion.

With Sir William Jury in charge of the Cinema Department, the trade was in effective charge of film propaganda. This was in consonance with the general pattern for mobilising Britain's war resources adopted by Lloyd George, who preferred to have a shipowner directing shipping, press barons in charge of written propaganda, and so on. Sir William Jury was a splendid personification of both the Cinema Department and the young film industry which he led into battle. The founder of Jury's Imperial Pictures, he started as a barely literate fairground operator and moved with ruthless energy and great natural ability to the top of the popular cinema's distribution and production structure, just as the cinema itself was gradually moving upwards out of the fairgrounds.[17]

In October 1918 the vigorous, if somewhat crude, propaganda film production programme ceased and the Department of Cinema was disbanded. It left behind a general acceptance of film as an effective new propaganda and communication medium. Soon other countries, principally Lenin's Russia, took a similar view and their films stimulated as well as continued the interest in the propaganda applications of film. At home during the 1920s, the British Board of Film Censors evolved and enforced an increasingly vigilant set of rules designed to ensure that films, including entertainment films, did not convey undesirable social or political propaganda to the growing millions of the cinema audience. Anti-government political propaganda in films was banned altogether and the ban extended to any portrayal of 'industrial unrest and violence'.[18] By 1928 evidence of the Board's increasing sensitivity to and understanding of film propaganda was provided by the inclusion of such rules as the ban on the portrayal of 'officers in British uniform in a disgraceful light', 'conflicts between the armed forces of a state and the populace' and 'British possessions represented as lawless sinks of iniquity'.[19] In the same year the government introduced protective legislation for the film industry, to ensure, among other aims, that this important means of communication in Britain and the Empire would not be monopolised by Hollywood and the Americans.

After the introduction of sound films at the beginning of the 1930s, the Board of Film Censors succeeded in 1932 in establishing that the addition of a commentary track to a film containing otherwise unobjectionable pictorial material, would nevertheless render it subject to censorship. In the same year, 1932, the Board secured Counsel's opinion that the mere juxtaposition of two or more sequences, originally recorded as scenes of real events, rendered the resultant film subject to censorship under the provisions relating to 'inaccurate, tendentious, objectionable or political presentations'.[20] This ruling effectively put paid to subversive propaganda by 'factual' compilation films in British cinemas. It was also evidence of the high level of expert understanding of film propaganda in the age of montage which existed among the officials of the BBFC whose services could be called upon in the event of war.

After the introduction of synchronised sound newsreels in 1929, many leading political figures also began making personal acquaintance with the new medium. The Conservative Central Office introduced the leaders of the party to sound film and saw to it that they appeared on newsreels as frequently as possible. Stanley Baldwin and Neville Chamberlain became not only frequent but also keen and effective projectors of a cinematic political image, carefully rehearsed and produced.[21] In 1934 Winston Churchill, chafing in the wilderness and denied access to the radio, planned to produce a series of political films with Alexander Korda on the gold standard, India, the rise of Japan, and other similar subjects.

Thus when the planning of the new Ministry of Information began after the 1935 election campaign, which saw the first large-scale use of film for party political purposes, it was taken for granted that the Ministry of Information should again have a Cinema Propaganda Department, to be called the Films Division. This assumption was reinforced by the first comprehensive survey into the size and composition of the cinema audience; it had been conducted the previous year and established the cinema as an unparallelled medium for reaching the mass of the ordinary people. Out of a total population of 46 million, a regular weekly audience of 18.5 million emerged.[22] But the planners soon found themselves on the horns of a dilemma. Although film was a tremendously pervasive medium of propaganda for reaching people at large, the cinemas were potential death-traps.

By 1935 the Air Staff had convinced themselves that the *Luftwaffe* also embraced their doctrine of strategic bombing and that the war would begin with an aerial knockout blow in the form of mass attacks on the heavily populated areas of Britain. They were also convinced that the Germans had, or would have by the outbreak of war, sufficient bomber capacity to effectively overcome whatever anti-aircraft defences might be provided, and that effective interception by fighters was not feasible.[23] If it was true that 'the bomber always gets through' then all public places of entertainment must be closed. Apart from the dreadful carnage which a direct hit on a cinema packed with women and children would cause, previous attempts at the rapid evacuation of auditoriums had led to panic and resulted in some of the worst peacetime disasters. It was precisely such cinema disasters at the beginning of the century which led to the cinema licensing powers of the local authority on which, by devious routes, the censorship powers of the BBFC came to rest. Thus if the Air Staff were right and if no new means of aerial defence were discovered by the outbreak of war, there would be little for the Films Division to do. There would be no cinemas to show its films – or only out in the country – and probably no studios, since they were mostly situated in the south east or in London.

Faced with the prospect that plans prepared for a Films Division might never be realised in the war, and aware of the paramount need to ensure that the BBC stayed on the air, most senior planners were unable to resist the strong temptation to push the planning of film propaganda to the bottom of their priorities. It was natural for overworked officials, however able and alive to new developments, to concentrate on producing new ideas for broadcasting and censorship and to readily accept that the Films Division need only be a reincarnation of the First World War Cinema Department. This did not mean that no plans were prepared – far from it – but it did mean that work on the Films Division was delegated to the less high powered staff who were allowed to rely uncritically on the advice of 'experts' from the Cinema Department of the First World War. The chief source of advice became Colonel A.C. Bromhead, Government Cinematograph Adviser since 1915, and a close friend of Sir William Jury. Bromhead was one of the pioneers of the early cinema, and founded the successful Gaumont (British) Company, in 1898.[24]

Therefore, a system of close cooperation with the commercial cinema industry, similar to the one used in the First World War, was planned for the new Ministry of Information's Films Division. The most important differences in the plans were that the Censor was to be given a more official position and that he was to take onto his staff Security Censors appointed by the Ministry's Censorship Division. It was clearly understood during the preparatory negotiations with Mr. J. Brooke-Wilkinson, the permanent chief official of the BBFC, that the powers of the Censorship Division in respect of film would extend beyond the mere excision of sequences showing military secrets. In all essentials, however, the organisational ideas of the First World War Ministry of Information were to be applied again for the production and distribution of official film in wartime. The history of British film propaganda during the Second World War would be very different if these plans had not been swept away almost as soon as the war broke out.

The first time the plans of the Ministry of Information were tested was during the Munich emergency. The result of that 'dry-run' was the disclosure of a state of dreadful unpreparedness, even in the priority areas. For example, it had been realised since the beginning of planning that quick-acting and effective censorship was essential to stem the manifold flow of free information which by 1938 characterised all democratic countries, particularly Britain. Much of this information was photographic and considered to be of special value to the enemy. Top priority had, therefore, been given to the organisation of censorship which, in accordance with the general policy for the organisation of all wartime information, was to be centrally exercised. Yet when the Munich emergency came in September 1938 it was found[25] that neither the planned system nor the supposedly trained personnel were ready and capable of doing their vital jobs. In the field of photographic and film censorship virtually no groundwork had been laid by the time of Munich. It was not until the following May that the censors and the Customs were brought together to establish how films for export were to be checked and certified. It was not until August 1939, a mere three weeks before the censorship machinery was called into action irrevocably, that the required seals, stamps and forms were received from the manufacturers.[26] The availability of such bureaucratic tools by the outbreak of war, even if only just in time, might seem to indicate that a great deal of progress had been made. Outwardly, the film censorship organisation was ready for action. However, the fact that no policy directive agreed by the Services and the Ministry of Information was available for the guidance of the censors when they took up their positions, indicates that much of the progress since Munich was apparent rather than real.[27]

On 28 July 1939, Sir Samuel Hoare, the minister in charge of planning the Ministry of Information, confidently unveiled to Parliament the outline of the MOI as a large, centralised and impressive organisation, ready for action. Key personnel were called up on 23 August, and on 4 September the Ministry and the Films Division emerged into full view, and, as

Lord Norwich (Duff Cooper) wrote, 'Nine-hundred and ninety-nine Civil Servants sprung to their office chairs'.[28] As planned, they occupied London University's new Senate House building, and regional offices were immediately set up all over the country. The emergence of such a large body from the chrysalis of war planning was meant to be an impressive public demonstration that the government had prepared thoroughly for war. Yet within a fortnight the Ministry of Information became the centre of an enormous row and a symbol of the failure to plan effectively – with the Films Division in the eye of the storm.

In his memoirs, Sir Samuel Hoare claimed that 'the Ministry assumed at once the bodily form that months of discussions with those best qualified to give their opinion had recommended, and that the experiences of the First World War suggested. The trouble which soon showed itself was that there were no devastating air attacks to prove the value of a regional organisation and no war news of first class value to disperse through a great machine of publicity'.[29] With two mighty, colourful empires moving onto a war footing there should have been no shortage of 'news of first class value'. It was, in fact, the censorship machinery which seized up almost at once, for lack of agreed and enforceable censorship criteria, just as it had threatened to do during the Munich emergency a year earlier. The absence of a place in the War Cabinet for the Minister of Information, and the omission of a chain of command for overcoming the inherent reluctance of the Service Department to release any news if they could avoid it, soon choked the News Division and strangled any chance of an effective propaganda offensive upon the outbreak of war. The Emergency Regulations issued by the War Office on subjects directly related to propaganda, such as photography (including 'moving pictures'), although prepared well in advance of the outbreak of war, had not been coordinated with the plans drawn up for the Ministry of Information. These regulations paralysed the newsfilm and the photo-journalistic coverage of the beginning of the war. None of these factors had much to do with the reluctance of the *Luftwaffe* to launch devastating air attacks, as Sir Samuel Hoare claimed in extenuation of the fiasco.

In fact, despite the year gained by the Munich settlement, the war exposed major planning errors in most of the Ministry's departments and in its placement in the wartime scheme of operations. The first three months of the war reduced the planned structure of the Ministry of Information to a state of incipient collapse, all the more spectacular because it was such a large edifice containing so many able, talkative and newsworthy people. The creaks and rumblings of this top-heavy structure provided the press with more column inches about the Ministry of Information than anything actually released by it. The storm of criticism and protest which broke out over the activities of this ill-prepared ministry extended especially to the activities of its Films Division. In fact the Films Division became the most bitterly and consistently attacked part of the Ministry, and it was forced to undergo a complete change of structure and personnel more than once during the first nine months of the war.

In terms of organisational planning, the major problem resulted from designing the Films Division to fight the previous war rather than the next one (a not uncommon type of error), and to operate under the technical and structural conditions of communications prevailing in 1918 rather than 1939. Once again, it was not to be equipped to be effectively the producer of its own films since it was not intended to have sufficient staff of scriptwriters and film directors. It was to commission films from commercial companies, leaving to them the realisation of subjects chosen by the Films Division. Since 1918, however, times had changed in the film world, both in terms of technology and the social composition of the audience, and both of these changes were fundamental.

'Propaganda' of the old crude sort, which anyone in the cinema industry could undertake, would no longer convince the new audience; this was not necessarily because the majority of the audience had become more sophisticated, for so had the commercial film producers. Rather, it was because the audience now included a more educated and critical section of the population, which was concerned that propaganda should not repeat the crudities and lies of the First World War. Modern versions of cartoon films of the Kaiser impaling babies on the spike of his helmet, or melodramas of innocent girls brutalised by 'Huns', or of Britannia warding off grasping hands reaching across the map, were no longer acceptable to the new audiences, however much such devices would be perfectly harmless within the different and more robust traditions of working class politics. Equally important was the fact that Britain was a more divided nation in 1939 than she had been in 1914. King, Country and Empire were no longer sufficient to unite the classes and the nations of Britain for total war. The emergent communist and fascist ideologies cut across national allegiance and created the spectre of treason on the grounds of ideological belief. Attitudes toward conscientious objection had also changed since 1918 and no one could be certain how far such objection would extend if war came. Much more sophisticated propaganda was called for under these circumstances, for which the Ministry was not initially equipped. What made the work of the Films Division, without its own staff of directors and scriptwriters, impossibly difficult, however, were the fundamental technological changes in film communications brought by the changeover to sound film.

The introduction of 'talkies' made vastly greater demands on the people using film for propaganda. Silent film could certainly convey a message, but it was a general one, a visual impression rather than a series of specific points. Captions only contributed a few words to specify the message, and they could be readily added or changed without remaking the entire film. A spoken sound-track, however, was precise. In a sound film an ill-judged phrase, or even an unfortunately chosen single word, can alter the effectiveness and the reception of the whole film. The additional precision of the talking film made the old system of commissioning films, by giving general guidelines to commercial studios, quite unworkable. The government, through the agency of the Films Division, could not leave the wording of what was, in effect, an 'official pronouncement', to a commercial film studio, however competent. The Films Division needed its own script-writers and it also required competent and experienced film directors with propaganda experience to ensure that its films, the government's films, said in words and pictures what was required. Since the Films Division was not planned to have this capacity, it was inevitable that films commissioned from well-meaning makers of entertainment films, and even from the highly specialised newsreel studios, would run into heavy criticism. They were bound to say the right things the wrong way and to barge unwittingly into all sorts of political intricacies. This was precisely what happened. Two-thirds of the films produced for the Ministry of Information during the first six months of war were either immediately withdrawn or never released; those which were shown ran the gauntlet of pungent and increasingly hostile criticism in the press, and produced constant complaints in and out of Parliament. While there was a measure of sympathy for the teething troubles of the complex censorship machinery, however infuriating its results may have been for hard-pressed editors at times, everyone accepted the need for it. The initial failings of the hapless Films Division, however, came to represent everything that the press and others felt was wrong with the Ministry of Information.

The official's inexperience of the film world and of international news communications was another factor in the disastrous début made by the Films Division. Sir George Villiers, for example, was put in charge of ensuring a flow of film pictures from the war fronts to the cinemas at home, and of even greater importance, to the cinemas of allies and allies-to-be, such as the United States of America. His experience of this complex business was confined to having run the propaganda section of the Indian Government in Britain, where he had some very limited contact with the film world. Inevitably, though an able man, he failed to grasp the complicated network of multinational corporations which by this time controlled the newsfilm companies. Together with the War Office, whose ideas remained comfortably rooted in their successful conduct of First World War film propaganda, Villiers vainly attempted to recreate the First World War system. This system, in which the War Office organised the supply of newsfilm, led to a comprehensive and embarrassingly comical lack of usable war footage. Less than ten per cent of the film shot by War

Office personnel during the first fortnight of the war was good for any purpose other than cinematic jokes. As a result, during the first vital month of the war, when British resolution, commitment and capacity for war needed to be demonstrated because of the loss of prestige and credibility incurred at Munich, newsfilm, the most convincing means for displaying military strength and determination, was missing altogether from the Allied propaganda armoury.

Instead, the Germans were allowed to score a resounding propaganda triumph. As virtually the only suppliers of war newsfilm, for the French were also poorly organised, the Germans could successfully impress and frighten the peoples of potential European allies of Britain. Moreover, the complete absence of news footage showing the British Expeditionary Force landing in France gave Goebbels a splendid start for his long-planned and well-prepared campaign against the French. The theme was to be that the British would fight to the last Frenchman, allowing Goebbels to inundate French trenches and supply depots with leaflets asking 'Where ARE Your British Allies?' Even British audiences, at home and in the Empire, were reduced to seeing the start of the war chiefly through German footage purchased in neutral countries. Naturally, this footage showed how the German army was comprised of splendidly prepared, fine, upright fellows, how devastatingly efficient their air force was, and how they were making mincemeat of the Poles. There was little help to be obtained at ministerial level in Britain: the Minister of Information, appointed in the absence of Reith (who was in Canada on a private trip, and perhaps for other reasons also), was a man of similarly unsuitable experience. Lord Macmillan had served in the Ministry of Information in 1918 and that was his last contact with propaganda work, for all practical purposes.

There was, however, another reason for the exceptionally bitter and intolerant tone of the attacks upon the Films Division, in the press and behind the scenes. This was the unfortunate choice of the person appointed to be head of the Films Division: Sir Joseph Ball.

His appointment was in line with the basic policy decision at the planning stage that, owing to the importance of the cinema as a means of propaganda, there should be much closer political control over the Films Division than over its First World War predecessors, which had been under the control of the joint War Office/Cinema Trade Committee, effectively run by Sir William Jury. Unlike Jury, Sir Joseph Ball was not a film distributor or producer; on the contrary, he was one of the Prime Minister's especially trusted officials, and had been so for many years.[30] However, he was not without recent experience in film propaganda; he could justifiably claim to be one of the few Englishmen well experienced in that novel field. As Director of Information at the Conservative Central Office and then Deputy Director of the National Publicity Bureau, he was responsible, with the help of Sir Albert Clavering, for the extensive, modern and highly successful Conservative film propaganda campaign in the 1935 general election. With a fleet of mobile projection vans equipped with sound, a large number of well-made, effective and biting films, and through excellent but confidential contacts with the newsreel companies, Sir Joseph's machine projected an efficient and modern image for the Conservative party. He was close to Neville Chamberlain and contributed to the successful cinematic portrayal of Chamberlain as Chancellor of the Exchequer and then as Prime Minister between 1932 and 1939. The Labour party complained a great deal about these campaigns, and they strongly suspected that, despite protestations to the contrary, the newsreels deliberately gave their huge and primarily working class audience a less than impartial presentation of the issues and personalities of both the 1931 and 1935 elections. Elated over the massive Conservative victory in 1935, some of the newsreels dropped their guard, in public and in private, and were happy to claim a share in 'the victory'. A more or less open partnership between some of the newsreels and the National Government was, again, much in evidence during 1938, and especially at the time of the Munich crisis. This was made more evident by the attempt of one newsreel company, British Paramount News, to present a critical view of the negotiations, which it was forced to abandon, as was subsequently admitted in Parliament, after strong pressure was brought upon it by decidedly devious and certainly not legal means. In the subsequent debate on the question of government interference with newsreels and on political censorship in the cinema, organised by Labour members in December 1938, speakers from the Left made clear their deep distrust of the relationship between the government parties and the newsreel and cinema companies.

While Sir Joseph Ball was justifiably proud of the achievements of the Conservative and Unionist Film Association and of the fruits of his contact with the newsreel companies, there was a great deal of bitterness felt not only by the official Labour Party but also by many members of the intellectual and artistic establishment for what they chose to see as unfair electioneering tactics and disgraceful 'propaganda' methods on the part of the Central Office, relying on the money and moneyed interests of the Conservatives. It made little difference to these observers that Labour's failure to use film for similar purposes was due as much to internal jealousies as to any lack of access to the means of production and distribution. The fact, on the other hand, that the British Board of Film Censors had also shown itself to have rather elastic rules over what to ban as 'political propaganda' and invariably failed to spot films known to have been sponsored by the National Publicity Bureau, added to their distrust.

It was supremely tactless, therefore, to appoint Sir Joseph Ball, the person most closely identified with Conservative propaganda in general and film propaganda in particular, to be the head of the Films Division of the very Ministry which was to be in charge of home propaganda. This was a not untypical example of the lack of sensitivity towards the feelings of Labour opponents which Chamberlain and his leading ministers – in this particular case, Sir Samuel Hoare – could display. Under these circumstances, nothing produced by the Films Division under Sir Joseph Ball, however good or effective, was likely to escape the charge of political bias, nor would it be accepted as a truly national statement.[31] His appointment seemed further to confirm the views of people who, like Clement Attlee, were 'not satisfied that the Ministry of Information was not part of the Conservative machine'.

His party-political background was not, however, the sole reason why Sir Joseph Ball's appointment was a bad mistake or why the films which originated under his régime were attacked with such vehemence. Along with charges of 'King and Country', paternalism and jingoism, there were accusations of general 'awfulness', 'vulgarity' and 'crudity'. These derived from the fact that Sir Joseph Ball was *persona non grata* as far as the literary and cultural establishment was concerned. It was, of course, from these circles that the reviewers in the quality press were recruited. When he had been Deputy Director of the National Publicity Bureau, Ball had identified himself too closely with the aspect of the film world which the *literati* detested most: the thoroughgoing populism shared alike by the newsreels and the 'commercial' cinema. From their point of view, there were good reasons for this detestation. Like the tabloid press, the newsreels and the commercial cinema bypassed the *literati*, and reached millions of the people directly and regularly. There was a deep feeling amounting to hatred for this new and vulgar culture of the cinemas, which anticipated the righteous fervour with which the idea of commercial television was resisted twenty years later. The successful harnessing of populism for Tory electoral purposes created, in the context of the prewar decades, political fears affecting a considerable proportion of the intelligentsia. The fact that the anti-egghead approach of the 'gutter press', the newsreels, and the 'Wardour Street films' manifestly appealed to the people, together with the prospect of an alliance, fostered through the media, between the masses and the Tories, gave rise to fears of a kind of fascism among some of the intelligentsia. What hurt most of them, however, and explained the bitterness of the opposition from all quarters of the literary, artistic and intellectual world, was the feeling that they, the thinkers, the teachers, 'the movers and the shakers', were being cut out of this new major channel of communication and persuasion. They felt that their right to be the educators of the plebeians and the determiners of national values was being undermined, and their function and importance in society threatened. And, personally, they loathed the vulgar 'Wardour Street types' who had the temerity to be making fortunes out of *not* trying to lead the people to Bloomsbury. Sir Joseph Ball shared the tastes as well as the views of these 'types' in the commercial cinema; he too loved expensive yachts and ostentatious parties and he too regarded the verdict of the box office as the final arbiter of values and of what the people should be provided with in their cinemas.

For all these reasons, the *literati* swung into furious attack when Sir Joseph Ball, as head of the Films Division, turned to newsreel companies, advertising agencies, and commercial production companies for personnel for the Films Division and also commissioned from them the first batch of its films. This was an entirely natural decision on his part since, as far as he was concerned, they had already proved their expertise in producing propaganda, and also because the people were known to him personally. The *literati* proved to be formidable opposition. They possessed their own journals, dominated the film reviews and literary sections of the quality press, and they were people with the finely honed pens needed to fill the correspondence columns of the influential newspapers. They also had influential political contacts through the aristocratic literary-political circle that disliked Chamberlain, of which Lady Margot Asquith and Harold Nicolson were typical.

It is against this background that criticisms voiced against the Films Division as it emerged in September 1939 need to be assessed, and also the charge that both the planners of the Ministry of Information and Sir Joseph Ball were ignorant of and failed to make use of what the critics claimed was the only body of fully trained and experienced film propagandists in Britain, the so-called 'documentary movement'. The outcome of this issue fundamentally affected the organisation and character of British film propaganda in the Second World War, and has coloured the views of everyone who has written since about the history of the British cinema.[32]

The British documentary movement in the 1930s, its origins, development and colourful personalities, have been the subject of a good deal of literature and need not be described here. By 1939 there were about sixty film-makers in Britain who could be said to belong to the documentary movement and who were proud to describe themselves not so much as film producers but as 'propagandists with a social purpose'. They worked outside the structure of the British 'commercial' cinema both in terms of production and exhibition. In production terms, there were three kinds of organisations in the late 1930s through which 'documentary' films were produced. First, there was the General Post Office Film Unit which, although small by commercial standards, was reasonably well equipped and had a core of technical staff as well as documentary directors. It could certainly be fairly described as a full-time government-owned film unit, founded for the purpose of propagandising the work of the Post Office and available, by commission, to other government departments for similar purposes (at least on a small scale, for the Treasury frowned on the practice). In the British context this did not mean, of course, that it was 'the government film propaganda unit'. Second, there were full-time documentary film units within the public relations departments of a few of the largest British companies, such as the Shell Film Unit, which were also well equipped, if very small by film industry norms. Finally, there were a number of independent documentary production companies, usually consisting of one or two producers who both owned the companies and directed the films. They worked on a hand-to-mouth basis, making films for industrial sponsors and occasionally for government agencies or public corporations. In terms of production equipment these small, independent documentary companies relied on a mixture of hired, second-hand and 'borrowed' equipment, and in terms of staff, on assembling a crew as and when they could obtain a commission. The largest of these companies were Realist, Strand and, later, Paul Rotha Productions, but even these could not be described as genuinely permanent production studios. They did, however, have an interesting and unique central organisation behind them. The Association of Realist Film Producers and Film Centre offered sponsors a measure of security in terms of production standards and accounting, and they functioned as a guild and friendly society for documentary film producers. And further, there was the extraordinary personality of the founder of the movement, John Grierson. He provided the producers with political and spiritual direction, drive and discipline, and also with the fruits of his singular genius for getting money out of large companies and even the Treasury. Until he left for Canada in 1938, he was the reality behind Film Centre's claim that it was 'a consultative and policy-making body, its purpose being not to produce films but . . . in general to guide the development of the movement as a whole'.[33] Nevertheless, there was also truth in what Sir Joseph Ball was reputed to have said when taxed with his 'failure' to give the documentary production companies commissions for Films Division films: that 'they were not production companies, just a name on the door and a typewriter'. It was a matter of perspectives and definitions.

Undoubtedly, there were talented and dedicated film-makers in the documentary movement, and it is also clear that the utilisation of those talents could have been advantageously planned for when designing the Films Division. Yet here again the case for this view can be seen much more clearly with hindsight than during the years 1936-39, when the plans were being prepared. At that time there were serious doubts about their usefulness for war propaganda work. In the first place, it was questioned whether they would be prepared to propagandise what they were told to project rather than to conduct their own propaganda with government resources. The 'documentary boys', as they were known to the trade, had distinguished themselves by, among other things, the skill with which they infused the industrial/commercial information films commissioned from them with their own political views. Many large business corporations and industrial associations found themselves unwillingly promoting what they regarded as left-wing propaganda through the films they had commissioned, but which bore little resemblance to the views of their boards. In some cases sponsors had even preferred not to use the finished film, despite the large sum which it had cost them and despite recognising the high artistic quality which the films also sometimes possessed. For example, *The Times* commissioned an exceptionally ambitious documentary film about itself from Paul Rotha, but preferred to lock the beautifully finished film and negative into its vaults in perpetuity. For twenty years *The Times* refused the most tempting as well as the most pressing offers for showing it because of the skill with which its maker managed unspokenly to convey his loathing for the Establishment as represented, *par excellence*, by *The Times.*[34] Even within the stricter confines of the GPO Film Unit, with its Civil Service rules and vigorous Conservative Postmaster General, the activities of its film-makers were only marginally fulfilling the official purpose of the Unit, that is, to advertise Post Office services. At one stage, it is said, even Special Branch was sufficiently alarmed by its films, writings and activities to put the Unit under observation.[35]

To make matters worse, several of the leading documentary film-makers had, at one time or another, been personally associated with antigovernment, anti-Chamberlain, or pacifist propaganda. Paul Rotha, among other exploits, fought a successful, much publicised and embarrassing campaign to extricate a certificate from the British Board of Film Censors for a pacifist, anti-rearmament film he had made. Edgar Anstey, a senior member of the documentary movement, became London Director of Production and then Foreign Editor of the American topical film series *March of Time*. Every one of the *March of Time* issues produced under him and dealing with Britain or British foreign policy ran into trouble with the British Board of Film Censors. In a single year, 1938, no fewer than four of his issues were banned altogether as unacceptable political propaganda. Although the films were successfully banned in England, *March of Time* had a very wide circulation and considerable influence in America and Canada. Not unnaturally, this made Anstey's involvement appear even worse in official eyes; antigovernment propaganda at home was one thing, but conducting it in a medium distributed widely in America and elsewhere in the world was another matter.

The members of the documentary movement not only communicated their views and politics through film, they were also masters of the pen – possibly the most literate group of men ever engaged in the visual arts. They owned a journal, *World Film News*, under the combative, mercurial and at times brilliant editorship of John Grierson, and most of the leading members of the documentary group wrote for it regularly. Their views, therefore, did not have to be deduced from their films. Their unambiguous prose could only confirm the doubts as to whether these talented, articulate and intensely serious young men would be prepared to carry out propaganda if they were not personally in agreement with every jot and nuance of it, and also whether they could be relied upon, at least, not to use the government's film propaganda machine against the government if they were in a position to do so and if they strongly disagreed with the government's policies. And they made no secret of their thorough detestation of the National Government in general and of war propaganda in particular. Nevertheless, should the planners of the Films Division and the Ministry of Information have been prepared to run this risk in order to mobilise their talents for the war effort? The answer to that question must substantially depend on how great those talents appeared at the time, and on how well justified, on the evidence available to the planners, were the claims for the effectiveness of documentary film as a medium of propaganda. The question of the effectiveness of the documentary film as a medium of persuasion lay at the core of the debate about the work of the Films Division. It was considered both before and after the eventual admission of the documentary approach during the war, and recurred at each of the turning points in the history of the Films Division and of the Crown Film Unit during the postwar period. The question is still alive and much debated within the context of television broadcasting, but for the purposes of this book it is only necessary to examine the evidence available by 1939.

By the time the final decisions were taken concerning the shape and personnel of the Ministry of Information, towards the close of 1938, the documentary movement was ten years old and had produced over two hundred films. No informed person could, by then, justifiably doubt the high artistic position achieved by the documentary film. Documentaries had won major international film awards in some of the most highly respected film festivals, such as Venice. In Britain the widespread critical acclaim which many of the major productions received was also beyond doubt. The films were good art – but were they also the best propaganda medium for the cinema-going public, and were they right for the working class people who formed the bulk of it? On the evidence available at the close of the 1930s, that claim was rejected as unanimously as the artistic eminence of the documentary film was accepted. The Cinematograph Exhibitors Association, the official body of the cinema owners, expressed the view that documentary films made no appeal whatsoever to ordinary viewers. The cinema trade's official journals, *Today's Cinema* and *Kinema Weekly*, repeated and articulated this view with impressive consistency over the years.[36] Trade associations, however, may not always accurately reflect their members' views. But the solid proof was the unwillingness, in practice, of the great majority of cinema owners and managers – who were, of course, in business to draw the maximum number of people to see the films they could hire at the cheapest rates – to take documentary films, despite the exceptionally advantageous terms on which they were usually offered. This was a fact, moreover, which the documentary movement admitted, although they angrily denounced the cinema owners as philistines unable to look beyond the window of the box office. Unwillingness to show documentary films was not due simply to a bias against factual films. The cinemas were perfectly willing to take many other kinds of informational films; for example, travelogues and even natural science films made in a nondocumentary style by commercial studios, such as Gaumont British Instructional Ltd., were widely shown. Only the documentary approach to such subjects was rejected.

The documentary movement countered the views of the cinema owners by arguing that they, being a part of the capitalist-commercial world, were prejudiced against the non-commercial approach which produced the documentary films. As for the claim that the documentary lacked popular appeal, they asserted that no fair trial had been given by the cinema-owners. Both of these claims are difficult to assess. Early on in the evolution of the movement, many cinemas did try out documentary films on their customers and dropped them when the response was unfavourable – but the examples shown were indeed early and therefore arguably not the best examples. A respectable number of cinemas did again take some of the fully developed documentary films – but precisely those examples, such as *Night Mail*,[37] which were the most romantic, most descriptive and in fact the least propagandist productions, the very films which were often attacked within the movement as examples of backsliding or of succumbing to the lure of the box office. Of the hard-core documentary films only a small proportion were shown as a regular feature and only by the handful of cinemas, in the West End of London and the corresponding districts of the largest cities, which were beginning just before the war to cater for the incipient middle-class cult of the art of the cinema. As far as the ordinary, industrial-urban viewers were concerned, the position was perhaps best summed up by the film critic of the *Northern Evening Dispatch*, writing in 1942: 'The pre-war documentary film though often excellent tended to be a little precious and tiresome and in any case the local cinema manager would have none of it.' After 1936, in fact, the documentarists themselves began to argue that their films were not suitable for the vulgar entertainment context of the ordinary cinema programme and that they needed to be shown in a properly educational context through a non-commercial distribution network. This was a view with which the cinema owners heartily agreed, adding that their patrons, having paid their sixpences, objected to being preached at for their money. But then, they did not much care for the message of the sermons either.

We need to look therefore beyond the cinema owners for evidence concerning the acceptability of the documentary approach, although there can be no doubt that had they been manifestly popular the cinema owners would not, in view of their cheapness, have objected so strongly to them. The majority of the cinema audience came from the industrial working class and the 'propagandist purpose' of the documentary movement was undoubtedly both socialist and also within the gradualist traditions of the Labour Movement. Yet Labour also did not accept the documentary film as a suitable medium of mass persuasion. The documentary movement made repeated attempts at persuading the Labour Party and the Labour Movement to use documentary films for propaganda amongst the working class at large, but without success. John Grierson's plan for a great Labour Party film propaganda machine was summarily rejected by Herbert Morrison in 1931. Five years later, at the 1936 Labour Party Conference, the documentarists organised a massive display of their films and presented a carefully prepared plan for a film campaign. The conference rejected the plan, although delegates recognised the merits of the documentary for educational purposes. Instead of the proffered documentary films the Conference decided to use travelling theatre shows, but it did support the setting up of a joint committee with the TUC for investigating the utilisation of the propaganda potential of film. On that committee, the documentary movement was represented and had every opportunity to make its case. In 1938 the report of the Film Committee was accepted by the TUC and funds were made available for the establishment of a Workers' Film Association – which promptly rejected the proposals submitted by the documentary movement for the production of films. Instead, the Workers' Film Association obtained its films from commercial studios, or from individual left-wing film producers who used the much more direct 'social realism' approach derived from Soviet propaganda films, an approach which, apart from the message, was very similar to the Conservative propaganda films produced by newsreel companies. Alternatively, the Association purchased films from abroad, largely from Comintern-financed sources. It was, however, the Co-operative and Wholesale Society which had the longest and widest experience in matters of film within the Labour Movement. The Society owned a substantial number of cinemas deep in the working-class districts and it had been using films for both publicity and propaganda purposes all through the 1930s. Yet the Co-op owned cinemas refused, like their privately owned competitors, to take documentaries and in this case we can be sure that that was not because of, but in spite of, their message. The Co-operative and Wholesale Society commissioned its own propaganda and advertising films not from the documentary producers, but from those whose approach was diametrically opposed to theirs and who were also used by Sir Joseph Ball's National Publicity Bureau: the advertising agencies, as a rule.

There was thus only one group of the population in whose case there was evidence for the popularity or effectiveness of the documentary film: the actual or aspirant intellectuals, the people who were members of the cinema societies, debating groups and the like; the same also applied to some extent at least in the case of those who attended evening schools, adult education classes or courses of various kinds. The view was taken that it was not worth the cost to prepare film propaganda for such small, atypical groups and that they were in any case literate people perfectly well catered for by the written media. Perhaps, with hindsight, it can be said that not enough weight was given to the argument, put forward often enough by the documentary movement, that the cinema society/WEA type of people possessed an influence greatly in excess of their numbers, that they were the natural leaders of opinion among their neighbours and workmates. However, the issues remained unresolved – it should be remembered that in the situation envisaged for the operation of the Ministry of Information, film propaganda was to be the medium for reaching ordinary people, the industrial and urban working men, their wives and their children, who would have to stand up to the enemy's aerial warfare. The decision to ignore the documentary movement in planning the work of film propaganda must thus be said to have been in accordance with the evidence available at the time and with the planned purpose.

In the course of 1938 and in the spring of 1939 selected film companies were thus invited to join confidential discussions of what they would be required to do in the case of war.[38] Gaumont British Instructional Ltd., the Newsreel Association (representing the five newsreel companies) and GB Screen Services Ltd. (an advertising and publicity films agency) were among those whose services were enlisted and with whom Ministry of Information plans were concerted. The GPO Film Unit and the private documentary film production companies were not invited and few plans were made for their wartime employment. In September 1939 they accordingly found that they, unlike commercial companies, were not 'called up'. Naturally, from their point of view, this came as a bolt from the blue. They had firmly expected that they would be the backbone and the main providers of film propaganda. They found it hard to believe that their exclusion from the Ministry of Information's plans for film propaganda could have been due to reasons other than sheer ignorance of their existence and achievements. 'On the political front' wrote Paul Rotha in *Documentary Diary* about the year 1939 'it was understood that the government had formed a shadow committee to draw up a policy and plans for a Ministry of Information to come into being if war should break out. A good deal of mystery naturally shrouded this committee and its activities but there is reason to believe that its membership included Lord Reith (later to be the first [sic] Minister of Information), Sir Joseph Ball (Director of the Conservative Research Department and the party's film adviser) and probably Mr. A. G. Highet (of the Post Office Publicity Department). As research for future use revealed, the committee appeared ignorant of the fact that there had been an efficient official machine for film-making (the GPO Film Unit) in being without interruption since the EMB Film Unit in 1929.'[39] This claim, that the planners of the Films Division were men ignorant of the existence and work of the documentary movement – a claim which is also generally found in current literature – cannot be substantiated by the evidence available. Mr. A. G. Highet, Assistant Controller, 1929-37, and Controller from 1937 of the Post Office Publicity Department could not possibly have been 'ignorant' of the existence of one of the most expensive constituents of his own department: the GPO Film Unit. Nor is it possible to argue that the other members of the committee might have been ignorant of the existence of the documentary film producers and productions. Sir Joseph Ball, for example, was a business associate as well as a friend of H. Bruce Woolf, and their company had actually produced several of the early documentary films, including Paul Rotha's award-winning *Shipyard*, before Bruce Woolf had come to the conclusion that the documentary was not suitable for the ordinary cinemagoer. As early as 1932, Sir John Reith, while he was Director General of the BBC, personally commissioned the Empire Marketing Board Film Unit, the original documentary film unit of John Grierson, to make a documentary about the BBC. Reith was not a man for small measures: *BBC: The Voice of Britain* emerged as one of the grandest and most expensive films ever produced by the documentary movement. It took over three years to complete, during which time Reith and the BBC came to know the documentary movement as thoroughly as the latter came to know the BBC. Reith, however, was bitterly disappointed with the caustic critical reception and virtually non-existent distribution of the film.

Sir Joseph Ball, Sir John Reith and Mr. A. G. Highet had indeed been involved at various levels and at various times in the planning of the work of the Films Division: unknown to the documentarists, Highet was in fact Assistant Director Designate. The ultimate decisions, and the responsibility for them, however, lay with Sir Stephen Tallents who, as the Director General Designate of the Ministry of Information, was in charge of its detailed planning. Sir Stephen Tallents knew the documentary movement and its members more intimately and for a longer period than anyone else. It was he who first employed John Grierson in 1927 and gave him his first chance to try his hand at actual film-making; until then Grierson had only been a film critic and the author of voluminous memoranda on the possible applications of film for propaganda purposes. The result was *Drifters*, the archetype of the British documentary film. It was Sir Stephen Tallents himself who established the Empire Marketing Board Film Unit, the cradle of the documentary movement, and it was he again who rescued it, when the Empire Marketing Board was closed down in 1932, by setting it up as the GPO Film Unit. On its behalf he had fought endless battles with a restive Treasury, and almost singlehandedly secured its survival and its freedom to experiment and to train documentary film-makers. Sir Stephen Tallents had been always credited in the most glowing terms by John Grierson himself with being the father of the documentary movement. Yet no evidence has so far come to light which would suggest that Sir Stephen Tallents as Director General Designate had intended to build the Films Division around the GPO Film Unit or that he intended to employ the documentary film producers in preference to the newsreel companies and the 'commercial' film producers. Although he probably remained personally fond of documentary films, as Director General Designate he was bound to act in the light of the evidence available, which he knew better than anyone, concerning the acceptability and effectiveness of the documentary film as a medium of propaganda for the ordinary, working-class people of the cinema audience. The fact that Sir Stephen Tallents, of all people, chose not even to consult Grierson, Rotha or other members of the documentary movement in the course of the preparation of the plans of the Ministry of Information, let alone invite any of them to work on the plans, is the most telling evidence of all for dismissing as a myth the charge of either a 'Tory plot' or of philistine ignorance as the cause of the exclusion of the documentary movement and the GPO Film Unit alike from the plans for conducting film propaganda in the war.

In the spring and summer of 1939, in accordance with the plans for the operations of the Films Division, there began the placing of commissions, initially for newsreel trailers for recruitment and for informational films concerning ARP and Civil Defence preparations. One such commission was in fact given to the GPO Film Unit.[40] The manifest distaste of its producers for the task of persuading the public to bear up confidently to the prospect of aerial bombardment, their success in turning the film into a macabre image of death and destruction for all, and the endless delays in actually completing the film, were not calculated to persuade Sir Joseph Ball to change the plans and make the GPO Film Unit the centre of wartime film propaganda. As soon as war was declared, and even while the cinemas were closed in expectation of the German attempt at an aerial knockout blow, the Films Division began to place commissions for a substantial number of propaganda films, for showing abroad and, if the cinemas were reopened, at home. In accordance with the plans, the commissions went entirely to the newsreel companies and to the other commercial film agencies. The release of these first Ministry of Information productions naturally commanded widespread attention, especially in the quality press, which was already irritated and dismayed by the unpreparedness and mistakes of the Ministry's News and Censorship Divisions.

The storm which broke over the first Ministry of Information films exposed at once the mistake of only planning film propaganda with the ordinary cinemagoers in mind and only employing the populist approach of the newsreel, advertising and entertainment film companies. In the *Spectator* on 29 September 1939, Mr. Graham Greene encapsulated the views widely expressed: 'Surely by now we should realise that art has a place in propaganda; the flat and worthy sentiment will always sound flat to neutral ears . . . "shoulder to shoulder to liberty", "baby-killers" . . . we want the technique used by Anstey in *Housing Problems.* America is more likely to listen with sympathy to the rough unprepared words of a Mrs. Jarvis of Penge faced with evacuation, black-outs, a broken home, than the smooth handled phrases of personalities. Above all we do not want the old commentators with their timid patronising jokes; this is a people's war'. This sort of criticism of the newsreels and other 'popular' productions had been made by aesthetes and reviewers such as Mr. Graham Greene himself for many years. As long as the cinema was a matter only for the cinema business, it could be ignored because the cinema owners knew that *Housing Problems* sold no seats at all to their 'regulars' – who, however, liked very much indeed the *Gaumont British News*, which was the best, or worst, exemplification of that other approach. However, with a ministry in charge of film propaganda, the material that went into the cinemas became a matter for public concern as expressed by the traditional organs of 'public opinion'. Whatever might have been the rights and wrongs of the case against employing the documentary with its 'aesthetic' and 'academic' approach, it was well enough known that the alternative, the populist approach represented by the newsreel companies and their associates, had long annoyed and irked the intelligentsia. In a national emergency such as war, it was a basic error to alienate them, the natural leaders of informed opinion.

The belated recognition of the importance of good relations with the *literati* was signalled by the abrupt replacement of Sir Joseph Ball[41] with Sir Kenneth Clark as Head of the Films Division. He was a much better choice in personal terms: politically uncommitted, popular with the quality press, and with proven ability in the field of management in the arts as a result of his work as Director of the National Gallery. He was also – and this was his main asset – fashionable in intellectual circles, in fact he was regarded as one of the most brilliant younger stars of the artistic and literary establishment. His experience of the film world, of propaganda, and of the information and news film structure was, to say the least, limited. He had a much greater sensitivity, however, for what might produce an outcry in the quality press and his arrival was soon followed by the scrapping of most of the films started under Sir Joseph Ball. Major changes in the organisation and orientation of the Films Division, however, did not take place at once.

The reconstruction of film propaganda began with a gradual replacement of personnel under the impact of Sir John Reith's energetic efforts to centralise and make more efficient the whole Ministry after his appointment as Minister, on 4 January 1940. Reith's first priorities were the administrative structure, which was chaotic and which he remodelled on BBC lines, and the reincorporation of the Press and Censorship Bureau, the real essence of the Ministry of Information, which had been made an independent body in a panicky attempt to counter the criticism of the MOI in the autumn of 1939. It was not until April 1940 that Reith could turn to the affairs of the Films Division. By that time military defeats and growing discontent with the conduct of the war had led to a weakening of Chamberlain's position and Reith assessed the situation accurately when he expressed the view that the government was bound to fall soon and that a coalition government was inevitable.[42] Thus, when Reith subjected the Films Division to a thorough reorganisation, the strong party instincts of the Chamberlain government were outweighed by the need for conciliating Labour and smoothing the feelings of the influential members of the literary and artistic establishment. Reith was very well aware of these needs. The result was a capitulation to the documentary movement and to its backers in the press. The GPO Film Unit was brought into the Ministry to become the hub of a large programme of direct film production by the Films Division and was subsequently renamed the Crown Film Unit. The largest and most modern commercial film studio, Pinewood, was eventually requisitioned for it. The independent documentary film units became the chief outside producers of the new programme of Ministry of Information films. Sir Kenneth Clark moved up to a more prominent position.[43] As Head of the Films Division, he was replaced by Jack Beddington, the former Director of Publicity for the Shell Group, who had been responsible for the establishment of the largest of the documentary film units in industry, the Shell Film Unit.[44] As head of the production section, later designated Supervisor of Films, Beddington brought in Sir Arthur Elton who, next to John Grierson himself, was already the most prestigious central figure of the documentary movement. He was the cofounder of Film Centre and, after the departure of Grierson to Canada, its moving spirit, as well as its director. Subsequently he became the most important single influence on the work of the Films Division and placed the stamp of his ideas and personality upon it.

Sir Arthur Elton,[45] with the background of a 10th Baronet educated at Marlborough and Jesus College, Cambridge, an immensely cultivated man, an historian and archaeologist, a captivating lecturer and gifted restorer of Clevedon Court, was among the first to join Grierson's movement in 1931. As a documentary film-maker he moved with equal facility from films poeticising the beauty of technological wonders, such as aero engines, to films of the social document type about such subjects as the appalling conditions in some of the slums, and to exceptionally clear filmic expositions of the workings of complicated machinery such as ancient windmills or the fluid flywheel. A 'good radical', with great charm and kindness of character, he appeared to be the least associated with the more extreme and dogmatic political activities of the documentary group. By background, personality and manner he was singularly well qualified to harmonise the high-minded approach of most of the 'production' divisions of the reconstructed Ministry of Information with the documentary movement. In fact, he personified the reconstructed Films Division of the second Ministry of Information as aptly as Sir William Jury had personified the Cinema Department of the first Ministry of Information in the rough, plebeian days of film propaganda during the First World War.

A little before the appointment of Sir Arthur Elton to the Films Division, Beddington had commissioned Film Centre to prepare a memorandum on the use of film for propaganda purposes. It is perhaps not altogether surprising to find that this memorandum became the 'basis of much of the Division's subsequent work',[46] and that the Second World War became the golden age of the British documentary movement.

Another important new appointment was that of Mr. Thomas Baird, who became the head of the newly created Non-theatrical Distribution Department. He came from the GPO/Imperial Institute Library, where he had led the documentary movement's experiments in trying to achieve a showing of their films outside the ordinary cinemas. The documentary approach to the use of film for persuasion had, as we have seen, been affected by the resistance of cinema owners to the inclusion of such films in their programmes. The first result of the documentary takeover of the Films Division was the direct reversal of the previous policy, which had concentrated on the production of films acceptable to the cinema owners. The principle behind the earlier policy was that the cinemas were the places where contact could be made with the maximum number of people who could not otherwise be reached. The new documentary-inspired policy placed maximum emphasis on developing a non-theatrical distribution system for their films which, it had to be realised, could not even in wartime be forced upon the cinemas, at least not in sufficiently large numbers. The documentary movement had claimed it as an article of faith that 'in Britain there were more seats outside the cinemas than in them'.[47] They saw the money-no-object conditions of wartime as the chance to prove it. Had this policy of reorientation from the cinemas to factory canteens, church halls, institutes, etc., fully succeeded, the history of British film propaganda in the Second World War would have been very different. As it happened, however, the policy ran into powerful opposition soon after it had been embarked upon.

The 13th Select Committee on National Expenditure conducted its enquiry into the affairs of the Ministry of Information and its Films Division during the spring and early summer of 1940. The Select Committee was not impressed by the claims made for the size of the non-theatrical audience, despite the grossly exaggerated 'estimates' provided by the Films Division. They were equally unconvinced by the powers claimed for the documentary type of film as a weapon of war propaganda.[48] They regarded such films as a cultural luxury, too esoteric and lacking in mass appeal; this was of course much the same view as was held by the cinema owners and indeed often expressed with force by working-class viewers and propagandists.[49] The Select Committee recommended, on 21 August 1940, the winding up of the whole new documentary film non-theatrical distribution setup. (Sir Joseph Ball's reactions upon reading the report are not recorded.) As it was, however, a mere four months since, with considerable fanfare, the documentary régime had been introduced and a clean sweep made of the original personnel of the Films Division, the report could hardly be welcomed by the Minister of Information. The Beddington/Elton/Baird régime and their appointees were far too closely committed, both to the documentary film and to the non-theatrical distribution policy, to be able to continue serving if orders were given for both to be dropped altogether, as the Committee had urged; and their departure would have been politically unacceptable. There had been enough resignations and dismissals – the Ministry of Information had been in the news too long already. The result was a compromise.

The Films Division was allowed to continue with a substantial, if reduced, programme of producing uncompromising documentary films. It was also allowed to continue with the attempt to create an audience for the documentaries outside the commercial cinema. But this was to be done on a more restricted budget which, in fact, never allowed them to compete at all seriously with the commercial cinema in terms of actual audience figures. While the cinemas reached over 24 million people each week, non-theatrical distribution scarcely reached 0.36 million per week at its peak in

1943-44. Despite the tremendous amount of work and the almost missionary zeal with which the staff of the Non-theatrical Distribution Department tried to make up for the relative scarcity of resources allocated to them, the 'great audience outside the cinemas' never materialised. There was however a hidden bonus in this failure: the documentary films produced for the non-theatrical circuit were of little interest to a busy Minister of Information or to the Cabinet. As a result the producers could do much as they liked, provided the Films Division's own chiefs approved. They could pursue, at first very obliquely, later quite evidently, a line of political argument which was unquestionably anti-Tory and which was in clear contravention of the rules adopted for propaganda by a coalition government in wartime.

On the other hand, the commercial film industry was brought back, if not in triumph at least as an unavoidable necessity, because of the report's insistence on the priority of theatrical mass distribution. A weekly programme of short propaganda films suitable for incorporation into cinema programmes was instituted in order to convey appropriate messages to a truly mass audience. In addition much emphasis was placed on a trailer programme attached to newsreels and produced chiefly by advertising film agencies, newsreel companies and other commercial studios. Many of the weekly propaganda films for the cinemas, called *Five Minute Films*, though in fact they tended to be much longer, were made by successful 'commercial' or 'feature' directors, such as the Boulting Brothers, Thorold Dickinson, Michael Balcon, Anthony Asquith and others. Since the cinemas were obliged to take these 'Ministry of Information shorts', this programme also enabled some of the liveliest of the documentary producers to explore ways of combining their principles with a popular presention. Paul Rotha, who had always had the edge over most of the others because of his superb visual sense and his belief in the need for art as well as message, was particularly successful in this field. So was Harry Watt, who used a more dramatised approach in order to reach the cinema audience and who for some time past had disagreed with Grierson's purist views on non-theatrical distribution. According to the canons of the documentary movement, many of the *Five Minute Films* fell far short of perfection, but by the more plebeian standards of popularity this programme was one of the most successful of the Films Division's productions.

The overall result of the compromise policy which emerged after the first nine months of war was a cross-fertilisation between the two approaches to film propaganda. It was admirably personified by Ian Dalrymple, the new head of the Crown Film Unit, who was an outstanding 'commercial' director and producer yet had genuine sympathy for the best of the work of the documentary film-makers. Under his patient, highly professional, yet sensitive guidance the Crown Film Unit produced a matchless series of films, the best of which, in the tradition of Renaissance art, elevated good propaganda of the moment into lasting works of art.

A particularly interesting result of the wartime cohabitation between 'commercial' and 'documentary' film-makers was the development of the 'true incident fiction film', or 'feature documentary' as the documentary producers preferred to call this genre. A typical example of this kind of film was *Western Approaches*, produced by Ian Dalrymple and Pat Jackson – both from outside the documentary movement; this employed the outward forms of a documentary, but was in fact a fully acted fiction film presenting the story of a single ship's struggle against enemy submarines. *Western Approaches* was produced by the Crown Film Unit, but similar and equally effective films in this genre were produced by commercial studios as private ventures and were thus outside the 'official films' category. Some of these 'feature documentaries', such as *In Which We Serve*, instilled exceptionally lasting propaganda messages in a very large proportion of the British people. They also contributed greatly to that wave of admiration for Britain which swept Europe after the war when an intelligent programme of political reeducation through film propaganda carried them into every part of the liberated continent.[50] Another example of effective cross-fertilisation emerged in the genre of the 'documentary compilation' film. *Desert Victory* was perhaps the finest of this kind of film, in which a 'commercial' director coordinated and directed the work of a large team drawn from the different worlds of both the documentary and the newsreel. *Desert Victory* owed its lasting appeal partly to its subject matter but also to the sense of balance required for a full-length film and which could be contributed by the best of the 'entertainment film' directors, in this case Roy Boulting, who was in overall charge of the production.

The compromise of 1940 remained in operation. No major changes in organisation or policy were made during the remaining four years of the war. Thereafter the Films Division showed a remarkable permanence in personnel as well as structure. All through the war it was commanded by Jack Beddington and Sir Arthur Elton. This stability was in marked contrast with the volatility of most of the other departments of the Ministry of Information – in August 1941, for example, no less than seven posts for departmental heads and controllers were vacant simultaneously.

From the summer of 1940 to the end of the hostilities, there was therefore a clear structure and consistent leadership in the Films Division, a leadership which operated the multi-faceted approach based on the compromise of 1940 always with competence and sometimes with brilliance. Both the aims and the methods and, above all, the criteria for what was fair even in war were very different from those of Dr. Goebbels and his Ministry of Propaganda. But in terms of consistent central direction, scale of production, talent and resources, the two largest film propaganda organisations of the Second World War were very well matched, and they afford a rewarding field for comparative historical study.

A full assessment of the working and achievements of the Films Division during the Second World War has yet to be made. The records of its policy-making and administration are now available for historical research in the Public Record Office, or at least as much of the records as appears to have survived a rigorous selection process after the war. Some additional and valuable records are located in the libraries and archives of the Imperial War Museum, the Post Office, the British Council and the newsreel companies. But it is in the nature of film propaganda that full historical judgement must primarily take into account the films themselves, the end-products of the processes documented by the written records. It is the purpose of the present catalogue to help the historian approaching this new extension of his work and to facilitate his task, in the same manner in which the lists, indexes and calendars of the Public Record Office help him in the domain of written records.

The British official film

What precisely was an 'official film' between September 1939 and March 1946? There is no simple definition which covers all cases and yet remains within the bounds of common sense. In strict theory, all films publicly exhibited in Britain during the war were official films because no film could be shown in a public cinema without official approval, expressed by a certificate issued by the British Board of Film Censors after careful and detailed scrutiny. Censorship extended to all kinds of film irrespective of length, subject, type or country of origin. In addition to the all-embracing powers of the Censorship Division and the Board of Film Censors to license or ban exhibition without reasons given, or to demand any kind of cuts or alterations in finished films as a prerequisite of exhibition, celluloid and acetate stock were declared war materials, and therefore were available only upon a licence issued by the Board of Trade. The Board of Trade reserved licences for those whose applications were supported by the Films Division of the Ministry of Information. Each proposed film production thus had to begin with the submission to the Films Division of the Ministry of Information of a detailed synopsis and also full information concerning the proposed production company and personnel; every production was thus conditional upon the approval of the Ministry of Information. A licence was again required for the film stock necessary for the making of release prints of the finished negative and even for new prints of a prewar film if someone wished to reissue it. The system built around the licensing of film stock enabled the government to add to the blunt (and overt) weapon of suppression through compulsory censorship, the more comprehensive and subtle weapon of controlling the apparently private production of films. The government could in effect determine what subjects would be made into films and could influence decisively the form of their treatment – without incurring the propaganda handicap of having to affix a 'Ministry of Information' label to the finished film. The Films Division certainly used these extensive powers widely and effectively. Professor Thorold Dickinson, who had personal experience of this system, has recorded the view that the Films Division's exercise of script and production supervision was not only comprehensive but served to improve greatly the artistic standards and efficiency of the British film industry as a whole.

Nevertheless it would be a mistake to regard all British films produced during the war as official propaganda. The Ministry of Information, through censorship and film stock licensing, was certainly invested with totalitarian powers. But the continuation of ingrained British attitudes, even in wartime, ensured that those powers were not applied with a totalitarian frame of mind. Just as the legal safeguards in the Nazi, or Soviet, constitution were in practice rendered meaningless by totalitarian habits of mind, so the absence of such habits of mind among the officials of the Ministry of Information and the members of the Cabinet itself ensured that the application of the Ministry of Information's wide powers stopped well short of a total direction of the film industry. It would go beyond common sense and reality, therefore, to describe the ordinary entertainment films produced in Britain during the war as 'official films'. No doubt, films questioning Britain's chances of victory, or the superior virtues of her system of government, or the desirability of associating with any of her actual allies, could not be produced, and all films were expected at least to combat 'gloom and despondency'. Nevertheless, there is a clear difference between the feature film *Blithe Spirit* and the Crown Film Unit's *Britain Can Take It.* The latter was an official film in which a government message was directly communicated to the public by the official agency of the Films Division, while the former was not, even though historians of British morale during the war might well regard them as equally effective propaganda.

There were therefore three types of films which were in practice 'official films', were so regarded by the Films Division itself, and are listed in this catalogue:

1) Films *produced* by the government's own film units, the GPO Film Unit, the Crown Film Unit, the Colonial Film Unit and the film units of the armed services.

2) Films *commissioned* from private film companies by the Ministry of Information, other ministries or government agencies. In most cases, though not in all, the Ministry of Information handled film commissioning for other ministries.

3) Films *distributed* by the government through the Ministry of Information, other ministries, and agencies such as the British Council. Such films may have been acquired by purchase from private companies in Britain or abroad, or by a gift or loan from other governments, or by capture from the enemy. A substantial proportion of films shown by the British government were in fact obtained in one of these ways and often from abroad. The degree to which such films were modified to suit government purposes varied from showing the film as it was, to complete reediting and redubbing, in which case the original film was used as little more than stock shots for an essentially new production. The majority of films of foreign origin fell in-between and were usually adapted by a few discreet cuts and perhaps a new soundtrack.

Films belonging to the last category are included in this catalogue because the purpose is to provide a comprehensive list of all the films which the government used for communicating its message to the public. Films from foreign sources were as integral a part of the British weaponry employed in the war as the tanks and aeroplanes and ships purchased from abroad. Apart from the saving of resources at home, the employment of foreign films played a very useful role which British-made films could not fulfil anywhere near as effectively. Putting Canadian, South African, Russian and even German films on the screen with a 'Ministry of Information Presents' caption at their head was both an effective illustration of some of the freedoms for which the country was fighting and an excellent opportunity for instilling the desired impressions without having to take overt responsibility for creating them. In the case of the enemy, for example, the War Office 'presented' Dr. Goebbels' *Feldzug in Polen* and the Ministry of Information released large batches of German newsreels, actually incorporating them in British newsreels showing in all the cinemas. *Feldzug in Polen* was shown with only a few very discreet cuts and complete with German commentary, while the newsreels were completely reedited with a continuous and often heavy-handed English commentary. Into the same category falls one of the most popular of all British propaganda films, *Germany Calling*, where Leni Riefenstahl's *Triumph of the Will* and some other German propaganda films were reedited and animated into a hilarious and biting parody to the tune of the Lambeth Walk. Prints of *Germany Calling* were subsequently scattered over occupied Europe by the Political Warfare Executive.

In the case of allies, the use of films made by them served the double purpose of publicising them at their own cost and of not involving the government in disputes over what the films actually said about them. Some Soviet films, for example, were taken over from the Soviet Film Agency and distributed by the Ministry of Information, but they wisely decided not to produce many films of their own about 'our Russian allies'. Soviet susceptibilities abroad, and the irreconcilable conflict between left-wing and right-wing susceptibilities about the Soviets within Britain would have made Ministry of Information films about the Soviet Union a source of trouble. A suitable selection from the offerings of the Soviet Film Agency worked much better, because the films would announce themselves as Soviet propaganda.

At the same time, not all films of an informational or propaganda character produced in Britain during the war were official films and their inclusion in this catalogue would be as misleading as the exclusion of films of foreign origin distributed by the Ministry of Information. Some political film units, such as that of the Workers' Film Association, continued to operate after the outbreak of war and some documentary film units, while working for the Ministry most of the time, could on occasion also 'find' film stock for other sponsors as well. Hence a small trickle of non-official political propaganda film production, which it was not politic to suppress through censorship, continued during the war. Some scientific and industrial units could also carry on with small-scale independent production, sometimes with stock left over from before the war (as in the case of Julian Huxley's films made at Dartington Hall), and sometimes by persuading the Ministry that the project was worthwhile. Such films were on occasion taken over by the Ministry while in production or bought after completion (in which case the film of course appears in this catalogue). Lastly, there was also a small-scale continuation of the prewar school film productions. These productions were encouraged but in most cases not directly sponsored by the Board (later Ministry) of Education, but film stock was allocated for them whenever the overriding needs of propaganda and wartime entertainment allowed. The crisis shortage of film stock prevailing in 1942-43, which led to the reduction of the Five Minute Film programme among others, virtually killed off all unofficial production, except some educational work. Thus while this catalogue includes all films distributed by the Ministry of Information and other government agencies as well as all those produced by them, it is not a catalogue of 'documentary films', as a genre, produced during the war.

One category of films, definitely both British and official, which regretfully could not be included in this catalogue, are the training and record films made for use by the three armed services. There are a large number of such films. They range from a few yards of camera-gun negative to large numbers of instructional films used for troop training, on such subjects as the visual recognition of enemy aircraft or tanks, and they also include a number of the military equivalents of the Ministry of Information propaganda films. No list of these films exists. The films themselves were deposited in the Imperial War Museum as and when someone remembered to declassify them. It will be a long time before a catalogue of these services' films can be produced. Most of the nontechnical propaganda films were, however, released for use outside the services by the Ministry of Information at one time or another, occasionally in a modified form, and thus they do in fact appear in the catalogue. *Next of Kin* is the most famous example: it was originally an army film. When these internal services' films have been catalogued, it is hoped that the resulting material will be published as a supplement to this catalogue.

The British Council operated under the joint supervision of the Ministry of Information and the Foreign Office, but very much as a semi-autonomous body, largely because of the accident that it was directed by Lord Lloyd. He was in the confidence of the War Cabinet, was long regarded as an expert in foreign propaganda and had been involved in the establishment of SOE 1 and of the Political Warfare Executive. His personal prestige secured a practical independence from the MOI. The British Council handled film propaganda in some areas in conjunction with, and in some areas on behalf of or instead of, the Ministry of Information, the Foreign Office and the Colonial and Dominions Office. It exercised a good measure of independence in its own selection of films, sometimes ignoring altogether MOI materials available to it. All the films distributed by the British Council are listed in the catalogue and their use by the British Council identified. They provide a ready record of what Sir Stephen Tallents had once called 'the projection of England' abroad during the war.

Sources of the catalogue

The Ministry of Information does not appear to have left a consolidated list of its films. No official history appears to have been commissioned, and it is quite probable that no such list was in fact prepared before the Ministry came to an end – at any rate no list has so far been discovered amongst the papers of the Ministry. The following five sources have, therefore, been used in the preparation of the catalogue:

1) The catalogues of the Central Film Library (CFL), which listed each year the films issued or reissued by the Ministry of Information for nontheatrical distribution.

2) The catalogues of the British Council, *Films of Britain* (FOB), which

listed the films issued for use abroad through the agency of the British Council.

3) The 'rosters' of the Ministry of Information films, including Colonial Film Unit productions, newsreel trailers and acquired films, which were printed periodically in *Documentary Newsletter* (DNL), from October 1940 to December 1947. *Documentary Newsletter* also produced a retrospective roster of films pertaining to the first year of the war. The rosters were prepared by Sir Arthur Elton's section in the Films Division and they were published by permission of the Ministry of Information. For all practical purposes they were fully official lists of Ministry of Information films, prepared with great care and considerable statistical finesse. The only problem these 'rosters' present is that they gave only the official relationship between the films and their makers. In some cases the producer assigned by the Ministry of Information had in fact little to do with the actual creation of a film. Wherever possible, this has been corrected in the catalogue.

4) The issue catalogues and indexes of the newsreel companies held in the libraries of Visnews Ltd., EMI-Pathe Ltd., and British Movietone Ltd., which provide an exact record of the date, length and constituent items of each newsreel issued by the company. Copies of these catalogues are now to be found in the library of the British Universities Film Council.

5) Information based on unpublished catalogues, viewing records and miscellaneous papers held in the National Film Archive, Imperial War Museum, the British Council and the Central Office of Information, supplied by courtesy of their officers. To the same category belongs the information collected originally by the Slade Films History Register and now located at the premises of the British Universities Film Council, and the information kindly provided by many former officers and producers of the Ministry of Information.

In addition, two general publications have been used to fill gaps and to provide checks:

1) *Monthly Film Bulletin* (MFB), published by the British Film Institute, which gave lists and short descriptions of films available for showing in commercial cinemas.

2) *Documentary Films, 1940-46,* published in *Cinema Yearbook 1949-50*, edited by Peter Noble.

Of the two wartime, government-issued lists of films, the British Council's *Films of Britain* and the *Catalogue of the Central Film Library,* the former were official publications which gave from the beginning an accredited list of what the government wished the public to see abroad. The status of the CFL catalogues is less clear and should be explained.

The Central Film Library of the Ministry of Information had originated as the film library of the Imperial Institute in the days of the Empire

Marketing Board. It distributed films about the Empire in Britain and, to a lesser extent, films about Britain within the Empire. After the dissolution of the Empire Marketing Board it continued as the distribution centre for the GPO Film Unit and pioneered the techniques of the non-theatrical showing of films on which the documentary movement substantially depended for continuing financial support. In addition, therefore, to government-originated documentary films in the shape of films made by the GPO Film Unit and sponsored by other ministries, it also distributed some films made by the documentary fraternity for commercial sponsors – the lines were deliberately blurred. In 1940 the Imperial Institute's film library and distribution personnel were taken over by the Ministry of Information and renamed the Central Film Library. For a short time a distinction was drawn between Ministry of Information and pre-Ministry of Information films. The Library continued to loan these latter films as well, but not all of them by any means. The 'official' status of the pre-Ministry of Information films was theoretically unclear – but in practice the disappearance of a large number of prewar films and their occasional reinsertion indicated that the whole of the Central Film Library list was in fact 'official'. The end of the war, the removal of close scrutiny, and also the availability of film stock for more marginal film propaganda efforts, were heralded by the reappearance of a very large number of prewar documentaries in the 1946-47 catalogues. To avoid ambiguity, we list separately, in Appendix 2, the prewar films distributed by the Central Film Library during the changeover period, 1939-42, but it must be emphasised that as far as the public was concerned all films appearing in the current catalogues of the Central Film Library were 'official' films representing what the government wished the public to see. The appearance of a single catalogue after 1942 indeed acknowledged it. Each successive issue of the CFL catalogue pointed out that films might have been withdrawn since the last issue and that such films would no longer be supplied, which also reinforced the point.

The catalogues of neither the Central Film Library nor the British Council were, apparently, deposited in the copyright libraries, and no effort appears to have been made by either the Ministry of Information or the British Council to preserve a complete set for archival purposes. Sustained search has eventually brought to light copies of all the wartime catalogues and their supplementary lists except for the first Central Film Library catalogue (December 1940) and the first and second supplementary lists issued in June 1941 and October 1942. We are indebted, for the catalogues which have been located, to the librarians of the City of Leeds, the Imperial War Museum, the British Council and the Central Office of Information; gratitude is also due to the many other librarians and departmental record officers who searched for them in vain. A set of photostat copies of the catalogues which were discovered has now been placed with the Film History Register, in the library of the British Universities Film Council.

The gradual procedure employed for the winding up of the Ministry of Information at the end of the war presents certain difficulties in cataloguing the 'official' British films of this period. The Ministry of Information was terminated officially on 31 May 1946, but the Crown Film Unit was kept in being within the newly formed Central Office of Information and some of the wartime arrangements for licensing and distribution were also maintained. Some of these arrangements and the Crown Film Unit were not finally abolished until the Conservative government came into power in 1951. On the other hand censorship and the compulsory showing of government films both came to an end as from 9 am, 2 September 1945. These powers were the twin essentials of a propaganda ministry – the rest was merely an exercise in publicity in a pluralistic society. Thus the real *terminus* of the wartime experiment in total propaganda was the morning of 2 September 1945. However, films could sometimes take a long time to materialise and many films not complete by this date, or not released by the time of the official winding up of the Ministry in the following May, were in fact part of the work of the Ministry of Information. All the films, therefore, which were issued up to June 1946, and also all the films for which a production date before January 1946 has been found, are included in the catalogue, even if some of these films were not issued until late 1946 and, in a few cases, not until 1947. The point should be borne in mind, however, in the case of films listed only with a 1946 or 1947 release date, that the reason for such late release might have been that the film did not turn out to represent propaganda policy at the time of its completion. In some cases films which appeared in the Central Film Library catalogue only after 1945 had been used abroad before, but were withheld from British audiences. Some of the more realistic film accounts of the extent of German bombing were a case in point. These were used abroad to strengthen sympathy and to stress urgency to potential allies, but were thought to be too strong meat for home audiences. Such films were hesitantly and gradually released in Britain after 1945. Appendix 3 lists films made during the war, but not released until after the war.

Both the Central Film Library and the *Films of Britain* catalogues provided a description of the contents of the films which they listed. These descriptions were not without a propaganda purpose and contain much of historical interest. They are reproduced without alteration irrespective of whether or not a viewer today would necessarily agree that they are 'a true record'. In the case of films for which no contemporary description could be found, a brief outline of its content is provided, wherever possible. These outlines were derived either from viewing ourselves surviving copies of the films, or from information supplied by film archivists. Such modern outlines are distinguished from contemporary descriptions by the use of parentheses.

The Dating and Classification of Films

Dating

The basis of the arrangement of the catalogue is chronological. The date which determined under which year a film should be entered was the date of release to the public, by analogy with publications. Only where this date was not available was the date of production used instead. Production dates are often unreliable as well as sometimes irrelevant in the case of film propaganda. A very long time may elapse between the completion of the creative production process and the appearance of the film as a propaganda weapon. Films can also be altered substantially during that time, not necessarily by the original production team, if the propaganda objectives have changed in the meantime. The release date is therefore the only meaningful historical date in the case of films produced as part of a continuous and large-scale propaganda campaign. After 1942, the 'rosters' prepared by Sir Arthur Elton's section in the Films Division and published in *Documentary Newsletter* themselves abandoned dating by the completion date of the production in favour of using the release date. Where no release date was available, as in the case of many of the films distributed by the British Council and in the case of some foreign-originated films, the date of the roster or catalogue in which the film appeared for the first time has been used. In these cases there is an additional dating problem due to the fact that the catalogues appeared at different times during the year and did not necessarily run from January to December. The *Documentary Newsletter* rosters themselves began with 'war years' – starting on 1 September – and only changed to a January-December pattern from the end of 1942. In most cases other evidence has helped to resolve the overlap problem, but there may well be some films entered for 1940, 1941 and perhaps 1942 which were in fact released during the last months of the preceding year.

Classification

Propaganda history is a seamless web in any age but especially so in the case of the Second World War. It was a total war fought on a global scale in the age of modern communications. The application of any system of classification to Second World War propaganda materials is likely to be a source of disagreement. It could be argued that even an alphabetical order is arbitrary.

An undifferentiated list of films would not be very helpful, however, from the point of view of the user of this catalogue who might wish to use it as a starting point for the study of a particular field of war propaganda, or for those who might wish to obtain a view of the types of films made by the Ministry of Information and of the proportions between them. We decided therefore to hazard unfavourable comment, abandon the approach of an undifferentiated chronological list, and group the films in categories, within a chronological framework. The categorisation was done on the basis of the primary purpose of the film during the war, as it appeared to us in the light of information now available.

The classification does not claim to be a definitive assessment of the place of any particular film in the scheme of wartime propaganda. Most films served several purposes and the most effective propaganda films operated on several different levels at once while ostensibly dealing with only one subject. A film apparently designed to provide straightforward 'instruction' on how to approach a government agency for relief might in fact be effective propaganda designed to show how comprehensively the government cared for those suffering from needs resulting from the war. Films apparently designed to give instruction on how to assist some wartime agency such as the auxiliary fire service might in fact be designed to show how thoroughly prepared, organised and capable the government was in dealing with all possible emergencies. Such films might also aim at party political propaganda beyond the war: 'Look what rapid and extensive advances in the provision of social services and political participation have been proved possible because there is a war on; let us make sure "they" cannot go back on them once the war is over'. Such messages were a common feature of many apparently 'instructional' documentaries. Many films could therefore be classified under several different categories and other people might well come to different conclusions from us. Another reason why our classification of some films might at first sight appear inconsistent is that good propaganda never allows its operations to settle into a readily recognisable pattern, for once the pattern is recognised it is no longer effective. It operates by mental associations and by the deliberate blurring of definitions. A series of strictly 'instructional' films, on how to dig, how to make a compost heap, and so forth, designed to instruct first-time gardeners, could be utilised for a compilation film which called upon all to *Dig for Victory*, which was an exhortation about the success of the campaign for self-sufficiency, not audio-visual instruction. Hence films ostensibly belonging to a single series on the basis of their titles need not appear in the same category.

A series of beautifully made 'educational' documentaries about the history of various medical discoveries with apparently no 'propaganda' purpose illustrates another point. These films were in fact part of a propaganda campaign designed to bring home to the public how many of the wounded in the present war were being saved by lavish medical attention, how many of the maimed and disfigured were at this very time being successfully rehabilitated, and how strongly and effectively the present government cared for the wounded soldiers and civilians. It was not a unique idea: Dr. Goebbels produced an identical campaign at almost the same time, also about surgical advances and the rehabilitation of wounded personnel. The German films were as apparently free of 'propaganda' as the Ministry of Information films. In both cases, however, the impetus for and the timing of the commissioning of these films arose from concern over mounting casualty lists in Africa for Britain, and in Russia for Germany. The fighting was increasingly turning into bitter slogging. It was feared that the casualties might recall memories of the human consequences of the failure of generalship in the First World War. The makers of these films might themselves have been quite innocent of the real propaganda purpose which gave them their commissions, and which gave them subjects and scripts quite free from any overt 'propaganda'. They might even resent now finding their films classified as 'Homefront Propaganda'. It was, however, not theirs to reason why the films were commissioned at one particular time rather than another.

Those films which were in the non-theatrical distribution scheme run by the Central Film Library were themselves classified in the CFL catalogues. The reasons why the Central Film Library's own categories are not retained in this catalogue should therefore also be explained. In the first instance, the classification scheme applied only to non-theatrically distributed films, thus providing a classification for only about 40 per cent of the films listed. Secondly, the Central Film Library classification system was itself designed to be a minor weapon in the propaganda war and to blur as much as to clarify. *Battle of the Books,* for instance, one of the very few examples to be produced of strident and Goebbels-like diatribes reminiscent of First World War film propaganda, was classified under 'Education and Youth' (to attract schools to show it) and was entered again under 'Government and Citizenship'. *Silent Village,* a terrifying reenactment by the inhabitants of a Welsh village of the German massacre at Lidice, a rare case of atrocity propaganda made by Humphrey Jennings and the Crown Film Unit in 1943, was classified in the Central Film Library catalogue under 'Government and Citizenship' as well as under 'United Nations: Free Fighting Forces'. We felt that the modern user of the catalogue would not be helped in finding films or surveying the work of the Films Division by the retention of these categories, despite their archival interest. In Appendix 4, however, we reproduce the classification list of the 1944 Central Film Library catalogue as an example, and it in fact contains most of the films listed in the CFL catalogue.

News, as Sir John Reith observed, was the shocktroops of propaganda. Without doubt, it was the newsreels which bore the brunt of the filmic part of the propaganda war. At the rate of ten newsreels per week, even a skeletal newsreel catalogue would take up a volume by itself. All that it was possible to do within the compass of this catalogue was to provide a statistical indication of the newsreel contribution. A full catalogue of British newsreels is badly needed, not only for the war years but also for the whole period between 1931 and 1956, during which the newsreels were perhaps the most important single medium of mass communications, only rivalled by radio after the outbreak of war and unmatched by television until the late 1950s.

Location of Copies of Films

Whenever a copy of a film is known to exist in the National Film Archive; the Central Film Library; the Imperial War Museum; the Library of Congress; the Museum of Modern Art, New York; the U.S. National Archives and Records service; or Public Archives Canada, its location is given. It appears that neither the British Council nor the Central Office of Information any longer possess copies of wartime films. An entry signifying that a copy is held in one of the archives listed does not necessarily imply that the copy is readily viewable, even less that it is available for hire. In some cases there is only a negative or an inflammable and possibly unstable print in existence – but it does mean that the film as such has not altogether ceased to exist.

Notes

1. Michael Howard. *The Continental Commitment,* London: Penguin Books, 1974, p. 110-19.

2. Planning began in 1935. By July 1937 there were some basic orders drawn up and the broad outline of the Ministry was in draft. Sir Stephen Tallents was appointed Director General Designate. The first 'progress report' was sent to the Cabinet on 31 January 1939, and it claimed that by then the organisation was substantially established (P[ublic] R[ecords] O[ffice] P.R.O. INF. 1/5 and P.R.O. INF. 1/178). However, the civil servants who were expected to provide the detailed planning were not relieved from other duties and they were too widely scattered, not only in Whitehall but also in the armed services and in the Royal Household. The Ministry was not only planned on a large scale, it also grew fast. By 1941 the Ministry employed 1,792 full-time officials and commanded a further 3,000 officials, many of them part-time in name only: Duff Cooper took the view that the Ministry had been planned on too large a scale: 'A monster had been created so large, so voluminous, so amorphous that no single man could cope with it'. (Lord Norwich, *Old Men Forget,* London, 1953, p. 285). From March 1937 Sir Samuel Hoare was in ministerial charge of the planning (Viscount Templewood, *Nine Troubled Years,* London, 1954, p. 120-2).

3. Beaverbrook and Northcliffe resigned in the first week of November, the dissolution of the Ministry was announced within a fortnight of the Armistice, and the process of winding up was concluded ahead of schedule on 16 December 1918. Much new evidence concerning the work of and the dissolution of the Ministry of Information, as well as the reasons for the British failure to maintain the lead in propaganda between the wars, can be found in P.M. Taylor, *The Projection of Britain: British Overseas Publicity and Propaganda 1914-1939.* Unpublished Ph.D. Thesis, University of Leeds, 1978.

4. For the more scholarly American view of British propaganda, see J. D. Squires, *British Propaganda at Home and in the USA; from 1914-1917,* Harvard, 1935; H. C. Petersen, *Propaganda for War – the Campaign Against American Neutrality,* Oklahoma, 1939; James R. Reid, *Atrocity Propaganda 1914-1919,* Yale, 1941. For a more sensational treatment of British propaganda in the U.S.A., see F. E. Lumley, *The Propaganda Menace,* New York, 1933.

5. Erich Ludendorff, *My War Memoirs,* London, 1920, vol. 2.

6. *Hitler's Mein Kampf,* with an introduction by D. C. Watt, London, 1969, p. 165, 167-9. Hitler used extraordinarily flattering terms to express his admiration for British propagandists wherever he referred to them: 'Their brilliant knowledge of the primitive sentiments of the broad masses is shown by their atrocity propaganda', etc.

7. *The Times' History of the War* shrewdly assessed the weight which should be placed on Ludendorff's views, as early as 1922, in what is still the best all-round account of the work of British propaganda during the First World War (*The History of the War,* vol. XXII, London, 1922, p. 348-58). A cool and balanced assessment of the causes of the collapse of German morale was also provided by Sir George Aston in *Secret Service,* London, 1930, p. 262-71. German assessments of the effectiveness of British propaganda remained consistent (even outside political circles) during the interwar years. See also, in particular, the scholarly volume of Hans Thimme, *Weltkrieg ohne Waffen,* Stuttgart, 1932, p. 127-38, and Herman Wanderscheck, *Weltkrieg und Propaganda,* Berlin, 1936.

8. Sir Arthur Ponsonby, *Falsehood in Wartime,* London, 1925. Republished in America in 1928, with considerable success.

9. A. J. Toynbee, *The German Terror in France,* London, 1917. See also his *The Evacuation of Belgium,* London, 1916. The postwar attempts to verify the sensational Bryce Report had little success on the whole and they caused considerable unease.

10. The fullest account of the use or broadcasting techniques during the General Strike is in Asa Briggs, *History of Broadcasting in Britain,* vol. 1, 1967, but see also very significant additions to the story in Robert Rhodes James, *Memoirs of a Conservative* (J.C.C. Davidson), London, 1969, p. 226-62.

11. Lord Reith, in *Into the Wind,* London, 1948, underplays the extent of the author's involvement in the planning of the Ministry. Although it does provide an accurate listing of Reith's functions the information is scattered all through the volume. *The Reith Diaries,* edited by C. Stuart, London, 1975, reinforce

but do not alter the ambivalence displayed there. Basically Reith could not make up his mind whether to accept the post of Minister of Information Designate and shape his own Ministry in the planning stage as he wished, or whether he should try to reach a more impressive and permanent ministerial position in some other capacity in case there should be no war, and no MOI. Also, by 1937, overweening ambition began to cloud his perception of the development of political events, and his own career prospects.

For an exceptionally clear and reliable account of the wartime working of censorship, including an excellent diagram of the system, see Rear Admiral George P. Thomson, *Blue Pencil Admiral,* London, 1947. Admiral Thomson was Assistant Chief Censor Designate 1937-1939; Assistant Chief Censor 1939-1941; Chief Censor 1941-1945.

13. For the development of political warfare as a separate concept and a separate organisation before and during the war, see Sir Robert Bruce Lockhart, *Comes the Reckoning,* London, 1947; Hugh Dalton, *The Fateful Years,* London, 1957; Sir Campbell Stuart, *Opportunity Knocks Once,* London, 1952; M. R. D. Foot, *S.O.E. in France,* London, 1966 (second edition). An exceptionally interesting insight into political warfare's genesis, for which much of the documentation is not yet available, and into the unofficial background to the development of British ideas on the subject during the interwar years (as well as accounts of some interesting wartime operations of PWE) can be found in John Baker White, *The Big Lie,* London, 1955. For the fullest treatment of PWE, see C. Cruikshank, *The Fourth Arm: Psychological Warfare 1938-45,* London, 1977.

14. *Nine Troubled Years,* p. 420.

15. Rachel Low, *The History of the British Film, 1914-1918,* London, 1950, p. 34-8.

16. The circulation figures of the press show that until the 1930s the press had failed to penetrate into working-class homes. In the years immediately preceding the First World War the circulation of the national daily press newspapers was under 5 million – no more than the *Daily Mirror* alone reached after the Second World War. By 1939 the circulation of national daily newspapers reached 10.4 million and together with the Sunday papers (12.3) now began to reach the majority of the working class.

17. Born in 1870, Sir William Jury lived through the whole history of the early cinema and its apotheosis in the years before and during the Second World War. He died as the doyen of the cinema trade in 1944.

18. British Board of Film Censors *Annual Report for 1933,* p. 7. Printed for private circulation. Copy from the files of British Paramount News Ltd. in Visnews Library.

19. Nicholas Pronay, 'British Newsreels in the 1930s: Their Policies and Impact', *History,* vol. 57 (Feb. 1972) p. 66.

20. BBFC, *Annual Report for 1932,* p. 18-23.

21. Alan Beattie, David Dilks, Nicholas Pronay, *InterUniversity History Film Consortium. Archive Series No. 1: Neville Chamberlain*, 1974, p. 1-3.

22. S. Rowson, 'A Statistical Survey of the Cinema Industry in Great Britain in 1934', *Journal of the Royal Statistical Society*, vol. 99 (1936), p. 67-119.

23. *The Continental Commitment*, p. 112-14.

24. Rachel Low and Roger Manvell, *The History of the British Film 1896-1906*, London, 1948, p. 21.

25. *Blue Pencil Admiral*, p. 2-6.

26. P.R.O. INF. 1/178/CNI provides a detailed account of the development of film censorship from 24 July 1936, the first draft regulation to be held in readiness for a contingency, until the first year of the war.

27. Not all the changes introduced after the Munich fiasco were for the better. Sir Stephen Tallents who, as Director General Designate, was in charge of planning in a full-time capacity – his office within the BBC was only a little more than nominal – was fired in December 1938 as the man responsible. He was replaced in the course of 1939 by a series of no more able but very much less experienced men, when in fact the inadequacy of the staff allocation given to Sir Stephen Tallents was the main problem. The sudden but fitful zeal displayed after Munich by Sir Samuel Hoare, the minister in control of the planning of the Ministry of Information, was also unconducive to effective planning.

28. *Old Men Forget*, p. 285.

29. *Nine Troubled Years*, p. 421-22.

30. Major Sir Joseph Ball, OBE, KBE, 1885-1967, graduated with First Class Honours in Law from London University. After a military career, largely in Intelligence, he joined the Conservative Central Office at the invitation of J.C.C. Davidson in 1927, and specialised in information and propaganda work. He was Director of the Research Department, 1927-39, and Deputy Director, National Publicity Bureau (under the 'National' governments of Macdonald and Baldwin and Chamberlain), between 1934 and 1939. He worked very closely with Chamberlain: he was for example the person entrusted with the secret mission of making contact between Chamberlain and Count Grandi, the Italian ambassador, behind the back of Sir Anthony Eden. According to his own account it was upon the personal invitation of Sir Samuel Hoare that he became Head Designate of the Films Division. (P.R.O. INF. 1/194). After his removal from that post he became Deputy Chairman of the Security Executive, until 1944. For other aspects of Sir Joseph Ball's varied career and background, which if they were known might also explain some of the heat generated against him, see *Memoirs of a Conservative*, p. 270-2.

31. Clement Attlee told Sir John Reith in the autumn of 1939 that he 'was not satisfied that the Ministry of Information was not part of the Conservative machine'. Sir Archibald Sinclair, the Liberal leader, took a similar line (*Into*

the Wind, p. 370). Mr. Phillip Noel Baker, on behalf of the Labour Party, and Mr. Charles Dukes, on behalf of the TUC, were however appointed as liaison officers to the Ministry of Information as early as 6th September 1939.

32. *The Report of the Dartington Hall Arts Enquiry: The Factual Film*, Dartington Hall, 1947, contains the earliest postwar exposition of this view and Paul Rotha's *Documentary Diary*, London, 1973, p. 233, is one of the most recent reiterations of it. See also the same view repeated by most members of the movement in E. Sussex, *The Rise and Fall of the British Documentary Movement*, London, 1975. Paul Rotha had been a member of the then anonymous body which prepared *The Factual Film*. (*Documentary Diary*, p. xix).

33. *The Factual Film*, p. 56.

34. *Documentary Diary*, p. 261-3.

35. John Grierson in conversation with the author, 4 September 1963.

36. For example: 'There is room for such "propaganda" films, but not on the cinema screens. It cannot be too strongly emphasised that the cinema's primary business is to entertain'. *Today's Cinema*, 2 March 1938.

37. *Night Mail* was the most successful documentary film of the period, and it alone achieved a cinema distribution almost comparable to one of the newsreels. Unlike a newsreel, however, *Night Mail* continued to be viewed for a generation, and became an acknowledged classic of the cinema. Paul Rotha's comments are revealing as well as just: 'If criticism can be made of *Night Mail*, not held by all, it is sentimentality towards the end of the film . . . its visuals are combined with sob-throated words spoken (and I suspect) written by Grierson himself . . . These examples of bathos may have been used by Grierson for what he perhaps foresaw as box-office appeal'. *Documentary Diary*, p. 133.

38. P.R.O. INF. 1/194.

39. *Documentary Diary*, p. 233.

40. This was the notorious film originally titled *If War Should Come*. It was eventually completed in August 1939, and withdrawn at once. It was reedited and released with the title *Do It Now*, but even in that version it had a short career.

41. The replacement of Sir Joseph Ball became the object of a fervent campaign run, in the traditions of aristocratic influence behind the scenes, by the redoubtable Lady Margot Asquith. For the best account of the affair, see R. J. Minney, *Puffin Asquith*, 1973, p. 102-3.

42. *Into the Wind*, p. 380.

43. Sir Kenneth Clark was promoted to be Controller of Home Propaganda and later Head of Planning, until he left the Ministry in 1941.

44. Jack Beddington, OBE. Educated at Wellington College and Balliol College, Oxford; he served in the Far East before he joined Shell-Mex and B.P. Ltd.

in 1927. Head of the Films Division, 1940-46. Returned to Shell after the war. Died in 1959.

45. Sir Arthur Elton died in 1973.

46. *The Factual Film*, p. 64.

47. *Documentary Diary*, p. 141, quoting John Grierson. On the other hand, in later life, John Grierson told the author in a conversation in 1962 that he saw his own greatest failure as his inability to find a formula which would have got his documentaries into the cinema, in order to reach the 'great audience'. He said that he came to realise by 1938 that the key was close topicality, and it was on that that the success of the Canadian Film Board during the war was based: with *World in Action*, a newsreel-cum-documentary, he did finally reach the masses. Grierson also rethought the non-theatrical idea; when he created the Canadian Film Board, the triumphant embodiment of his frustrations in England, he laid it down that it must operate within the framework of the commercial cinema. Non-theatrical distribution was to play a part only as an extension of the cinema into the distant and isolated places and communities of Canada.

48. *XIIIth Report of the Select Committee on National Expenditure*, HMSO, 21 August 1940, p. 10. The committee's chairman was Mr. John Silkin, M.P.

49. Even such a committed working man and lifelong advocate of films for working-class propaganda as Alderman Joseph Reeves took the view that showing over an hour of documentary films, unrelieved by a cartoon, newsreel or something similar, 'was more than human nature could endure'. Reported in *Glasgow Herald*, 21 January 1941.

50. This campaign was jointly organised by the Psychological Warfare Department of SHAEF in Western Europe, the Psychological Warfare Branch of the Allied Forces Headquarters for the Mediterranean, the Ministry of Information and the Political Warfare Executive. It was almost entirely based on theatrical distribution with the accent on newsreels – specially prepared in most cases – and feature films. For accounts see: *The Factual Film*, p. 87-91; Roger Manvell and Heinrich Fraenkel, *The German Cinema*, London, 1971, p. 101-3. Heinrich Fraenkel was himself one of the organisers of this highly successful campaign.

Abbreviations

Review Sources

BFY	British Film Yearbook
DNL	Documentary Newsletter
FoB	Film of Britain, British Council
KW	Kine Weekly
KYB	Kine Yearbook
MFB	Monthly Film Bulletin, British Film Institute
MPH	Motion Picture Herald
S&S	Sight and Sound, British Film Institute
TC	Today's Cinema

Credit Abbreviations

adap	adaptor
anim	animator
assoc	associate
asst	assistant
comm s	commentary speaker
comm w	commentary writer
d	director
ed	editor
m	composer
nar	narrator
p	producer
ph	photographer
pc	production company
sc	scriptwriter
sp	sponsor

Archive Abbreviations

BFI	British Film Institute, Distribution Library, 81 Dean Street, London W1
CFL	Central Film Library, Government Building, Bromyard Avenue, London W3
IWM	Imperial War Museum, Film Department, Lambeth Road, London SE1 6HZ
LC	Library of Congress, Motion Picture, Broadcasting and Recorded Sound Division, Washington, D.C., 20540, USA
MOMA	Museum of Modern Art, Department of Film, 11 West 53rd Street, New York, N.Y. 10019, USA
NARS	National Archives and Records Service, Motion Picture and Sound Recording Branch, Audiovisual Archives Division, Washington, D.C., 20408, USA
NFA	National Film Archive, 81 Dean Street, London W1
PAC	Public Archives Canada, National Film Archives, 395 Wellington, Ottawa K1A ON3, Canada

1939

HOMEFRONT – General

Carrying on
(British railways in wartime)
Review MFB VII 45
MoI *pc* British Foundation

Do it now
(Wartime precautions for the public. Alternative titles *If war comes* or *If war should come)*
Review MPH 30 Sept 1939
MoI *pc* GPO
11 mins IWM NFA

Factory front
(Munitions production)
MoI *pc* GPO
NFA

The first days
(Impressionistic compilation of scenes filmed during the first days of war by several members of the GPO Film unit. Also known as *A city prepares*)
Reviews DNL I Jan 6, MFB VI 214
MoI *pc* GPO *p* Cavalcanti *d* Humphrey Jennings, Harry Watt, Pat Jackson *ed* R Q McNaughton
23 mins IWM NFA

The green
(National Savings and how they help preserve England's rural scenery)
Review FoB 1940
pc Merton Park *d* R Smart
14 mins MOMA NFA

The lion has wings
(Compilation film showing the events of the war to date and the strength of the Allies' cause)
Reviews DNL I Jan 8, MFB VI 20
dist United Artists *pc* London *p* Alexander Korda *assoc p* Ian Dalrymple *d* Brian Desmond Hurst, Michael Powell, Adrian Brunel *comm s* E V Emmett *cast* Ralph Richardson, Merle Oberon, Anthony Bushell, Derrick de Marney, Brian Worth
90 mins NFA

North Sea
How the ship-to-shore radio service safeguards the lives of seamen. (Film made in 1938. Short silent version entitled *Distress call*)
Reviews FoB 1940, MFB XII 10
pc GPO *p* Cavalcanti *d & sc* Harry Watt *ph* Jonah Jones, H E Fowle *ed* S McAllister *m* Ernst Meyer
30 mins MOMA NFA

The first days. *Flowers brought as a goodbye gift on call-up.*

The first days. *Girl checks her appearance in ambulance mirror.*

SS Ionian
A voyage aboard a freighter of the British Merchant Service. (Short version entitled *Cargoes* made in 1940)
pc GPO *d* Humphrey Jennings
20 mins NFA

FIGHTING SERVICES & CAMPAIGNS

Battlefleets of Britain
(Survey of the strength, organisation and tradition of the Royal Navy. *March of time* 5th year no 6, British series; vol 6 no 2, US series)
Review MFB VI 215
pc March of Time
18 mins IWM NFA

OVERSEAS DISTRIBUTION

Do it now

The first days

The first days. *East End street scene.*

1940

HOMEFRONT – General

Albert's savings
(National Savings campaign)
National Savings Ctte & MoI *pc* Merton *p* W H Williams *d* Harold Purcell *cast* Stanley Holloway
5 mins IWM NFA

All hands
Anti-gossip. A sailor in a café tells his girl when his boat is due to leave. The information is passed step by step to a U-boat commander. (Part of a series which includes *Now you're talking* and *Dangerous comment*)
Review DNL I May 17
MoI *pc* Ealing Studios *p* Michael Balcon *d* John Paddy Carstairs *cast* John Mills
12 mins IWM NFA

Ashley Green goes to school
(School services in wartime. Shortened version of *Village school*)
MoI *pc* Strand *d* John Eldridge *p* Alexander Shaw *assoc p* Arthur Elton
5 mins

Behind the guns
A broad impressionistic survey of work in the furnaces and foundries, the shipyards and munition factories of Britain
Review DNL I Aug 12
MoI *pc* Merton Park *p* Cecil Musk *d* Montgomery Tully *m* Francis Chagrin
21 mins IWM LC NFA

Big city
A picture of living and working in London, seen through an examination of the London Transport system and some personal stories of men who depend on it
Review DNL I Aug 13
MoI *pc* Strand *p* Alexander Shaw *d* Ralph Bond
12 mins LC NFA

Bringing it home
(Food convoys. Intended for theatrical

distribution. Non-theatrical version entitled *Food convoy*)
Review FoB 1941
sp Cadbury *pc* Merton Park *d* John Lewis
19 mins NFA

Britain at bay
Made in September, 1940, this film, with commentary by J B Priestley, summed up the spirit of Britain after the fall of France. Compiled from library material. (Identical overseas version entitled *Britain on guard*)
MoI *pc* GPO *comm s* J B Priestley
8 mins IWM NFA

Britain can take it
(This is a shortened version of *London can take it* for British distribution)
Review DNL I Nov 14
MoI *pc* GPO *d* Harry Watt, Humphrey Jennings *comm s* Quentin Reynolds
5 mins IWM NFA

Britannia is a woman
(Women's war work. Intended for theatrical distribution. Non-theatrical version entitled *Women in wartime*)
Review DNL I July 6
sp British Council *pc* British Movietonews
9 mins IWM

The call for arms!
(The contribution to the war effort of two women munition workers. Anti-gossip campaign)
Review DNL I Oct 15
MoI *pc* Denham & Pinewood *d* Brian Desmond Hurst *cast* Jean Gillie, Rene Ray
5 mins NFA

Dangerous comment. *A lady indulges in some careless talk about a bombing mission.*

Channel incident
(A story set at Dunkirk)
Review DNL I Nov 5
MoI *pc* Denham & Pinewood *p* Dallas Bower *d* Anthony Asquith *cast* Peggy Ashcroft, Gordon Harker
5 mins IWM LC MOMA NFA

The circus
(National Savings)
pc Merton Park

Civilian front
(The civilians' part in winning the war)
MoI *pc* GB Instructional *d* Mary Field *comm s* E V Emmett
10 mins NFA

Coal front
A picture of coal production in a modern mine
Reviews DNL II 9, MFB VIII 7
MoI *pc* GB Instructional *d* Francis Searle *p* D Woolfe
10 mins IWM

Common heritage
(A review of the political histories of the Mediterranean countries and the present war situation)
Reviews DNL II 209, MFB VIII 139
pc World in Action *p* John Hanau *comm s* Leslie Howard, Kent Stevenson
22 mins

Curse of the swastika
(Newsreel compilation on the rise of the Nazi Party in Germany, ending with the first sea battle between the *Admiral Graf Spee* and the *Ajax* and *Exeter*)
Review MFB VII 62

pc Pathé *d* Fred Watts *sc* Vernon J Clancey
45 mins NFA

Dangerous comment
Anti-gossip. A young pilot, annoyed at not going on a raid, grouses to his fiancée, who tells a friend, who chatters at a cocktail bar. The raiders are recalled just in time. (Part of a series which includes *Now you're talking* and *All hands*)
Review DNL I May 17
MoI *pc* Ealing Studios *p* Michael Balcon *d* John Paddy Carstairs
13 mins IWM LC

Fear and Peter Brown
(Fighting fear to defeat Germany)
p Ivan Scott *d* Richard Massingham *pc* Spectator Films
16 mins IWM NFA

Food convoy
A picture of routine life, alert and tense, on board a merchant ship in convoy bringing food to Britain. (Non-theatrical version of *Bringing it home*)
Review DNL I Oct 9
sp Cadbury *pc* Merton Park *p* A Taylor *d* John Lewis
10 mins IWM

From family to farm
(Turning waste food into feeding stuffs for animals)
pc John Page *p & d* John Page *comm s* Morton King

The front line
A visit to Dover during the first month of bombardment from France, including interviews with C.D. workers and townspeople
MoI *pc* GPO *d* Harry Watt *ph* Jonah Jones
7 mins IWM NFA PAC

Furnaces of industry
The story of the production of different steel alloys for different types of munitions
MoI *pc* Merton Park *p & d* Cecil Musk
12 mins IWM LC NFA

Harvest help
(Bringing in the harvest)
MoI *pc* Merton Park

Health in war
An exposition of the plans put into operation on the outbreak of war to clear hospitals for emergencies while maintaining peacetime services. In a prologue and epilogue the film relates this story to the efforts being made before the war to improve the health services and to what must be done after the war
Reviews DNL I Dec 9, MFB VIII 111
MoI & Min of Health *pc* GPO *d* Pat Jackson *p* Harry Watt
13 mins IWM LC MOMA NFA

Her father's daughter
(Women in industry)
MoI *pc* Butcher's *d* Desmond Dickinson *cast* Alastair Sim, Jennifer Gray
5 mins NFA

Home front
(Effect of war on homes during the last nine months)
Review DNL I April 7
sp & pc CWS *d* Jiri Weiss
19 mins

A job to be done
(How the Schedule of Reserved Occupations works and the best use of civilian manpower in wartime)
Review DNL I Oct 8
MoI *pc* Shell *p* Arthur Elton *d* Donald Alexander *ph* Stanley Rodwell
10 mins LC MOMA NFA

Love on the wing
(Cartoon advertising GPO letter services)
Review DNL I Feb 12

pc GPO *d* Norman McLaren *ph* Jonah Jones, Fred Gamage
Dufaycolour

Men of the lightship
In September, 1939, the East Dudgeon Lightship in the Thames estuary was bombed and machine-gunned. The crew took to boats and died. The film re-creates this story as it happened
Review DNL I Sept 12
MoI *pc* GPO *p* Cavalcanti *d* David Macdonald
25 mins IWM LC MOMA NFA

Miss Grant goes to the door
(Shows the precautions which can be taken to hinder any enemy infiltration. Two elderly sisters help outwit a German invasion)
MoI *pc* Denham & Pinewood *d* Brian Desmond Hurst *story* Thorold Dickinson, Donald Null
7 mins IWM NFA

Miss Grant goes to the door. *Miss Grant confronts a German paratrooper disguised as a British officer.*

Musical poster no. 1
(Abstract film on the theme of careless talk)
Review DNL I Oct 14
MoI *pc* Crown *d* Len Lye
5 mins colour NFA

Neighbours under fire
A picture of how, after the first raids, people got together and improvised food, clothes, shelter and rest for their bombed-out neighbours
Review DNL I Dec 7
MoI *pc* Strand *d* Ralph Bond *assoc p* Basil Wright
7 mins IWM LC MOMA NFA

The new Britain. *Children in a play-school.*

The new Britain
(Twenty years of British achievement)
Review DNL I Aug 13
MoI *pc* Strand *p* Alexander Shaw *d* Ralph Keene *comm w* Graham Greene
10 mins IWM NFA

Now you're talking
The first of three anti-gossip films made for the Ministry of Information in 1939 by Ealing Studios. Each film tells a dramatic story of disaster caused or narrowly avoided. In *Now you're talking* a worker at a government research station talks about some guns salvaged from a German plane for examination. (See also *All hands* and *Dangerous comment*)
Review DNL I May 17
MoI *pc* Ealing Studios *p* Michael Balcon *d* John Paddy Carstairs *cast* Sebastian Shaw, Dorothy Hyson
12 mins IWM LC NFA

Nurse!
A survey of the work being done by women in all branches of nursing in peace and war and of the training given to them
Reviews DNL I Oct 8, MFB VIII 111
MoI *pc* Pathé
9 mins IWM NFA

The new Britain. *Bridges in Newcastle—examples of Britain's prowess in the field.*

On guard in the air
(Britain's air defences)
pc GB Instructional
14 mins NFA

Owner comes aboard
(National Savings. A visit to a destroyer to see how the money is spent)
MoI *pc* Spectator *p* Ivan Scott *d* Alex Bryce *cast* Charles Doe
5 mins IWM

Ports
(British ports)
MoI *pc* GB Instructional

Religion and the people
(Religion in a democracy; social work carried out in Britain by the different religious faiths)
Review DNL I Oct 8
MoI *pc* British Films *assoc p* Arthur Elton *p & d* Andrew Buchanan
15 mins LC NFA

Salvage with a smile
A serious appeal, in light form, to housewives to save paper, bones and metal
Review KW 29.8.40
MoI & Min of Supply *pc* Ealing Studios *p* Cavalcanti *d* Adrian Brunel
7 mins IWM NFA

Save your way to victory
('Lend to defend' slogan of the National Savings Ctte)
Review KW 25.7.40

The scaremongers
(Anti-gossip. Also known as *Miss Know-all*)
MoI *pc* Denham & Pinewood *d* Graham Cutts *ass d* E J Holding *ed* Sidney Stone *ph* C Friese-Greene *cast* Mark Daly, Martita Hunt
5 mins IWM NFA

Seedtime to harvest
The year's work on an English farm
pc Tida
13 mins NFA

Shipbuilders
Key workers from a number of shipyards discuss with Emmett, of GB News, their job of building the ships to win the war at sea
MoI *pc* GB Instructional *d* Leon Schauder
10 mins IWM

66 northbound
(Road transport in wartime)
MoI *pc* Spectator

Speed up and welfare
Workers in an aircraft factory organise their own discipline and welfare and defence against raids and invasion. (Overseas version entitled *Wartime factory*)

Review DNL I Nov 14
MoI *pc* Strand *assoc p* Arthur Elton *p* Alexander Shaw *d* Edgar Anstey
10 mins NFA

These children are safe
(How British children were being cared for during the autumn of 1939)
Reviews DNL I Feb 12, FoB 1940
British Council *pc* Strand *p* Alexander Shaw *ph* Jo Jago *m* William Alwyn
18 mins NFA

They also serve
A tribute to women doing their ordinary work to keep a home going for husbands and children at work and in the Forces
MoI *pc* Realist *p* John Taylor *d* Ruby Grierson *ph* A E Jeakins
8 mins IWM LC MOMA NFA PAC

Thoroughbred
(The many roles of the horse in British life—farming, racing, transport)
Review DNL I Feb 6
British Council *pc* Pathé *d* A Curtice

Tomorrow is theirs
Two stories of the ways in which secondary schools faced the problem of providing a good education in spite of the war
Review MFB XI 84
MoI & Board of Educ *pc* Strand *assoc p* Arthur Elton *p* Alexander Shaw *d* James Carr
10 mins IWM LC NFA

Transfer of skill
Skilled craftsmen of peace-time apply their skill to essential war production. The film shows in detail half-a-dozen examples of this transfer of skill
Review DNL I Nov 15
MoI *pc* Shell *p* Arthur Elton *d* Geoffrey Bell
10 mins IWM LC NFA

Village school
A picture of the school at Ashley Green, Bucks, increased in size by evacuated children and looked after by a woman teacher (who wrote and speaks the commentary) and one woman assistant. (Shortened version *Ashley Green goes to school*)
Reviews DNL I Oct 8, MFB XI 110
pc Strand for Min of Information with Board of Educ *d* John Eldridge *p* Alexander Shaw *asst p* Arthur Elton
10 mins IWM LC MOMA NFA

War and order
The story of the police in war-time, from routine work at the station helping people in trouble to the special jobs done during a raid
Reviews DNL II 9, MFB VIII 7
MoI *pc* GPO *d* C Hasse *p & sc* Harry Watt
12 mins IWM LC MOMA NARS NFA PAC

War comes to London
(The situation in London immediately before the declaration of war and the first days after, showing the evacuation of children, distribution of gasmasks etc)
Reviews DNL I March 6, FoB 1940
British Council *pc* British Movietonews *p & d* Gerald Sanger
10 mins NFA

Welfare of the workers
(The Ministry of Labour's efforts to safeguard workers in wartime)
Review DNL I Nov 14
pc GPO *d* Humphrey Jennings *p* Harry Watt
9 mins LC MOMA NFA PAC

Westward ho!
(The evacuation of children during the early years of the war)
Review KW 18.7.40

MoI *pc* Denham & Pinewood *d* Thorold Dickinson *ph* Desmond Dickinson
5 mins IWM

White battle front
The story of the unceasing fight carried on by scientists and the army medical services to prevent diseases and to look after the wounded
Reviews DNL 1 Oct 8, MFB VIII 111
MoI & War Office *pc* Seven League *d* Hans Nieter *assoc p* Basil Wright *ph* Bernard Browne *comm w* Arthur Calder Marshall
10 mins 1WM LC

Women in uniform
Reviews KW 8.2.40, TC 6.2.40

Women in wartime
(Non-theatrical version of *Britannia is a woman*)
Review FoB 1940
British Council *pc* British Movietonews
9 mins LC NFA

Yesterday's over your shoulder
(Encourages men to attend the government-organised, free 6-month courses in engineering so that they can make a greater contribution to the war effort)
MoI *pc* Denham & Pinewood *d* Thorold Dickinson *ph* Desmond Dickinson *cast* Robertson Hare, Joyce Barbour
7 mins MOMA NFA

HOMEFRONT – Scotland

Dundee
(How the jute industry has caused first the prosperity and then the decline of Dundee)
Review DNL I May 6
pc Scottish Films *d* Donald Alexander *ph* Graham Thomson
19 mins

HOMEFRONT – Instructional

Britain's youth
A talk by C B Fry on the value of games in promoting health, discipline and pleasure
Review DNL I Sept 13
MoI *pc* Strand *p* Alexander Shaw *d* Jack Ellitt *comm w* C B Fry
13 mins IWM NFA

Choose cheese
(Food value of cheese)
Reviews DNL I Sept 12, MFB VII 116, MFB XI 49
sp British Commercial Gas Company *pc* Realist *p* John Taylor *d* Ruby Grierson *ph* A E Jeakins *comm s* Alec Clunes
5 mins IWM

Food for thought
(The nutritional value of various foods)
MoI *pc* Ealing Studios *p* John Croydon *d* Adrian Brunel *cast* Mabel Constanduros, Muriel George
5 mins NFA

Mr Borland thinks again
(The importance of silage to farmers)
Review KW 29.8.40
MoI *pc* British Films *d* Paul Rotha *cast* Herbert Lomas, Emlyn Williams, Beatrix Lehmann
5 mins NFA

Oatmeal porridge
The film stresses the food value of oatmeal and shows how to make good porridge
Reviews DNL I Dec 7, MFB XI 36
MoI & Min of Food *pc* Verity *d* Jay Gardner Lewis *sc* Maxwell Munden *ph* S D Onions
7 mins NFA

The obedient flame
(The theory and practice of domestic gas cooking)
Reviews DNL I Jan 8, MFB IX 95

British Commercial Gas Assoc *pc* Science Films *p* Arthur Elton *d* Norman McLaren *ph* Frank Goodliffe
18 mins NFA

Odd jobs in the garden
(Weedkilling and use of fertilisers for cuttings)
Reviews DNL I Dec 9, MFB VII 193
pc Plant Protection
7 mins silent colour

Oh, whiskers!
A film made to teach children under ten the importance of cleanliness and eating good food
Min of Health *pc* GPO
10 mins NFA

Plan for living
(What everyone should know about diet)
British Commercial Gas Assoc *pc* GB Instructional *d* Donald Carter
20 mins NFA

Raw material is war material
(Waste paper)
Min of Supply *pc* Crighton Film & Radio Publicity

Six foods for fitness
(The value and preparation of milk, cheese, fish, oatmeal, green vegetables and potatoes)
Review DNL I Oct 8
MoI *pc* Realist *p* John Taylor *d* Ruby Grierson *ph* A E Jeakins *comm w* Geoffrey Bell
10 mins

Steaming
How to improvise a steamer so as to save fuel and time
Reviews DNL I Dec 7, MFB XI 144
MoI & Min of Food *pc* Verity *d* Jay Gardner Lewis *ph* S D Onions *sc & comm s* Maxwell Munden
7 mins NFA

Thrift
(How waste products on the farm can be put to good use)
Reviews DNL I Apr 6, MFB VII 137
National Federation of Women's Institutes *pc* GB Instructional *d* Mary Field *comm w* Peter Herbert
14 mins

Transfer of power
(The transfer of power by means of the lever from the wooden cog-wheels of wind- and water-mills to the case-hardened gears of motor-cars and turbines)
Reviews DNL I Feb 12, MFB VII 142
sp & pc Shell *p* Arthur Elton *d* Geoffrey Bell *ph* Sidney Beadle *anim* Francis Rodker
20 mins NFA

We've got to get rid of the rats
(The rat menace)
Reviews DNL II 9, MFB VIII 7
MoI *pc* Strand *d* James Carr *assoc p* Arthur Elton, Bill Dalton
5 mins

What's for dinner?
(Casserole cooking)
Reviews DNL I Sept 12, MFB VII 167
British Commercial Gas Company *pc* Realist *p* John Taylor *d* Ruby Grierson *ph* A E Jeakins *assoc p* Edgar Anstey *comm s* Alec Clunes
10 mins NFA

Winter storage
(Storing roots and seeds during the winter)
Reviews DNL I Dec 9, MFB VII 193
pc Plant Protection
7 mins silent colour

Young folks show the way
(School savings)
Review KW 25.7.40
pc British Movietonews

HOMEFRONT – Specialised instructional

Airscrew
An exposition of the making of an airscrew, from the inspection of the raw material to the final check by the Aircraft Inspection Department, and of the mechanism of a variable-pitch airscrew
Review DNL I Sept 12
pc Shell *sp* Petroleum Films Bureau *p* Arthur Elton *d* Grahame Tharp *diagrams* Francis Rodker *ph* Sidney Beadle
22 mins MOMA NFA

Farm tractors
(Mechanised agriculture)
pc Shell

Silage
An instructional film for farmers on how to make and use silage for winter cattle feeding to make up for shortages of imported feeding stuffs
Review DNL I Oct 8
MoI & Min of Ag *pc* Films of GB *p & d* Andrew Buchanan
21 mins

HOMEFRONT – Air raid precautions

Fire
(Training and functions of the AFS)
pc British Films

Fire bombs–how to fight them yourselves
pc GPO Film Unit
IWM

Incendiary bomb training
(The best way to deal with this type of bomb)
Review MFB VIII 24
MoI & Home Security *pc* Universal
17 mins

HOMEFRONT – Wartime social services

Mother and child
A story of the maternity and child-welfare services, showing their increased importance in wartime
Reviews DNL I Oct 9, MFB VIII 111
MoI & Min of Health *pc* Realist *assoc p* Basil Wright *d* Frank Sainsbury *ph* A E Jeakins *cast* Barbara Mullen
10 mins LC NFA

FIGHTING SERVICES & CAMPAIGNS

AA gun emplacements
(Equipment and procedure at typical gun sites in Britain's anti-aircraft defences)
MoI *pc* GB News
9 mins IWM

Air communique
(Checking up enemy plane casualties by RAF intelligence)
Review DNL I Dec 7
MoI *pc* Crown *d* Ralph Elton *p* Harry Watt
5 mins LC MOMA NFA

Coastal defence
A survey of the part played by each of the Services in the defences against invasion
Review DNL I Oct 9
MoI *pc* British Movietonews *p* Gerald Sanger *comm s* John Snagge
11 mins IWM LC NFA

Fighter pilot
The Spitfire pilot in action, his machine, equipment and job. Commentary written and spoken by Air Chief Marshal Sir Philip Joubert
MoI *pc* British Movietonews *p* Gerald Sanger *d* Raymond Perrin
8 mins IWM LC NFA

Fighting pioneers
pc GPO Film Unit
IWM

Into the blue
Training men in classroom, link trainer, and in the air to be pilots and observers in the RAF
MoI *pc* GB Instructional
10 mins IWM LC

Italy beware
(Describes Allied strength in the Mediterranean. Overseas version entitled *Drums of the desert*)
Review DNL I July 7
MoI *pc* British Paramount News *p* G T Cummins
14 mins NFA (overseas version)

The King's men
The King reviews men of the Army, Royal Navy and Royal Air Force
MoI *pc* British Movietonews *p* Gerald Sanger
7 mins IWM NFA

A nation springs to arms
(The beginning of the war and the Army in training)
MoI *pc* British Movietonews
11 mins NFA

Squadron 992. *Training in balloon handling procedures.*

Raising soldiers
First stages in training men for the Army
MoI *pc* British Movietonews *sc* Gerald Sanger *comm s* Leslie Mitchell
12 mins IWM

Sea fort
Life on one of the sea forts, garrisoned by a surprising mixture of units, that guard the approach to important ports
MoI *pc* Ealing Studios *p* Cavalcanti *d* Ian Dalrymple *ph* Ernest Palmer *comm s* Patric Curwen
7 mins IWM LC NFA

Squadron 992
(The balloon barrage in training in England and their defence of the Forth bridge. Film made in 1940)
Review DNL I May 6
MoI *pc* GPO *p* Cavalcanti *d* Harry Watt *ph* Jonah Jones *ed* R Q McNaughton
25 mins IWM MOMA NFA

Undersea patrol
(Submarines)
MoI *pc* British Paramount News *p* G T Cummins
6 mins NFA

The voice of the guns
(Armaments and the different types of guns in use by the Allies)
Review DNL I July 6
MoI *pc* Pathé
10 mins NFA

DOMINIONS & COLONIES – General

African skyway
The air route pioneered by Imperial Airways from Cairo to Cape Town including visits to some of the towns along the route
Review DNL I Feb 12
sp Imperial Airways *pc* Strand *p* Donald Taylor *ph* Jo Jago *ed* Jack Ellitt
30 mins NFA

Children of the Empire
An Empire tour. From the Port of London to Africa, India, Malaya, British New Guinea, Australia, New Zealand and Canada, and back again to London. (Intended for African audiences)
pc Colonial Film Unit
9 mins silent

Food from the Empire
(The Dominions' and Colonies' contribution to British food supply)
Review DNL I Oct 9
MoI *pc* Merton Park *p & d* Theodore Thumwood
10 mins IWM NFA

Wings over the Empire
(How aviation helps the administrator, agricultural expert, businessman and the man who wants to keep in touch with his friends on the other side of the earth)
Reviews DNL I Jan 7, MFB VI 177
pc Strand *p* Alexander Shaw *ed* Stuart Legg
MOMA

DOMINIONS & COLONIES – Africa

Men of Africa
The principles of British colonial administration are shown in the health, education and agricultural services in East Africa. British administrators try to maintain native traditions when they are valuable and to associate Africans in the administration so that their peoples shall be able to assume full responsibility for their own well being
Reviews DNL I June 7, FoB 1940, MFB XIII 72
sp Colonial Office *pc* Strand *p* Basil Wright *d* Alexander Shaw
20 mins IWM NFA

DOMINIONS & COLONIES – Canada

Atlantic patrol
Life on board a Canadian destroyer on patrol guarding the North Atlantic route. (*Canada carries on* series)
pc National Film Board of Canada *d* Stuart Legg
10 mins IWM

Canada at war
A picture of how Canada in 1940 was mobilising its war resources, showing recruiting and training of men, industrial

resources and production, and administrative planning. Canada's relations with the United States, at that time neutral, are also reviewed. (*March of Time* fifth year no 12, British series; vol 6 no 8, US series)
Reviews DNL I May 7, MFB VII 69, KYB 1941
pc March of Time
18 mins IWM NFA

Front of steel
(Canada's munitions drive)
pc National Film Board of Canada *p* Stuart Legg *d* J McDougall
5 mins

Home front
(Canada's industrial effort and the part played by women. *Canada carries on* series)
Review DNL I Nov 14
pc National Film Board of Canada *d* Stanley Hawes
10 mins

Letter from Aldershot
(The Canadian Expeditionary Force in Britain. *Canada at war* series)
Review DNL I Nov 14
pc Realist & National Film Board of Canada *d* John Taylor
10 mins IWM LC

Wings of youth
The story of the growth of the Royal Canadian Air Force in the years between the wars and of the operation of the Empire Air Training Scheme, showing the first stages in training of men from all parts of the Empire. (*Canada carries on* series)
Reviews DNL I Dec 9, MFB VIII 21
pc National Film Board of Canada & Audio Pictures *p* Raymond Spottiswoode, Stuart Legg *d* Roger Barlow
18 mins IWM

DOMINIONS & COLONIES – South Africa

Fighters of the Veld
Men of South Africa's Army, Navy and Air Force in training before going into action in East and North Africa and on the vital sea route round the Cape of Good Hope; with a speech by the Prime Minister, Field-Marshal Smuts
Review DNL I Nov 15
sp South African Govt *pc* African Film Productions
22 mins IWM NFA

OVERSEAS DISTRIBUTION

Air communique

All hands

America moves up
This film was not issued in Britain. (The first of a series of on-the-spot reports of Americans in the firing line entitled *Front line camera*)
pc Crown *d* Ralph Elton *ph* E Catford *ed* D Ginsberg
13 mins IWM LC

Ashley Green goes to school

Behind the guns

Big city

Britain on guard
(Identical overseas version of *Britain at bay*)

Britain shoulders arms
(Britain between the wars and the preparations for the new struggle. Overseas distribution only)
Reviews DNL I March 6, FoB 1940
sp British Council *pc* British Paramount News *p & d* G T Cummins
10 mins NFA

Britain's youth

The British Army
(Overseas distribution only)
pc Colonial Film Unit
23 mins

British made
How, as a result of technical developments in the last century, the old apprenticeship system, foundation of British craftsmanship, merged into an even closer application of skill to material
Reviews MFB XV 148, FoB 1940
sp British Council *pc* Tida *d* George Pearson *ph* Jonah Jones *ed* R Q McNaughton *sd* Ken Cameron *m* Ernst Meyer
9 mins NFA

British power
(This newsreel compilation was not seen in Britain)
MoI *pc* Universal News *p* Clifford Jeapes
10 mins IWM NFA

The call for arms!

Cargo for Ardrossan
(The importance of oil in the modern world with examples from Scottish life)
Reviews DNL I 12, FoB 1940, MFB XIV 104
pc Realist *d* Ruby Grierson *asst d* Gerald Keen *ph* A E Jeakins
18 mins NFA

Channel incident
(A story set at Dunkirk)

Children from overseas
(Part of the *Canada carries on* series. Only distributed overseas)
pc National Film Board of Canada *p* Stuart Legg *d* Stanley Hawes
9 mins

The city
(The need for planning in London and especially the proper planning of the city's transport system)
Reviews DNL I Jan 7, FoB 1940, MFB VI 151
pc GPO *p* Cavalcanti *d* Ralph Elton *ph* H E Fowle *comm s* Herbert Hodge

Coal front

Coastal defence

Copper web
The conversion of the trunk telephone system to underground working
Reviews FoB 1940, S&S VI 203
sp GPO *d* Maurice Harvey *ph* H E Fowle *ed* G Diamond
11 mins NFA

Dangerous comment

Drums of the desert
(Overseas version of *Italy beware*)
IWM (silent version)

Empire around the Atlantic
(Diagrams show the development of the countries around the Atlantic Ocean since 1815)
Review FoB 1940
pc GB Instructional
11 mins

The Empire at work
(Intended for African audiences)
pc Colonial Film Unit
21 mins

English and African life
(By using a series of familiar African subjects as pictorial captions to their English counterparts, this film imparts elementary knowledge of some features of life in England. Intended for African audiences)
pc Colonial Film Unit
6 mins silent

Fighter pilot

Foretelling the weather

From the seven seas
Overseas distribution. (Britain's west coast ports and their role in keeping open Britain's vital links with the outside world)
MoI *pc* GB Instructional *d* Leon Schauder
11 mins IWM

The front line

Furnaces of industry

Goofer trouble

The green

Healing waters
The Romans discovered the healing properties of the waters at Bath, but the Roman baths were forgotten until the early 18th century when they were rebuilt and the city replanned. Before long Bath had become the best planned city in Europe
Review FoB 1940
sp British Council *pc* Strand-Tida *d* W B Pollard *sc* Donald Taylor *ph* George Noble, Fred Gamage *cast* Nina Keech & Bath Operatic Dramatic Society
10 mins NFA (Under title *Of all the gay places*)

Health in war

Her father's daughter

Heritage for defence
(Intended for African audiences)
pc Colonial Film Unit
10 mins

How the telephone works

The islanders
The importance of communications in the development of island communities. Contrasting Eriskay in the Outer Hebrides with Guernsey
Review FoB 1940
sp & pc GPO *p* J B Holmes *d* Maurice Harvey *asst d* S McAllister *ph* Harry Rignold, Jonah Jones *m* Darius Milhaud
23 mins MOMA NFA

Italy beware

Job in a million

A job to be done

The King's men

London can take it
(Intended for overseas distribution. Shorter British version entitled *Britain can take it*)
Review DNL I Nov 14
MoI *pc* GPO *d* Harry Watt, Humphrey Jennings *ph* Jonah Jones, H E Fowle *comm s & w* Quentin Reynolds *ed* S McAllister
10 mins BFI IWM NFA PAC

London can take it. *A street scene after a night of bombing.*

London river

London's reply to Germany's false claims
(Possibly not released)

London can take it. *A woman looks through her broken window.*

MoI *pc* GB News *nar* Quentin Reynolds
8 mins NFA

Men of the lightship

Men who work

Merchant ship
Showing in detail the loading of cargo into merchant ships in London docks. (Film made pre-1940)
Review FoB 1940
16 mins silent

Miss Grant goes to the door

Mr English at home
(Life in an ordinary English home. Intended for African audiences)
pc Colonial Film Unit
27 mins silent

Modern Bath
The history of this city to the present day. Film made pre-1940
Review FoB 1940
15 mins

Mother and child

Musical poster no. 1

Neighbours under fire

Night mail
A dramatic account of the journey of the 'Postal Special' to Scotland. Film made in 1936. Silent version entitled *Postal special*
Reviews FoB 1940, MFB III 36
pc GPO *supervision* John Grierson, Harry Watt *d* Basil Wright *m* Benjamin Britten *sc* W H Auden
23 mins MOMA NFA

Now you're talking

Nurse!

Progress in the colonies—African hospital
(Reception and treatment of a street accident case, with a look at the X-ray Dept. in a Lagos hospital. Intended for African audiences)
pc Colonial Film Unit
14 mins silent

Protection of fruit
The story of co-operation between entomologists, mycologists, chemists and farmers in controlling and destroying insects and diseases which destroy fruit
Reviews DNL I Feb 12, FoB 1940, MFB VII 138
sp Technical Products *pc* Shell *p* Arthur Elton *d* Grahame Tharp *ph* Stanley Rodwell, Erwin Hillier
19 mins

Raising air fighters
(Training pilots)
Review FoB 1940
British Council *pc* British Paramount News
17 mins IWM NFA

Raising soldiers

Religion and the people

Ring of steel
Not seen in Britain. (British defences)
Review DNL I June 8

MoI *pc* British Paramount News *p* G T Cummins
40 mins

Royal review
(The King and his people—events in the national life where the King was present, between 1937-39)
Review FoB 1940
pc British Paramount News
13 mins IWM NFA

Salvage with a smile

Sea fort

Shipbuilders

Silage

6.30 collection
The work of a city sorting office. Film made in 1934
Review FoB 1940, MFB I 37 76
GPO *pc* GPO *p* John Grierson *d* Edgar Anstey, Harry Watt
15 mins NFA

Squadron 992

The story of cotton
Intended for African audiences. (Film made in 1939)
pc GPO (Colonial Film Unit)
11 mins NFA

Swinging the Lambeth Walk
(An experimental film setting colour to music)
Reviews DNL I Mar 6, FoB 1940
British Council *pc* Realist *p & d* Len Lye
3 mins colour NFA

These children are safe

They also serve

Tomorrow is theirs

Transfer of skill

Ulster
A survey of the natural and industrial resources of Northern Ireland from flax and linen to shipbuilding and aircraft manufacture
Reviews DNL II 9, FoB 1941, MFB VIII 49
sp British Council *pc* Strand *p* Alexander Shaw *d* Ralph Keene *ph* Jo Jago, George Noble
12 mins NFA

Undersea patrol

Voice of the guns

War and order

War comes to London

Wartime factory

Welfare of the workers

What of the children?
American version of *These children are safe*
LC

White battle front

Women in wartime
Non-theatrical version of *Britannia is a woman*
Review FoB 1940
British Council *pc* British Movietonews
9 mins LC NFA

World exchange
The international telephone exchange in London
Review FoB 1940
GPO
11 mins silent

Yesterday's over your shoulder

NEWSREEL TRAILERS

Anderson shelter (1)
MoI & Home Security *pc* Pathé

Anderson shelter (2)
MoI & Home Security *pc* Universal

ARP services
MoI

Britain's citizen army
MoI

Do the job well
MoI

Gas masks
MoI & Home Security *pc* GB Instructional

Get under cover
MoI

Goofer trouble
(Take cover trailer)
MoI *pc* Denham & Pinewood *d* Maurice Elvey
5 mins MOMA NFA

How you can deal with incendiary bombs
MoI

Local Defence Volunteers
MoI & War Office *pc* British Movietonews

Nurses urgently wanted
MoI

Our island fortress
MoI

Post early
MoI & GPO *pc* Pathé

Speed the plough
MoI

The WAAFs are proud today
MoI

What to do in an air raid
MoI & Home Security *pc* separate version made by each newsreel company

Women wanted
MoI

You can't be too careful
MoI

Your home as an air raid shelter
MoI & Home Security *pc* Universal

1941

HOMEFRONT – General

Any old iron
An appeal to works managers, farmers and householders to turn out scrap metal for munitions. Intended for theatrical distribution. (Non-theatrical version entitled *Feed the furnaces*)
MoI & Min of Supply *pc* Merton Park
5 mins NFA

Battle of the books
While the Nazis try to destroy knowledge by burning books, in Britain ways are found of making more books available to more people. Mobile libraries, books for the Services, cheap editions and books by specialists at popular prices all serve to meet the increasing demand for knowledge
Reviews DNL II 207, MFB VIII 139
MoI *pc* Rotha Productions *p* Paul Rotha *d* Jack Chambers *ph* Peter Hennessy *comm w* Henry Ainley
7 mins IWM NFA

Buried treasure
The lay-out of faces, roads and ventilation systems is shown by diagrams and the work done by each type of mineworker is explained. The mechanised pit shown is worked on a three-shift system. During the first shift the coal is undercut with electric cutters; during the second the coal is loosened, moved by conveyor belt from the face and taken in tubs along the main haulage roads to the cages and thence to the surface, where it is sorted and washed. The third shift moves all the machinery into position for the next day's work
sp Coal Utilisation Joint Council *pc* GB Instructional *supervision* John Grierson, Arthur Elton *d* Donald Carter
33 mins NFA

Canteen on wheels
A night in a blitz with a YMCA mobile canteen bringing refreshments to an AA battery, ARP workers, firemen and shelterers. (Shorter theatrical version titled *Mobile canteen*)

Reviews DNL II 47, MFB VIII 36
Empire Tea Bureau & MoI *pc* Verity *p* Basil Wright *d* Jay Gardner Lewis *ph* Bernard Browne
10 mins IWM

Cargoes
A voyage aboard a freighter of the British Merchant Service. (Short version of *SS Ionian*)
Review DNL I Oct 14
pc Tida *d* Humphrey Jennings
8 mins NFA

Christmas under fire
(London during the Christmas of 1940)
Reviews DNL II 29, MFB VIII 7
MoI *pc* Crown *p* Harry Watt *d* C Hasse *comm s* Quentin Reynolds
5 mins IWM LC NFA

The dawn guard. *Home Guard men, Bernard Miles and Percy Walsh discuss the values that Britain is fighting for.*

Citizen's army
An account of the duties and elementary training of the Home Guard. (Longer, modified version of *Home Guard*)
MoI *pc* Strand *p & d* Donald Taylor *assoc d* Ivan Moffat *ph* Charles Marlborough
10 mins IWM MOMA

The dawn guard
Two Home Guards on duty in the country talk about the war and the new world we are fighting to build
Reviews DNL II 28, MFB VIII 21
MoI *pc* Charter *p* John Boulting *d* Roy Boulting *ed* Jack Harris *original idea* Anna Reiner *cast* Bernard Miles, Percy Walsh
7 mins IWM NFA

Dig for victory
An appeal to everyone to get some land and grow vegetables for the good of the country and their own better health
Review MFB VIII 139
MoI & Min of Ag *pc* Spectator *p* Michael Hankinson *assoc p* Edgar Anstey
7 mins IWM LC NARS NFA

English village
Life in an English village
pc Colonial Film Unit
14 mins

Farmer's day
A day's work on a modern English dairy farm
Reviews FoB 1941, KW 28.11.40
pc Selwyn *p* C A Ridley *d* Brian Smith
16 mins NFA

Feed the furnaces
An appeal to works managers, farmers and householders to turn out scrap metal for munitions. Theatrical version entitled *Any old iron*
MoI & Min of Supply *pc* Merton Park
9 mins IWM

A few ounces a day
A demonstration, by means of animated Isotype diagrams, of the importance of salvage in offsetting shortages of materials for war factories due to loss of merchant ships in the Battle of the Atlantic
Reviews DNL II 207, MFB VIII 140
MoI *pc* Rotha Productions *p* Paul Rotha *designs* Isotype Institute *sd* Ernst Meyer *comm w* Henry Hallatt *d* Donald Alexander
7 mins IWM LC NFA

Germany calling
(A film ridiculing the Nazis by editing sequences of goose-stepping soldiers, Hitler and party rallies to the music of the 'Lambeth Walk'. Released through the newsreels without MoI acknowledgement)
MoI *pc* Spectator *ed* C A Ridley
2 mins IWM MOMA NFA

Goodbye yesterday
MoI *pc* Realist *p* Basil Wright *d* John Taylor *ph* A E Jeakins *comm w* Colin Wills

Healing waters

The heart of Britain
A visit to the blitzed areas in the industrial Midlands and North. A factory firewatcher and a Coventry WVS official talk about their jobs. Lancashire mill girls show how to pass the time in a shelter. In Manchester the Hallé Orchestra plays Beethoven's Fifth Symphony; and the Leeds Choral Society sings 'The Messiah'. War production never stops. (Film made in 1941. Released in the USA as *This is England*)
Reviews MFB VIII 21, DNL II 48 (under the title *This is England*)
MoI *pc* Crown *d* Humphrey Jennings *comm s* Ed Murrow *p* Ian Dalrymple *ph* H E Fowle *ed* S McAllister
10 mins IWM NFA

Home Guard
In a Hertfordshire inn Bernard Miles, as a Home Guard, talks about a week's course at a Home Guard training school. (Longer modified version made entitled *Citizen's army*)
Reviews DNL II 107, MFB VIII 60
MoI *pc* Strand *p & d* Donald Taylor *assoc d* Ivan Moffat *ph* George Noble *cast* Bernard Miles
8 mins NFA

Hospital nurse
An appeal to young girls to take up nursing as a wartime job and a career for life, showing in outline the training given and the work to be done
MoI & Min of Health *pc* GB Screen Services *d* Francis Searle
8 mins LC NFA

Island people
How six people representative of various types spend Saturday
Review DNL I April 6
sp British Council *pc* Realist *p* John Taylor *d* Philip Leacock, John Taylor *ph* A E Jeakins
10 mins NFA

It comes from coal
An essay on synthetic substances derived from coal, dealing particularly with plastics used in aircraft gun-turrets and M and B 693, the famous medical drug
Review DNL I Nov 14
sp British Commercial Gas Assoc *pc* Realist *p* Edgar Anstey *d* Paul Fletcher
12 mins

Lady be kind
(Billeting civilian workers)
Reviews DNL II 147, MFB VIII 106
MoI *pc* British National *p* John Corfield *d* Rodney Ackland *script* Rodney Ackland, Arthur Boys *cast* Muriel George
8 mins NFA

Living with strangers
A discussion of some of the problems of evacuation and of various solutions which were attempted
Review DNL II 149
MoI & Min of Health *pc* Realist *assoc p* Basil Wright *d* Frank Sainsbury *ph* A E Jeakins, Jo Jago *p* John Taylor
12 mins IWM NFA PAC

London river
The River Thames, key to London's importance as a centre of commerce and government
Reviews DNL I April 7, FoB 1940
sp British Council *pc* British Films
10 mins NFA

Machines and men
From a blitzed factory to four Yorkshire engineers came the corroded, distorted remains of an essential machine imported from America. The men had never worked with it and there were no blue-prints. The film shows how they got the machine to work again so that production should not be held up
sp CWS *pc* CWS Film Unit *d* George Wynn *sc* John Baines *comm s* Wilfred Pickles
10 mins IWM LC

Mediaeval village
At Laxton the main features of the communal, open-field system of the Middle Ages still survive and function efficiently. The film shows how the land is farmed and the work of the Juries elected by the tenants to see that the land is farmed properly and the rights of each tenant protected. It presents a picture of the beginnings of self-government as well as of farming. (Film made in 1936)
Reviews DNL I Oct 15, MFB IV 22
pc GB Instructional *d* Mary Field
20 mins NFA

Merchant seamen
A merchant ship in convoy is sunk by torpedo. The crew are rescued and later join another ship. A youngster in the crew has meanwhile taken a gunnery course. After a nerve-racking night, fogbound, the convoy is again attacked by a submarine
Reviews DNL II 88, MFB VIII 60
MoI *pc* Crown *p* Cavalcanti *d* J B Holmes *assis d* Ralph Elton *ph* H E Fowle *ed* Richard McNaughton *settings* Edward Carrick *m* Constant Lambert
24 mins IWM NFA

Merchant ship
Showing in detail the loading of cargo into merchant ships in London docks. (Film made pre-1940)
Review FoB 1940
16 mins silent

Mr Proudfoot shows a light
A warning to those who think black-out is not really so important
Review MFB VIII 49
MoI *pc* 20th Century Fox *d* Herbert Mason *sc* Sidney Gilliatt *ph* Arthur Crabtree *cast* Sidney Howard, Muriel George, Irene Handl, Michael Wilding *p* Edward Black
8 mins IWM MOMA NFA

Mobile canteen
(Providing meals during the blitz. See also *Canteen on wheels*, longer non-theatrical version)
MoI *pc* Verity *assoc p* Basil Wright *d* Jay Gardner Lewis *ph* Bernard Browne
14 mins NFA

Modern Bath
The history of this city to the present day. Film made pre-1940
Review FoB 1940
15 mins

New acres
The story of the second great ploughing-up campaign of millions of acres, illustrated by typical examples in several parts of the country
Reviews DNL II 167, MFB VIII 122
MoI & Min of Ag *pc* Shell *p* Edgar Anstey *d* R K Neilson Baxter *ph* Stanley Rodwell *sd* W S Bland *cast* Herbert Lomas
9 mins IWM LC NFA

The new bread
The national wheatmeal loaf
MoI *pc* Merton Park
7 mins

Night watch
(ARP workers)
Reviews DNL II 128, MFB VIII 90
MoI *pc* Strand *p & d* Donald Taylor *assoc p* Ralph Bond *sc* Rodney Ackland, Reg Groves *ph* George Noble, Lionel Banes *cast* Ann Firth, Cyril Chamberlain
5 mins IWM.

Our school
Bampton School, Devon, is a kind of rural senior school where lessons spring from and are related to the character and work of the village. A London school was evacuated to Bampton and found it had something to learn about education
Reviews DNL II 47, MFB VIII 37
MoI & Board of Educ *pc* Realist *p* Paul Rotha *d* Donald Alexander
17 mins NFA

Out of the night
Training of blind people in Britain for interesting and useful careers
Reviews DNL II 48, MFB VIII 37, FoB 1941
British Council *pc* Realist *p* John Taylor *d* Max Anderson
10 mins NFA

The owner goes aloft
(National Savings. The visit of a citizen to an RAF station to see how his savings are used)
Review MFB IX 51
MoI *pc* Spectator *d* Ivan Scott *cast* Charles Doe
6 mins IWM LC NFA

Oxford
Student life in the university city
Review FoB 1941
pc Strand *exec p* Donald Taylor *p* Alexander Shaw *d* Ralph Bond *asst d* Charles de Lautour *sc* Hugh Gray *comm w* Reg Groves *comm s* Leslie Mitchell
8 mins NFA

Post 23
At their wardens' post men and women get to know each other and the people living in their district. They see what they can do for each other in wartime and realise that the future will also depend on the co-operation of ordinary people like themselves
Review DNL II 209
MoI & Min of Home Security *pc* Strand *p* Donald Taylor *d* Ralph Bond *ph* Charles Marlborough *cast* John Longden
10 mins IWM NFA

Protection of fruit

Queen's messengers
The story of the mobile canteens organised by the Ministry of Food which are rushed to blitzed areas to provide food for the bombed-out
Reviews DNL II 129, MFB VIII 90
MoI & Min of Food *pc* Strand *p & d* Jay Gardner Lewis *assoc p* Basil Wright
7 mins IWM LC NFA

Red Cross in action
A survey of the work done by the Red Cross and St John War Organisation, including the work done for prisoners of war
Review MFB VIII 60
Red Cross & St John *pc* British Movietonews *p* Gerald Sanger
10 mins

Sailors without uniform
From fishing villages and towns come the men who know the dangers of the sea in peace-time to face the greater danger of war-time
Review FoB 1941
British Council *pc* Spectator *p & d* Ivan Scott
9 mins IWM NFA

Salute to farmers
On the farms of Britain farmers are increasing the production of wheat, milk, vegetables and fruit by turning over land from unessential crops, ploughing up new land and using modern machines. The Women's Land Army, school children and townspeople at week-ends help to get the work done
Cadbury *pc* Merton Park *d* Montgomery Tully
17 mins LC NFA

Sam Pepys joins the Navy
(Finance and the Navy seen through the eyes of a young recruit)
Reviews DNL II 229, MFB VIII 156
MoI & National Savings Ctte *pc* GB

Screen Services *p & d* Francis Searle *ph* Walter Harvey
7 mins IWM NFA

Shunter Black's night off
The story of a shunter who, during a blitz, by good sense and courage prevented a disastrous explosion in a marshalling yard
Reviews DNL II 167, MFB VIII 106
MoI *pc* Verity *p* Sydney Box, James Carr *d & comm w* Maxwell Munden *ph* Bernard Browne *comm s* John Slater
8 mins IWM LC MOMA NFA

SOS
At stations all round the coast lifeboats and voluntary crews are ready to help any ship in distress. Behind them is the Royal National Lifeboat Institution to see that spare parts are ready for instant despatch anywhere
Reviews DNL I Aug 12, FoB 1941, MFB VIII 21
British Council *pc* Tida *p & d* John Eldridge *ph* Michael Curtis *m* William Alwyn
14 mins IWM LC NFA

Spring offensive
The story of the work done by a Suffolk War Agricultural Committee in reclaiming a derelict farm, typical of the first ploughing-up campaign of 1939-40. (Theatrical release title *Unrecorded victory*)
Reviews DNL I Dec 7, MFB VII 191
MoI *pc* GPO *d* Humphrey Jennings *comm s* A G Street *p* Cavalcanti
21 mins IWM LC MOMA NFA

Steel goes to sea
Another ship is built to help win the war at sea. The film shows each stage in construction and emphasises the importance today of the traditional skill of British shipbuilders
Reviews MFB VIII 123, FoB 1941
British Council *pc* Merton Park *d* John Lewis
16 mins IWM NFA

Tank patrol
(A RAC sergeant tells factory workers the story of a trapped tank's breakout from behind the Italian lines to illustrate the importance of the components they are making)
MoI *pc* Strand *p* Alexander Shaw *d* John Eldridge
35 mins IWM LC

The team—it all depends on me
George Allison, with the Arsenal Club, shows what team work means in football and in the field of war production
Reviews DNL II 167, MFB VIII 106
MoI *pc* Welwyn Studios *d* Leslie Arliss, Norman Lee *ph* Walter Harvey, Ronald Anscombe
6 mins IWM

Telefootlers
(Don't gossip on the phone)
Reviews DNL II 47, MFB VIII 21
MoI *pc* Verity *p* George E Turner, Sydney Box *d* John Paddy Carstairs *cast* Muriel George, Barbara Everest
5 mins

War front
A team of photo-journalists record some outstanding stories of the War Front, in the air, in factories, in Civil Defence and on the Home Front
Reviews DNL II 68, MFB VIII 41
Odhams Press *pc* Strand *d* John Eldridge *ph* Jo Jago *m* Ludwig Brav
16 mins IWM NFA

Winter on the farm
The first of four films on farming through the seasons. *Winter on the farm* was made at Upton Manor Farm, Uploders, Dorset. It shows the different kinds of jobs done all the year round on a mixed farm and the various skills demanded of the farm workers
Reviews DNL III 90, MFB X 94
MoI & Min of Ag *pc* Green Park *assoc p* Edgar Anstey *d* Ralph Keene *ph* Erwin

Hillier *m* William Alwyn *agricultural adviser* Ralph Wightman
15 mins NFA MOMA

Words for battle
Extracts from Camden's 'Britannia', Milton, Blake, Browning, Kipling, Churchill and Lincoln; spoken by Laurence Olivier
Reviews DNL II 89, MFB VIII 60
MoI *pc* Crown *p* Ian Dalrymple *d* Humphrey Jennings *comm s* Laurence Olivier *ed* S McAllister
8 mins BFI IWM MOMA NFA

Yellow Caesar
(Sarcastic comic compilation about Benito Mussolini)
Reviews DNL II 67, MFB VIII 37
pc Ealing Studios *p* Michael Balcon *d* Cavalcanti *sc* Frank Owen, Michael Foot
24 mins NFA

You're telling me
A small boy threw a stone and by evening a war factory had been destroyed. The film shows how the story grew and appeals to everyone not to spread rumours on hearsay
Review DNL II 68, MFB VIII 37
MoI *pc* Rotha Productions *p* Paul Rotha *d* Bladon Peake
7 mins IWM

HOMEFRONT – Scotland, Ulster & Wales

Dai Jones
(A Welsh miner joins a rescue squad)
Reviews DNL II 67, MFB VIII 36
MoI *pc* Verity *d* Dan Birt *ph* Roy Fogwell *p* Jay Gardner Lewis
5 mins MOMA NFA

Fighting fields
The story of wartime farming in Scotland
Reviews MFB IX 92, KYB 1942
MoI & Scottish Dept of Ag *pc* Scottish Films & GB Instructional *p* Mary Field *d* S Russell
12 mins IWM LC NFA

Scotland speaks
A picture of Scotland at war, showing Scots regiments in training, workers in the Clyde shipyards and steel foundries, crop and sheep farmers and fishermen
Review MFB VIII 49
MoI *pc* Strand *p* Alexander Shaw *d* Jack Ellitt
17 mins IWM LC NFA

Scotland's war effort
Review DNL I Dec 9
pc Strand *p* Alexander Shaw *d* Jack Ellitt

They made the land
The history of agriculture in Scotland. (Film made in 1938)
Films of Scotland Ctte *pc* GB Instructional *d* Mary Field
20 mins MOMA NFA

Ulster
A survey of the natural and industrial resources of Northern Ireland, from flax and linen to shipbuilding and aircraft manufacture
Reviews DNL II 9, FoB 1941, MFB VIII 49
British Council *pc* Strand *p* Alexander Shaw *d* Ralph Keene *ph* Jo Jago, George Noble *m* Richard Addinsell *comm w* St John Irvine *comm s* Robert MacDermot
12 mins LC NFA

Wealth of a nation
Scotland's industrial problems in the years following the 1914-18 War and the efforts made to solve them. (Film made in 1938)
Films of Scotland Ctte *pc* Scottish Films *p* Stuart Legg *d* Donald Alexander
14 mins MOMA NFA

Welsh plant breeding station
An account of Sir Reginald Stapledon's

work at Cahn Hill, Aberystwyth, in producing special grasses to improve grasslands
Imperial Relations Trust *pc* GB Instructional *assoc p* Arthur Elton *d* J W Durden
17 mins NFA

HOMEFRONT – Instructional

All about carrots
How to grow carrots and a number of ways to serve them
MoI & Board of Educ *pc* British Foundation *p & d* Ronald Haines
9 mins NFA

A-tish-oo
(Combating the common cold)
Reviews DNL II 89, MFB VIII 36
MoI *pc* Verity *p* Jay Gardner Lewis *d* Maxwell Munden *ph* Bernard Browne
5 mins NFA

Backyard front
(How to grow vegetables in the backyard)
Reviews DNL I Apr 7, MFB VII 85
sp Min of Ag *pc* British Films *p & d* Andrew Buchanan *ph* Charles Francis *cast* Claude Dampier, C H Middleton
20 mins

Bampton shows the way
The village of Bampton, Devon, shows how to organise a Food Education Week
MoI & Min of Food *pc* Realist *p* Paul Rotha *d* Bladon Peake
6 mins NFA

Breath of danger
The common cold is a menace. This film shows how it is spread and how everyone can help to protect himself and his neighbours
Review MFB XIII 69
sp Central Council for Health Educ *pc* GB Instructional *p* Bruce Woolfe *d* Stanley Irving
9 mins NFA

Casserole cooking
Review DNL I Dec 7
MoI & Min of Food *pc* Verity *d* Jay Gardner Lewis *ph* S D Onions
7 mins

Crust and crumb
Housewives have a part to play in the Battle of the Atlantic by not wasting bread. The film shows how odd crusts can be used to improve various dishes
Review MFB XI 63
MoI & Min of Food *pc* A & D Productions *d* Alex Bryce *cast* Hay Petrie
6 mins

Dairying in the Cotswolds
Work on a dairy farm including cleaning and feeding of cows, cleaning and sterilization of utensils and cooling of milk. (Film made in 1939. Shorter version entitled *Milking*)
Review MFB VIII 125
pc Cadbury
12 mins

Dangers in the dark
A pedestrian, cyclist, despatch rider, motorist and lorry driver in an accident which each could have prevented. (Alternative title *This wouldn't have happened*)
Reviews DNL II 207, MFB VIII 156
MoI & Min of War Transport *pc* Public Relationship *d* Richard Massingham, Lewis Grant Wallace
7 mins IWM NFA

Defeat diphtheria
Thousands of children die every year from diphtheria. The disease could be stamped out if all young children were immunised. The film explains, by some simple diagrams, the nature of the disease, tells how the anti-toxin was discovered and shows parents the part they must play in protecting their children. (Re-edited in 1945)
Reviews DNL II 107, MFB VIII 111
MoI & Min of Health *pc* Rotha Produc-

tions *p* Paul Rotha *d* Bladon Peake *ph* Erwin Hillier
12 mins NFA

Emergency cooking stoves
After a blitz gas and electricity may be cut off. The film shows how a simple and efficient outdoor stove can be quickly made to cook hot food for a large number of people
MoI & Min of Food *pc* Films of GB *d* Andrew Buchanan *ph* Henry Cooper
9 mins IWM

Fine feathers
(How to achieve a balanced diet in wartime)
Review MFB IX 11
sp Central Council for Health Educ *pc* Films of GB *p* Andrew Buchanan *d* Henry Cooper *ph* Charles Francis *cast* Jeanne de Casalis
12 mins NFA

Fitness for service
Exercises and games to maintain fitness in spite of longer hours and harder work
MoI *pc* GB Instructional *d* J Warren
9 mins IWM

Green food for health
Green vegetables and plenty of them are essential for health. It is important to know which are the most nutritious and how to get full food value from them
Reviews DNL I Sept 12, MFB VII 166
sp British Commercial Gas Assoc *pc* Realist *p* John Taylor *d* Ruby Grierson *ph* A E Jeakins *comm s* Alec Clunes *assoc p* Edgar Anstey
6 mins NFA

Handicraft happiness
The first of four films produced in 1940 for the National Federation of Women's Institutes by GB Instructional to show countrywomen how to relearn useful home crafts. (Others entitled *Rugmaking, Quilting, Thrift*)
Review DNL I April 6
sp National Federation of Women's Institutes *pc* GB Instructional *d* Mary Field
12 mins

Herrings
How to cook, bone and serve herrings
Reviews DNL I Dec 7, MFB XI 36
MoI & Min of Food *pc* Verity *d* Jay Gardner Lewis *ph* S D Onions *comm w & s* Maxwell Munden
7 mins NFA

Hot on the spot
In winter sandwiches or bread-and-cheese are not an adequate midday meal. The film shows how to make, from materials easily available, a 'thermos' for a hot meal
Review MFB XI 63
MoI & Min of Food *pc* Films of GB *p* Andrew Buchanan *d* Henry Cooper *ph* Charles Francis
10 mins

How to dig
The first of six instructional films on food production in gardens and on allotments. They were made in collaboration with the Royal Horticultural Society. *How to dig* demonstrates the best methods of breaking up new ground and of dealing with established plots
Review DNL II 191
MoI & Min of Ag *pc* Selwyn *assoc p* Edgar Anstey *d* Jack Ellitt *ph* Jack Parker *comm s* Roy Hay
14 mins CFL IWM MOMA NARS NFA

Kill that rat
Rats in the country destroy ricks, stored crops and poultry. The film shows how farmers can protect their crops and wipe out the rats
Review DNL II 107
MoI & Min of Ag *pc* Publicity *assoc p* Edgar Anstey *d* Terence Bishop *ph* Alan Dinsdale
9 mins NFA

Milking
(Shorter version of *Dairying in the Cotswolds*)
Review MFB VIII 159
8 mins

Miss T
A simple exposition of the principles of a good diet illustrated in the growth of Miss T from birth to adolescence
sp Electrical Assoc for Women *pc* GB Instructional *d* Mary Field
13 mins LC

Potatoes
The right ways to cook potatoes so as to get full value from them
Reviews DNL I Dec 7, MFB XI 64
MoI & Min of Food *pc* Verity *d* Jay Gardner Lewis *ph* S D Onions
7 mins NFA

Pots and pans
A film for women on how to mend aluminium, tin and enamelled pans and kettles, showing the simple tools and materials required
MoI & Board of Trade *pc* Films of GB *p* Andrew Buchanan *d* Henry Cooper *ph* Charles Francis
12 mins

Quilting
(The craft of quilting and where it is still practised)
Reviews DNL I Apr 6, MFB VII 137
National Federation of Women's Institutes *pc* GB Instructional *d* Mary Field *comm s* Peter Herbert
12 mins silent

The rabbit pest
Rabbits cause vast damage to essential food crops and pasture land and must be exterminated. The film shows how, by modern methods, this can be done
Review DNL II 128
Plant Protection *pc* Strand *p* Donald Taylor *d & ph* Gerald Gibbs *comm s* Bernard Miles
6 mins NFA

Roots of victory
(Use of spring vegetables)
Min of Food & Min of Ag *pc* Verity *p* Jay Gardner Lewis

Simple soups
Housewives from Scotland, Yorkshire and Wales explain how they make soup
MoI & Board of Educ *pc* British Foundation *p & d* Ronald Haines
9 mins

Simplified first aid
Some elementary hints on what anyone can do to alleviate pain and prevent further injury until the doctor arrives
MoI *pc* Films of GB *p* Andrew Buchanan *d* Henry Cooper *ph* Charles Francis
11 mins

Sowing and planting
Preparation of the soil and sowing and planting of shallots, parsnips, onions, peas, brussels sprouts, cabbages, leeks and potatoes
Review DNL III 6
MoI & Min of Ag *pc* Selwyn *assoc p* Edgar Anstey *p* Jack Ellitt *ph* Jack Parker *comm s* Roy Hay
13 mins CFL IWM MOMA NARS NFA

Storing vegetables indoors
How to store shallots, runner beans, onions, haricot beans and tomatoes
Review DNL III 71
MoI & Min of Ag *pc* Realist *assoc p* Edgar Anstey *p* Frank Sainsbury *d* Margaret Thomson *ph* A E Jeakins *comm s* Roy Hay *m* Ernst Meyer
12 mins LC MOMA NFA

Storing vegetables outdoors
How to store potatoes and carrots in clamps
Review DNL III 71
MoI & Min of Ag *pc* Realist *assoc p* Edgar Anstey *p* Frank Sainsbury *d* Margaret Thomson *ph* A E Jeakins *comm s* Roy Hay *m* Ernst Meyer
8 mins LC MOMA

This wouldn't have happened

Two cooks and a cabbage
There is a good and a bad way of cooking a cabbage. It is worth knowing the good way
Review DNL II 168, MFB XI 36
MoI & Min of Food *pc* A & D Productions *p* Alex Bryce *ph* Stephen Dade
6 mins NFA

When the pie was opened
'All the season's vegetables baked in a pie' by Len Lye; a simple recipe presented with lively ingenuity
Review DNL II 147
MoI & Min of Food *pc* Realist *p* John Taylor *d* Len Lye *ph* A E Jeakins
9 mins BFI NFA

Wisdom of the wild
Some useful food hints from animals, presented in light form by Emmett of GB News
Reviews MFB VII 195, MFB XI 84
sp Electrical Development Assoc *pc* GB Instructional *d* Mary Field
12 mins IWM NFA

HOMEFRONT – Specialised instructional

The turn of the furrow
Tractors are enabling farmers to speed up food production. The film shows the jobs that can be done by different types of tractors suited to the needs of different types of farms
Reviews DNL II 28, FoB 1941, MFB VIII 21
Petroleum Films Bureau *pc* Shell *p* Edgar Anstey *d* Peter Baylis *ph* Sidney Beadle *comm s* Bernard Miles
20 mins MOMA

A way to plough
An instructional film on a way to plough which is efficient and economical of land, fuel and time. The scenes of Land Girls being taught are supplemented by diagrams illustrating how the field is divided and the course of the tractor determined
Reviews DNL III 54, MFB XIII 177
MoI & Min of Ag *pc* Verity *assoc p* Edgar Anstey *p* Sydney Box, James Carr *d & ph* Clifford Hornby *ed* J Durst *adviser* S J Wright *comm s* Freddie Grisewood
16 mins MOMA

HOMEFRONT – Air raid precautions

September, 1940
pc London Fire Brigade

HOMEFRONT – Wartime social services

Carry on, children
The story of the health services for children from birth to adolescence
Reviews FoB 1941, MFB IX 10
sp Central Council for Health Educ *pc* Spectator *p* Ivan Scott *d* Michael Hankinson
11 mins

Citizens' Advice Bureau
(The work of the Citizens' Advice Bureau shown through typical cases)
Review MFB VIII 90
MoI *pc* GB Screen Services *p* Leslie Arliss *d* Francis Searle
8 mins NFA

Eating out with Tommy Trinder
(British restaurants)
Reviews DNL II 107, MFB VIII 60
MoI *pc* Strand *d* Desmond Dickinson *ph* George Noble *p* Donald Taylor *cast* Tommy Trinder, Jean Colin
5 mins NFA

FIGHTING SERVICES & CAMPAIGNS

Ack ack
An explanation of the function of AA in defeating enemy raids given in a visit to a gun site on active service
Review DNL II 67
MoI & War Office *pc* Shell *p* Edgar Anstey *d* Peter Baylis *ph* Sidney Beadle *anim* Francis Rodker
9 mins IWM LC MOMA NFA

Airwoman
A story of the part played in a bomber raid by the various sections of the WAAF at an operational station
Reviews DNL II 149, MFB VIII 90
MoI & Air Min *pc* GB Screen Services *d* Francis Searle *ph* Roy Fogwell
8 mins IWM LC NFA

ATS
A survey of jobs done by women in the Army, from cooking to AA detector work, and of living conditions in camps and hostels
Reviews DNL II 128, MFB VIII 75
MoI & War Office *pc* Army Film Unit *d* Hugh Stewart *ed* R Verrall
7 mins IWM LC NFA

Britain's RAF
The story of the RAF in 1940. The film outlines the function of Fighter, Bomber and Coastal Command, and shows the Air Council in session. It refers to the Empire Air Training Scheme and American aircraft, and reviews the Battle of Britain. (*March of Time* 6th year no 6, British series)
Review DNL I Dec 7
pc March of Time
18 mins IWM

Carrier pigeons
(Longer theatrical version of *Winged messengers*)
Reviews BFY 365
IWM

Corvettes
Corvettes are a special type of warship designed for protecting convoys from submarines and aircraft. Life on them, as the film shows, is exacting and tense
Review MFB VIII 122
MoI & Admiralty *pc* Spectator *d* Ivan Scott
8 mins IWM LC NFA

Ferry pilot
(The story of the ATA which provides personnel to fly newly completed aircraft from factory to service airfield)
Reviews DNL III 37, MFB IX 8
pc Crown *p* Ian Dalrymple *d* Pat Jackson *ph* H E Fowle *ed* Richard McNaughton *m* Brian Easdale
35 mins IWM LC NFA

Guards of the north
Iceland is of prime strategic importance to the United Nations. This film shows how Canadian troops, with British troops, arrived and set about building camps, air bases, and gun sites for the larger forces that were to come. (Part of the *Canada carries on* series)
pc National Film Board of Canada *d* Tennyson d'Eyncourt
10 mins IWM

HM minelayer
A minelayer sets off to lay mines off the enemy coast. An enemy aircraft passes over but the job is done without interruption and the ship returns
Reviews DNL II 191, MFB VIII 140
MoI & Admiralty *pc* Verity *p* Sydney Box, James Carr *d* Henry Cass
8 mins IWM LC

The lion of Judah
The story of the liberation of Abyssinia, from the formation of the Patriot army which helped the British Army to drive out the Italians, to the entry of Haile Selassie into Addis Ababa
Reviews DNL II 109, MFB XI 111

MoI & War Office *pc* Army Film Unit *d* Eric Boothby
15 mins IWM NFA

Lofoten
An eye-witness account of the Lofoten raid, by Lt-Commander Anthony Kimmins
Reviews MFB VIII 49, DNL II 68
MoI & War Office *pc* Army & Crown Film Units *p* David Macdonald *d* Tennyson d'Eyncourt *comm s* Anthony Kimmins
7 mins IWM LC NFA

Naval operations
(Warships and sea battles of the early war years illustrate the character of contemporary naval combat)
Reviews DNL III 5, MFB VIII 171
MoI *pc* Shell *p* Edgar Anstey *d* Grahame Tharp *anim* Francis Rodker
9 mins IWM LC MOMA

Northern outpost
The story of the arrival in Iceland of British troops to guard the North Atlantic routes
Reviews DNL II 47, MFB VIII 21
MoI & War Office *pc* Army Film Unit *p* David Macdonald *d* Tennyson d'Eyncourt
9 mins IWM NFA

The pilot is safe
The story of how a fighter pilot returning from a daylight sweep was rescued from the Channel
Reviews DNL II 191, MFB VIII 123
MoI & Air Min *pc* Crown *p* Ian Dalrymple *d* Jack Lee *ph* Skeets Kelly
9 mins IWM LC NFA

Raising air fighters
(Training pilots)
Review FoB 1940
British Council *pc* British Paramount News *p* G T Cummins
17 mins IWM NFA

Raising sailors
First stages in training of men called up and young boys entering the Navy as a career
Review MFB VIII 7
MoI *pc* Pathé *p* Fred Watts, A V Curtice *ph* A Farmer *comm s* C F Danvers Walker
10 mins IWM NFA

Royal Observer Corps
The movements of every aircraft towards and over Britain must be detected and plotted. Doing this work the men of the Royal Observer Corps help to defeat enemy raiders
Review MFB VIII 171
MoI *pc* Spectator *p* Michael Hankinson *d* Gilbert Gunn
7 mins IWM LC NFA

Sea cadets
An outline of the training for the Royal Navy given in the Sea Cadets. (Also known as *Nursery of the navy*)
Reviews DNL II 149, MFB VIII 106
MoI *pc* Strand *p* Jay Gardner Lewis *ph* Charles Marlborough *comm s* Bernard Miles
8 mins IWM LC NFA

Special despatch
A typical job of work for an Army motor-cycle despatch rider—twelve hours to take a secret message from London to Clydeside
Review DNL II 207
MoI & War Office *pc* Army Film Unit *d* Hugh Stewart *ed* Edward Carrick
8 mins IWM LC

Target for tonight
Review DNL II 147
MoI & RAF *pc* Crown *p* Ian Dalrymple *d & sc* Harry Watt *ph* Jonah Jones *sd* Ken Cameron
50 mins IWM NFA

Venture adventure
An outline of the training for the RAF

available for boys of fourteen to eighteen in the Air Training Corps
Reviews DNL II 207, MFB VIII 156
MoI & Air Min *pc* Crown *p* Ian Dalrymple *d* C Hasse *ph* E Catford *sd* A Valentine
7 mins IWM LC NFA

Target for tonight. *Air Crew are briefed on the night's raid.*

War in the east
(Eastern war zone)
Reviews DNL III 5, MFB IX 8
MoI *pc* Shell *p* Edgar Anstey *d* R K Neilson Baxter *intro* J F Horrabin
6 mins IWM

Winged messengers
The story of how carrier pigeons were mobilised and trained to play an important part in military communications. (Longer non-theatrical version titled *Carrier pigeons*)
Reviews DNL II 128, MFB VIII 75
MoI & War Office *pc* GB Instructional *d* Mary Field *ph* Frank North *comm s* Colin Wills
11 mins IWM LC

WRNS
Work and life in the Women's Royal Naval Service
Reviews DNL II 209, MFB VIII 156
MoI & Admiralty *pc* Strand *p* Donald Taylor *d* Ivan Moffat *ph* Jo Jago
8 mins IWM LC

DOMINIONS & COLONIES – General

Alert in the East
On guard from Suez to Singapore, from Singapore to Hong Kong
Review KYB 1942
MoI *pc* Movietonews *p* Gerald Sanger *ed* Raymond Perrin
10 mins IWM

The Empire's new armies
A newsreel compilation showing the mobilising of the fighting forces of the Dominions and the Colonies and the kind of equipment and tactics in which they were trained
MoI *pc* Pathé
9 mins IWM LC

From the four corners
Leslie Howard shows London's past to an Australian, a Canadian and a New Zealander and discusses with them why their countries chose to declare war against Germany, and send them and thousands of their countrymen to Britain to fight
Review MFB VIII 65
MoI *pc* Denham and Pinewood *p & d* Anthony Havelock-Allan *cast* Leslie Howard
16 mins IWM NFA

Wheat fields of the Empire
Different methods of wheat harvesting in the Empire
6 mins

DOMINIONS & COLONIES – Africa

Gold Coast
Native life in a Gold Coast village, showing the men landing and preparing their catch of fish and working in a cocoa-bean plantation
sp Cadbury *pc* Merton Park *p* W Crichton
12 mins NFA

DOMINIONS & COLONIES – Australia

Australia at war
Australia's war effort and strategic position in the Pacific. (*March of Time* 6th year no 14, British series)
Reviews DNL II 107, MFB VIII 65
pc March of Time
18 mins NFA

Australia marches with Britain
A picture of the natural and industrial resources of Australia for the production of food and munitions of war
sp National Film Council of Australia *pc* Cinesound *p* K Hall
16 mins IWM

It's the Navy
The men and ships of the Royal Australian Navy. (Re-edited version released later entitled *Royal Australian Navy*)
sp National Film Council of Australia *pc* Branch Studios *d* R Smart
12 mins IWM

Keeping the fleet at sea
A visit to the King Edward Naval Dock, which keeps men and ships of the Royal Australian Navy equipped with everything they need
sp National Film Council of Australia *pc* Argosy *d* Alan Mill
11 mins IWM

Royal Australian Navy
(Guarding Australia's shores. Re-edited from *It's the navy*)
Reviews MFB VIII 123
pc Commonwealth Cinema, Melbourne *d* R Smart *ed* Sylvia Cummins
13 mins LC NFA

Wealth of Australia
The story of the development of the wool industry, mining for gold, silver and lead and wheat growing, re-edited from *A nation is built*
Govt of New South Wales *p* Frank Hurley *re-ed* Horace Shepherd
11 mins

DOMINIONS & COLONIES – Canada

Canada in London 1941
MoI *pc* Realist *p* John Taylor *d* Hans Nieter *ph* A E Jeakins

Peoples of Canada
The story of the peoples of many nationalities who have migrated to Canada and have built a new nation in which they still preserve their own national characteristics: French in Quebec; Scots, Americans, Dutch and Germans in the Maritime Provinces; Englishmen, Orangemen and Scots in Toronto; and in the prairie towns peasants from Central and Eastern Europe
Reviews MFB IX 92, MFB XI 95
pc National Film Board of Canada *p* Stuart Legg *d* G Sparling
21 mins

A visit from Canada
The men of Princess Patricia's Light Infantry make themselves welcome in a South of England village in which they spent the winter
Reviews DNL II 107, MFB VIII 60
MoI & National Film Board of Canada *pc* Realist *p* Basil Wright *d* John Taylor *ph* A E Jeakins
8 mins IWM

DOMINIONS & COLONIES – India

Arms from India
A picture of India's war production of trucks, tyres, cloth, tents and medical supplies. (Original title *Tools for the job*)
sp Films Advisory Board of India *pc* Indian Film Unit *p* Alexander Shaw *d* Ezra Mir, Sherraz Farrukhi
11 mins IWM

The handymen
Without the Sappers and Miners no advance is possible. This film shows the work of the Royal Bombay Sappers and Miners, Kirkee
Review DNL III 9
sp Films Advisory Board of India *pc* Indian Film Unit
11 mins IWM

India marches
An Indian infantry regiment in training
Reviews DNL II 149, MFB VIII 37
sp Govt of India *pc* Bombay Talkies/ Crown *comm s* Z A Bokhari
5 mins IWM

DOMINIONS & COLONIES – New Zealand

New Zealand has wings
Men in training for the Royal New Zealand Air Force. (Re-edited from *Wings over New Zealand*)
Review MFB VIII 122
New Zealand Govt *pc* New Zealand National Film Unit *re-ed* Sylvia Cummins
6 mins IWM

Rainbow river
River scenes, catching rainbow trout and cooking in neighbouring hot-water springs
10 mins

DOMINIONS & COLONIES – South Africa

Sinews of war
How South Africa's factories produced the munitions and equipment for the South African forces which fought through Italian East Africa into Egypt
South African Govt *pc* African Film Productions
16 mins IWM

South Africa marches
(South Africa's war effort. Re-edited version of *Sinews of War* and *Road to victory*)
Review MFB VIII 106
MoI *pc* South African Film Unit *ed* Sylvia Cummins
5 mins LC

ALLIES – General

Guests of honour
(Our allies from occupied countries and their fighting efforts)
Reviews DNL II 167, MFB VIII 122
pc Ealing Studios *p* Cavalcanti *d* Ray Pitt *ed* Charles Crichton *ph* Douglas Slocombe
25 mins

ALLIES – Poland

Polish bomber's holiday
(Polish bomber squadron in the RAF marks the anniversary of the first raid by Polish bombers against Germany. Distribution arrangements unknown)
pc Polish Film Unit
10 mins IWM

The shortest route
(Polish soldiers train as paratroops in Britain. Distribution arrangements unclear)
pc Polish Film Unit
10 mins IWM

This is Poland
The story of the invasion of Poland up to the fall of Warsaw and of the re-forming of Polish forces in Britain. The film opens in Polish towns and country in peace
Review MFB VIII 21
Polish MoI *pc* Concanen *p* Derrick de Marney *d* Eugene Cekalski
18 mins NFA

The White Eagle
The Poles in Britain work to preserve their intellectual and cultural traditions, while Polish fighting forces take their place in the Battle of the Atlantic and air battles and train for the time when they will help to liberate their country
Reviews DNL II 149, MFB VIII 146
Polish MoI *pc* Concanen *p* Derrick de Marney *d* Eugene Cekalski *comm w* Val Gielgud *comm s* Leslie Howard
12 mins IWM NFA

ALLIES – USA

Adventure in the Bronx
The story of a small boy who went off to the Zoo by himself in search of adventure, of the things he saw and how he learnt to stand on his own feet
pc Film Associates
12 mins

America speaks her mind
A review of the development of American public opinion from the invasion of Poland to the passing of the Lease-Lend Act. The film shows and records speeches by President Roosevelt, Mr Wilkie and Senator Wheeler. It contains scenes of the Nazi occupation of France. (*March of Time* 6th year no 11, British series)
Review DNL II 67
pc March of Time
21 mins IWM

The children see it thru'
(The work of the American Save the Children Committee with child victims of the London bombing)
Review DNL II 189
pc Rotha Productions *p* Paul Rotha *d* Yvonne Fletcher *comm s* Arthur Mann
7 mins NFA

ALLIES – USSR

Odessa besieged
The last newsreel report sent out from Odessa before it fell, showing preparation for the final battles
Soviet Film Agency *pc* Central Studio, Moscow
11 mins NFA

One day in Soviet Russia
Scenes of fighting units of the Red Army in action
Reviews DNL II 168, MFB VIII 122
Soviet Film Agency *pc* Central Studios, Moscow
8 mins NFA

Our Russian allies
(The armed strength of the Soviet forces)
Review DNL II 229
pc Soviet Central Newsreel Studios *p & compilor* Herbert Marshall *comm s* J B Priestley, Major A S Hooper, Charles Garner
57 mins NFA

Salute to the Soviet
A picture of the peoples and lands of the Soviet Union with an epilogue by M Maisky, the Soviet Ambassador; produced shortly after the Nazi invasion
Soviet Film Agency *pc* Pathé
11 mins IWM

Soviet harvest
The rich harvests of the USSR coveted and soon to be devastated by the Nazis
Soviet Film Agency *pc* Central Studio, Moscow
8 mins IWM

Soviet women
(Work being done by women in Soviet Russia)
Soviet War News Film Agency
7 mins

Three in a shellhole
The story of an encounter between a Soviet soldier, a Soviet Red Cross girl and a Nazi army doctor. (Dialogue in English)

Reviews DNL III 5, MFB VIII 172
MoI & Soviet Film Agency *pc* Mosfilm *d* Lioniel Leonov
10 mins IWM LC

ALLIES – Yugoslavia

100 for 1
In a small town in Jugoslavia a Nazi soldier is killed. A hundred men and women are taken by the Nazis to be shot, but they escape to join the guerrillas. (Not suitable for children)
Review MFB IX 25
sp Soviet Film Agency *pc* Lenfilm
16 mins IWM

OVERSEAS DISTRIBUTION

A1 at Lloyd's
A description of Lloyd's services to world shipping, and the story of a voyage from Valparaiso to Hull, ending with the ringing of the famous Lutine Bell at Lloyd's to signal the safe arrival of a missing vessel
Reviews DNL II 149, FoB 1941
sp British Council *pc* Strand *p* Alexander Shaw *d* Ralph Bond *sc* Reg Groves *ph* Jo Jago *comm s* Leslie Mitchell *m* John Greenwood
11 mins

Ack ack

Adeste fideles
(Christmas in war-ridden Britain. Overseas distribution only)
Review DNL II 88
MoI *pc* Strand *p* Basil Wright *d* Ralph Keene, Ralph Bond *ph* Charles Marlborough, Gerald Gibbs *md* Muir Mathieson
14 mins LC NFA

An African in London
(An African visitor to London. Intended for African audiences)
pc Colonial Film Unit *d* George Pearson *cast* Robert Adams
12 mins silent

Airwoman

Alert in the East

The answer
(The spirit of Britain in the face of Hitler's threat of invasion)
Review FoB 1941
sp British Council *pc* Spectator *d* Alex Bryce
16 mins NFA

Architects of England
13 mins CFL

Battle of the books

Blitzkreig tactics
MoI
NARS

Bringing it home

Carry on, children

Christmas under fire

Citizens' Advice Bureau

City bound

Corvettes

Dai Jones

Dangers in the dark

The dawn guard

Defeat diphtheria

Eating out with Tommy Trinder

Emergency cooking stoves

The Empire marches
(Overseas distribution only. The armed solidarity of the British Empire)
MoI *pc* Universal News
9 mins IWM

The Empire's new armies

Farmer's day
A day's work on a modern English dairy farm
Reviews FoB 1941, KW 28.11.1940
pc Selwyn *p* C A Ridley *d* Brian Smith
16 mins NFA

Ferry pilot

A few ounces a day

Fighting fields

Five and under
(The problem facing working mothers during the war of where to leave their children during working hours. Overseas distribution only)
Review MPH 19.7.1941
MoI *pc* Rotha Productions *p* Paul Rotha *d* Donald Alexander *ph* John Page
16 mins LC NFA

From the four corners

Germany calling

Green girdle
(London's 100 square miles of publicly-owned countryside)
Reviews DNL II 108, FoB 1941, MFB VIII 106
sp British Council *pc* Strand *p* Basil Wright *d* Ralph Keene *ph* Jack Cardiff *m* Richard Addinsell *comm s* Bruce Belfrage, Robert MacDermot
10 mins colour NFA

The gun
(Not shown in Britain. Wartime life of British merchant seamen and their urgent need for anti-aircraft guns)
Review MFB VIII 106
sp Admiralty *pc* British Paramount News
p & d G T Cummins *with* Ed Murrow
20 mins IWM

The heart of Britain

HM minelayer

HM Navies go to sea

Home Guard

Hospital nurse

How to dig

Hydraulics
(The principles and practice of hydraulics)
Reviews DNL II 28, FoB 1941, MFB VIII 21
pc Shell *p* Arthur Elton *d* Ralph Elton
13 mins NFA

Indian Ocean
(History of the Indian Ocean and the activities of European nations on its shores)
Review FoB 1941
pc GB Instructional *p & d* Mary Field
22 mins colour

India's Navy grows
(This was not shown in Britain)
MoI *pc* British Movietonews *p* Gerald Sanger
6 mins IWM NFA

Into the blue

Kill that rat

Land of invention
From Scotland, nurse of many inventors, came the macadamised road, the first locomotive engine, gas lighting for our cities, the steam-hammer, the Caledonian canal, the electric telephone, chloroform and a host of other enterprises
Reviews FoB 1941, MFB XII 90
sp British Council *pc* British Films *d* Andrew Buchanan *ph* Henry Cooper *ed* James Anderson
11 mins NFA

Learning to live
(An introduction to state education through the lives of three children)
Reviews DNL II 129, FoB 1941, MFB X 19
sp British Council *pc* Merton Park *d* Harold Purcell *ph* James Rogers
15 mins NFA

Living with strangers

Locomotives

Men of Africa

Merchant seamen

Mr Proudfoot shows a light

Naval operations

New acres

Our school

Out of the night
10 mins NFA

Oxford

The pilot is safe

Post 23

Queen's messengers

RAF commentary
pc Colonial Film Unit

Raising sailors

The Royal Air Force
Intended for African audiences
pc Colonial Film Unit
11 mins

Royal Observer Corps

Sailors without uniform

Scotland speaks

Sea cadets

Sea scouts
(How the Sea Scouts are trained to carry on Britain's seafaring tradition)
Reviews MFB IX 51, FoB 1941
British Council *pc* Technique *d* Julian Wintle
11 mins

Shunter Black's night off

SOS

Sowing and planting

Steel goes to sea
Another ship is built to help win the war at sea
Reviews FoB 1941, MFB VIII 123
sp British Council *pc* Merton Park *d* John Lewis
16 mins NFA

Storing vegetables indoors

Storing vegetables outdoors

Target for tonight

These are London firemen
(How firemen are trained in London)
pc Colonial Film Unit
13 mins silent

These are paratroops
pc Colonial Film Unit

This is a barrage balloon
pc Colonial Film Unit
7 mins

This is a searchlight
pc Colonial Film Unit
5 mins

This is a special constable
pc Colonial Film Unit
9 mins

This is an anti-aircraft gun
pc Colonial Film Unit
6 mins

This is an ARP warden
pc Colonial Film Unit
10 mins

The turn of the furrow

Unrecorded victory

Venture adventure

A visit from Canada

War in the east

A way to plough

We won't forget
(An expression of Britain's gratitude for American aid during the Blitz. Intended for American distribution)
MoI *pc* Realist *assoc p* Basil Wright *p* John Taylor *d* Frank Sainsbury *ph* A E Jeakins, Reginald Wyer
12 mins LC MOMA NFA

Winged messengers

Winter on the farm

Women at war
(Work done by women on the railways in wartime. Overseas distribution only)
Review MFB XII 106
MoI *pc* Commercial & Education Films *d* John Oliver *ed* Louise Birt
9 mins LC MOMA NFA

Words for battle

WRNS

You're telling me

NEWSREEL TRAILERS

Address clearly
GPO *pc* Universal

Carry your gas mask
MoI & Home Security *pc* Universal

Coals and the war

Diphtheria
MoI & Min of Health *pc* GB Instructional

Economical use of coal
MoI & Mines Dept *pc* British Movietonews

Empty houses
MoI & Home Security *pc* Pathé

Fire fighting

1941
NEWSREEL TRAILERS

Fire prevention

Food advice centre
MoI & Min of Food *pc* Verity

Fuel economy (heating)
MoI & Mines Dept *pc* Films of GB

Harvesting fruit

Help for the homeless
MoI & Min of Health & Home Security *pc* GB News

Morning blackout
MoI & Home Security *pc* GB Instructional

Munitions

Paper saving
MoI & Min of Supply *pc* Universal

Post early
GPO *pc* Publicity

Recruits for munitions
MoI & Min of Labour *pc* Andrew Buchanan

Save your waste paper

Shelter at home
(Turning a house into a reasonably safe shelter, a refuge room)
MoI & Home Security *pc* British Movietonews
4 mins IWM

Stop that fire
MoI & Home Security *pc* Crown
MOMA

Swinnerton
MoI & Min of Supply *pc* Publicity Pictures

To all mothers and fathers

1942

HOMEFRONT – General

All those in favour
Arthur Mann, reporter for the Mutual Broadcasting System, sees how a rural district council in Devon dealt with various problems arising from the war and discusses with some of the members of the council the implications of their experiments for the future of democratic local government. This film was made for exhibition in America
Reviews DNL III 5, MFB XII 41
MoI *pc* Rotha Productions *p* Paul Rotha *d* Donald Alexander *ph* Geoffrey Faithfull
22 mins LC NFA

Architects of England
The past and present of England's architecture
Reviews DNL II 29, FoB 1941, MFB VIII 21, MFB XI 37
sp British Council *pc* Strand *p* Donald Taylor *d* John Eldridge
13 mins CFL MOMA

Arms from scrap
From the blitzed towns have been salvaged great quantities of steel for munitions. The film shows this work being done and appeals to everyone to help in collecting every bit of scrap metal to be turned into ships, guns and tanks
Review MFB IX 23
MoI & Min of Supply *pc* British Movietonews *p* Gerald Sanger *comm s* Leslie Mitchell
9 mins IWM LC

Atlantic Charter
The newsreel account of the meeting between Mr Churchill and Mr Roosevelt
pc British Movietonews *p* Ian Dalrymple
9 mins NFA

BBC Brains Trust
3 issues
Review DNL IV 166
pc Strand *p* Howard Thomas, Donald Taylor *ph* Jo Jago, Charles Marlborough, Harold Young, Moray Grant *with*

Commander Campbell, Professor C E M Joad, Jennie Lee, Colonel Walter Elliot, Doctor Julian Huxley & others and Question Master Donald McCulloch
33 mins each NFA

Birth of a tank
From workshops and garages small tank parts pass to the first sub-assemblies at larger factories and from them to larger factories still, where the tank is finally built and armoured. Thence the tanks go to be tested before going overseas to fight
MoI & Min of Supply *pc* Spectator *p* Michael Hankinson *d* Gilbert Gunn *ph* Cyril Bristow
13 mins IWM LC

Builders
A bricklayer, a navvy and a crane-driver building a new war factory talk about their jobs and the kind of building they expect to do after the war
Reviews DNL III 54, MFB IX 51
MoI *pc* Crown *p* Ian Dalrymple *d* Pat Jackson *ph* C Pennington-Richards *ed* Francis Cockburn *comm s* John Hilton
8 mins IWM LC NFA

Chiang Kai-shek in India
(Original title *Our gallant neighbours*)
Reviews DNL III 125, MFB IX 120
MoI *pc* Indian Film Unit *d* Ezra Mir
5 mins

Churchill the man
MoI *pc* British Movietonews
10 mins NFA

City bound
London's transport system
Reviews FoB 1941, MFB XII 42
sp British Council *pc* Spectator *d* Robin Carruthers *p* Ivan Scott *ph* B Luff
10 mins NFA

City of progress
(London's government. Non-theatrical version of *The Londoners*)
Reviews FoB 1941, MPH 25.1.41
pc Realist
10 mins LC NFA

The countrywomen
Through a talk between a countrywoman and a woman evacuated from a town the film describes the history of the Women's Institutes and their aims and methods of working, and indicates how they can promote projects of local and national importance
Reviews DNL III 55, MFB XIII 26
MoI *pc* Seven League *assoc p* Paul Rotha *d* John Page
14 mins LC NFA

The day that saved the world
(Looking back two years to the climax of the Battle of Britain)
MoI *pc* Crown *compiled by* Jack Chambers *p* Ian Dalrymple
5 mins IWM

Dockers
(The industrial effort)
Review DNL III 100
MoI *pc* Realist *p* John Taylor *d* Frank Sainsbury *ph* A E Jeakins
5 mins

Down our street
(National Savings)
Review MFB IX 77
National Savings Ctte & MoI *pc* Merton Park *d* Terence Bishop
5 mins IWM

Essential jobs
A story, with a moral, of half-a-dozen seemingly unimportant jobs
Reviews DNL III 113, MFB IX 104
MoI & Min of Labour *pc* Rotha Productions *p* Paul Rotha *d* John Page *ph* Stanley Redwell *sc* V S Pritchett *sd* Leo Wilkins *ed* Sylvia Cummins
6 mins IWM LC

Filling the gap
An appeal to everyone, in an animated

cartoon, to grow vegetables on every possible bit of land in order to leave farm land free for other crops
Reviews DNL III 55, MFB IX 51
MoI & Min of Ag *pc* Realist *assoc p* Edgar Anstey *p* Frank Sainsbury *p* John Halas, Joy Batchelor *m* Ernst Meyer
6 mins IWM LC NFA

Food flashes
(Series of short message films with themes such as 'Eat potatoes not bread', 'Give your children cod liver oil and orange juice', 'How to use your ration book' etc.)
MoI & Min of Food
2-5 mins each, B&W and colour NFA

Give us more ships
Reviews DNL II 229, MFB VIII 156
sp National Savings Ctte *pc* Merton Park *sc* Gilbert Frankau *comm s* Leslie Banks
5 mins

A good landfall
On a night train is a Scots sailor going to join his ship. In Edinburgh his child lies critically ill. By a stratagem against time a stranger makes it possible for him to join his ship in peace of mind
Review DNL II 189
sp Salvation Army *pc* Strand *p* Basil Wright *d* Michael Gordon *ph* Lionel Banes *cast* Caven Watson, Cyril Chamberlain
10 mins IWM

The great harvest
The story of the great harvest of 1942, showing how it was made possible by the work throughout the year of the farmers and farmworkers and at harvest time by the added efforts of children, townspeople and British and American soldiers. (Library compilation)
Review MFB IX 149
MoI & Min of Ag *pc* Rotha Productions *p* Paul Rotha *d* Jack Chambers *m* Francis Chagrin *assoc p* Edgar Anstey *sc* A G Street *comm s* Rex Warner
8 mins IWM LC NFA

It all depends on you
An appeal to everyone to save waste paper and turn out unwanted magazines and books
sp Thames Board Mills *pc* Merton Park *d* Theodore Thumwood
8 mins

Jane Brown changes her job
The story of a girl who gave up shorthand typing in an office to go to work in an aircraft factory
MoI & Min of Labour *pc* Verity *p* Sydney Box, James Carr *d* Harold Cooper *cast* Anne Firth
9 mins IWM LC

Job in a million
The recruitment and training of Post Office messenger boys. (Film made in 1937)
Review FoB 1940
d Evelyn Spice *ed* Norman McLaren *pc* GPO *ph* S D Onions
15 mins NFA

Knights of St John
An example of the kind of work done by the members of the St John Ambulance Brigade
MoI *pc* Strand *p* Donald Taylor *d* Jay Gardner Lewis
7 mins IWM

Land girl
A Land Girl shows that she can learn the job, stand up to hard work and adapt herself to the ways of life on a farm
Review DNL III 21
MoI & Min of Ag *pc* Rotha Productions *p* Donald Alexander *d* John Page *ph* Graham Thomson
8 mins LC NFA

Life begins again
An account of new methods of rehabilitation for men injured in industry or in the Forces. The most advanced medical treatment, planned physical exercise, and freedom from worry about the

future are essential if injured men are to resume a useful and happy life
MoI & Min of Health *pc* Rotha Productions *p* Paul Rotha *d* Donald Alexander *ph* Wolfgang Suschitzky *m* William Alwyn
20 mins IWM NFA

Listen to Britain
'The music of a people at war. The sound of life in Britain by night and day.' The film records the roar of Spitfires and tanks, the noise of furnaces and factories, the march of miners and soldiers, music and songs in trains, dance halls, canteens and the National Gallery. With Flanagan and Allen, and Dame Myra Hess and the RAF Orchestra. (Film made in 1942)
MoI *pc* Crown *p* Ian Dalrymple *d* Humphrey Jennings, S McAllister
19 mins BFI CFL IWM MOMA NARS NFA

London, 1942
(London during 1942)
Reviews DNL IV 181, FoB 1942-3, MFB X 105
sp British Council *pc* Green Park *p* Ralph Keene *d* Kenneth Annakin
14 mins NFA

The Londoners
The story of the progress achieved in London's housing, health and education services during fifty years of democratic local government, made to celebrate the jubilee of the LCC. (Shorter non-theatrical version for overseas distribution called *City of progress*)
Review MFB VI 61
sp British Commercial Gas Assoc *pc* Realist *p* Basil Wright *d* John Taylor
18 mins MOMA NFA

Market town
Human Geography series. Market day in an old Nottinghamshire town. The film shows something of the importance of a market town as the centre of life of the surrounding countryside
Review FoB 1942-3
sp British Council *pc* GB Instructional *d* Mary Field *ph* Jack Parker
11 mins NFA

Men of tomorrow
MoI *pc* Technique *p* Sydney Box, James Carr *d* A Travers
8 mins LC

Mobile engineers
The work of the National Industrial Mobile Squads which go from place to place training new workers, getting new factories into production and evolving methods for speeding up production
Reviews DNL III 71, MFB IX 37
MoI & Min of Supply *pc* Strand *p* Donald Taylor *d* Michael Gordon *ph* Bernard Browne *sc & comm w* Reg Groves
5 mins IWM LC

Morning paper
The preparation and printing of a national daily newspaper in wartime
Reviews FoB 1941, MFB IX 51
sp British Council *pc* GB Instructional *ed* Darrell Catling

New towns for old
A visit to 'Smokedale' to see what has been done and the opportunities that now exist for replanning towns after the war. There are problems too. The responsibility for the future rests finally, not with expert planners, but with every citizen
Reviews DNL III 90, MFB IX 92
MoI *pc* Strand *p* Alexander Shaw *d* John Eldridge *ph* Jo Jago *sc* Dylan Thomas
7 mins NFA

Newspaper train
A story of how newspapers, necessary for informed public opinion, were delivered during the blitz in spite of bombs on London railway stations and machine-gunning of trains. (Film made in 1941)

Review DNL III 37, MFB IX 8
MoI *pc* Realist *p* John Taylor *d* Len Lye *ph* A E Jeakins *sound* Ernst Meyer *comm w* Merril Mueller
6 mins IWM NFA

Next of kin
(Originally made as an army training film on the dangers of careless talk, in the context of a fictional air-raid. A re-edited version was successfully released in the cinema at home and overseas)
War Office *pc* Ealing *d* Thorold Dickinson *p* Michael Balcon *cast* Mervyn Johns, Nova Pilbeam, Stephen Murray
99 mins IWM NFA

Next of kin. *Landing craft with British soldiers on raid on an occupied French port.*

Night shift
Ten hours on a night shift at an ordnance factory making guns for tanks, described by one of the two thousand girls on the job. (Film made in 1942)
Review MPH 6.2.43
MoI & Min of Supply *pc* Rotha Productions *p* Paul Rotha *d* Jack Chambers *ph* Harold Young *sc* Arthur Calder-Marshall
15 mins IWM LC NFA

Out and about
Walking at the week-end is one of the best ways for boys and girls to relax and keep fit: the Youth Hostels are still open for walkers
MoI & Board of Educ *pc* GB Instructional *d* Stanley Irving
9 mins

Night shift. *Factory supervisor inspects completed gun barrel straight off the production lines.*

Partners in crime
(The black market)
Review MFB IX 77
MoI *pc* Gainsborough *sc & d* Frank Launder, Sidney Gilliat *cast* Irene Handl, Robert Morley
8 mins LC NFA

Power to order
The development of the railway system and the construction of a modern locomotive
Review FoB 1942-3
pc Spectator
10 mins NFA

Proof positive
pc British Movietonews *p* Gerald Sanger
7 mins

Rush hour
(Shoppers must travel between 10 and 4)
Review MFB IX 8
MoI *pc* 20th Century Fox *p* Edward Black *d* Anthony Asquith
6 mins NFA

Seaman Frank goes back to sea
(The broadcaster Frank Laskier is shown returning to work in the Merchant Service and appealing for more contribu-

tions to National Savings)
Reviews DNL III 21, MFB VIII 171
National Savings Ctte & MoI *pc* Concanen *p* Derrick de Marney *d & ph* Eugene Cekalski *comm s* Terence de Marney, Frank Laskier
7 mins IWM NFA

A seaman's story – people at war
(The story of the courage of merchant seamen, as seen in the case of one seaman from Newfoundland whose boat has been torpedoed four times)
MoI *pc* Realist *d* John Taylor *ph* A E Jeakins
14 mins IWM

Speed-up on Stirlings
A story of the kind of problem which must be faced in the early stages of work on any new type of aircraft. The film shows how production of the Stirling was speeded up by breaking it down into numerous sub-assemblies which could be brought together for the final assembly. The people of the film are the people who built the first Stirlings and who are still building them
Review DNL III 151
MoI & Min of Aircraft Production *pc* Shell *p* Edgar Anstey *d* Grahame Tharp *ph* Sidney Beadle
20 mins IWM NFA

Spring on the farm
This film was made with farmers and farm workers of Ross-on-Wye, Herefordshire. It shows the preparation of the land, spring sowing and rolling, the purpose of each operation and the use of various implements. It shows how the agricultural research stations help the farmers. As spring ends the farm workers see the first signs of the harvest to come
Reviews DNL III 151, MFB X 94
MoI *pc* Green Park *assoc p* Edgar Anstey *d* Ralph Keene *ph* Erwin Hillier *m* William Alwyn
15 mins NFA

Summer on the farm
With hay making in June farmers begin to get in the harvests which give the towns food and which the farmers must sell in order that country people may buy the products of the towns. For the extra labour required to harvest the crops the country depends on the Land Clubs, and the schools. The film shows, with the help of maps and diagrams, how one industrial area–Manchester–gets its green vegetables, potatoes, fruit and milk from the surrounding farms of Lancashire and Cheshire
Reviews DNL IV 182, MFB X 116
MoI *pc* Verity-Greenpark *assoc p* Edgar Anstey *d* Ralph Keene *ph* Raymond Elton *ed* Julian Wintle *m* William Alwyn
12 mins NFA

A tale of two cities
The people of Moscow and London stand united by their common resistance to Nazi raids and in their determination to strike back
Review MFB IX 37
MoI & Soviet Film Agency *pc* Crown *p* Ian Dalrymple *compiler* John Monck
8 mins LC NFA

They keep the wheels turning
A story of six of the girls who, by taking the place of men in the repair shops, are helping to maintain essential road transport services
Review DNL III 113
MoI & Min of War Transport *pc* GB Screen Services *d* Francis Searle *ph* Walter Harvey *sound* John Douglas *ed* Enid Mansell
9 mins IWM

They met in London
At the 1941 meeting of the British Association statesmen and scientists of the United Nations discussed plans for victory and a New World of freedom and plenty. The speakers included Anthony Eden, John Winant, Maisky, Wellington Koo, Benes, John Orr, and Julian Huxley
Review DNL III 5

MoI *pc* Rotha Productions & British Paramount News *p* Paul Rotha *ph* Jack Harding
12 mins NFA

They speak for themselves
A report of a discussion by a group of young people of the war and the future for themselves and Britain
Reviews DNL III 113, MFB XIII 26
MoI *pc* Seven League *p & sc* Hans Nieter, Paul Rotha, Miles Malleson, Rex Warner
9 mins IWM

Twenty one miles
(Britain's front line, revisited by Ed Murrow. Also known as *Dover revisited.* Overseas title *Front line camera*)
Reviews DNL III 113, MFB IX 121
MoI *pc* Army Film Unit *d* Harry Watt
8 mins IWM NFA

Victory over darkness
The story of the work done at St Dunstan's in looking after the blinded and training them for work
Review MFB IX 37
MoI *pc* Realist *p* John Taylor for St Dunstan's *d* Max Anderson *ph* A E Jeakins
6 mins NFA

Water
Pure water consisting of hydrogen and oxygen never occurs in Nature. Among other things, water contains solids such as calcium, and chemists study the constituents of water so that use may be made of the valuable solids and the bad effects of others may be counteracted
Reviews DNL III 94, FoB 1942-3
ICI *pc* GB Instructional *d* Mary Field *ph* Jack Parker, F Percy Smith
11 mins

When we build again
A film about rehousing and town planning based on the survey published by the Bourneville Village Trust. The film surveys the still widespread slums and the congested inner suburbs of big industrial towns. It examines the faults of housing estates and flats built since the last war and shows how some of these can be avoided. An architect explains how he would re-plan a built-up area and plan a new town for the people who should be moved from the old town. Comments and opinions on the problems are provided by interviews with people living in the places shown in the film
Reviews DNL IV 182, MFB XVI 132
Cadbury Brothers *pc* Strand *d* Ralph Bond *ph* Charles Marlborough
30 mins MOMA

Women away from home
Three girls are moved to Birmingham to do war work. Two are billeted and one goes to live in a hostel. The film follows them until they have settled down in their new homes
MoI & Min of Labour *pc* Spectator *p* Michael Hankinson *d* Gilbert Gunn
10 mins IWM LC

Work party
(The factory effort)
Reviews DNL III 95, MFB IX 78
MoI *pc* Realist *p* John Taylor *d* Len Lye *ph* A E Jeakins *m* Ernst Meyer *asst d* Albert Pearl
6 mins

WVS
Stories of some of the hundred and one jobs done by the million members of the Women's Voluntary Services. The film shows them at work in a dozen different places, running clothes depots, rest centres and billets, driving ambulances, organising salvage collections, making hot tea for mobile canteens
Review DNL III 5
MoI *pc* Verity *p* Sydney Box, James Carr *d* Louise Birt *m* William Alwyn
22 mins IWM LC

Young farmers
Every boy and girl should grow up in knowledge of the land. In Young Far-

mers' Clubs in town and village they can learn the first lessons in what for some will be their future career and for others can be a constant source of interest and enjoyment
Reviews DNL III 152, MFB XII 142
MoI & Min of Ag *pc* Strand *assoc p* Edgar Anstey *d* John Eldridge *ph* Jo Jago
14 mins NFA

Young veterans
(The growth and development of the army from the viewpoint of a new recruit)
Reviews DNL I Dec 9, MFB VII 191
pc Ealing Studios *p* Cavalcanti *d* Charles Crichton *comm w & s* Michael Balcon
25 mins IWM NFA

Youth takes a hand
How a Youth Service Corps came to be formed and the work it undertook
MoI & Board of Educ *pc* Films of GB *p* Andrew Buchanan *d* Henry Cooper *ph* Charles Francis
12 mins

HOMEFRONT – Scotland, Ulster & Wales

Cally House
At Cally House the Glasgow Education Committee established a new kind of co-educational boarding school for boys and girls evacuated from Glasgow secondary schools
Review MFB XIII 129
MoI & Scottish Office *pc* Scottish Films *d* S Russell
10 mins LC

Western isles
(The making of Harris tweed and the contribution of the people of the Hebrides to the war effort)
Reviews DNL III 37, FoB 1942-3, MFB IX 24
British Council *pc* Merton Park *d* Terence Bishop *ph* Jack Cardiff *m* William Alwyn
14 mins colour NFA

HOMEFRONT – Instructional

ABCD of health
A simple exposition of the importance of the four Vitamins A, B, C, D, of what each contributes to health and the foods to eat to get them
MoI & Min of Food *pc* Spectator *p* Michael Hankinson *d* Jack Ellitt
9 mins LC NFA

Cultivation
How to thin dwarf french beans, carrots, parsnips, turnips, onions and transplant cabbages, cauliflowers and leeks; the proper use of three kinds of hoes; and how to stake peas, beans and tomatoes
MoI & Min of Ag *pc* Realist with Royal Horticultural Society *assoc p* Edgar Anstey *p* Frank Sainsbury *d* Margaret Thomson *m* Ernst Meyer *comm s* Roy Hay
12 mins CFL

Harvesting and storing
comm s Roy Hay
12 mins

He went to the cupboard
Hay Petrie and Joan Sterndale Bennett get to work on the store cupboard and save themselves food and trouble
MoI & Min of Food *pc* Films of GB *p* Andrew Buchanan *d* Henry Cooper *ph* Charles Francis *cast* Joan Sterndale-Bennett, Hay Petrie
8 mins

How to file
(Metal filing)
Review DNL II 229
pc Shell *p* Edgar Anstey *d* Kay Mander *ph* Sidney Beadle
7 mins NFA

How to thatch
George Wise, a Berkshire thatcher, shows how anyone who will take the trouble can do a first-class job of thatching

Reviews DNL III 5, MFB XVI 126
MoI & Min of Ag *pc* Strand *assoc p* Edgar Anstey *d* Ralph Bond *ph* Charles Marlborough *comm s* Freddie Grisewood
12 mins NFA

Making a compost heap
Review KYB 1943
MoI & Min of Ag *pc* Realist *assoc p* Edgar Anstey *p* Frank Sainsbury *d* Margaret Thomson
4 mins IWM NFA

No accidents
Accidents in factories cause personal suffering and loss of production. Most of them can be prevented by care and forethought. The film shows the kind of accident risks that exist in factories and how they can be prevented
MoI & Min of Labour *pc* Scottish Films *d* S Russell
10 mins CFL

The nose has it
With a wealth of surprising illustrations Arthur Askey shows why the British Public must not be sneezed at
Reviews DNL III 152, MFB IX 120
MoI & Min of Health *pc* Gainsborough *p* Edward Black *d* Val Guest *cast* Arthur Askey
8 mins CFL NFA

Rat destruction
A description of the methods by which local Rodent Officers, given essential assistance by shopkeepers, can track down and destroy rat infestations which threaten the food and health of the nation
Review DNL III 100
MoI & Min of Food *pc* Rotha Productions *p* Paul Rotha *assoc p* Bladon Peake *d* Budge Cooper *ph* Peter Hennessy *m* William Alwyn
10 mins NFA

Start a land club
The agricultural effort
Reviews DNL III 100, MFB IX 92
MoI & Min of Ag *pc* Films of GB *assoc p* Edgar Anstey *d* Andrew Buchanan *ph* Charles Francis
5 mins NFA

HOMEFRONT – Specialised instructional

Blood transfusion
This film tells the story of how doctors and scientists of many nations made possible modern methods of preserving blood and using it far from the places where the blood was given. It traces the development and present operation of the blood donor system in Britain and appeals to everyone to give blood to save the lives of others. The long version is available only for showing to groups of doctors, medical students and trained nurses
Review MFB X 118
MoI & Min of Health *pc* Rotha Productions *p* Paul Rotha *d* Hans Nieter *ph* Harry Rignold *diagrams* Isotype Institute
21 & 38 mins CFL IWM NFA

Ditching
Good, well-kept ditches and drains are essential to good farming. In this film a Hertfordshire ditcher and his mate show how the work should be done
MoI & Min of Ag *pc* Realist *assoc p* Edgar Anstey *p* John Taylor *d* Margaret Thomson *ph* Alex Strasser *m* Ernst Meyer *comm s* Roy Hay
10 mins MOMA NFA

Hedging
Mr Deighton, farmer, of Moulton, Northamptonshire, shows how to cut back and lay a hedge
MoI & Min of Ag *pc* Realist *assoc p* Edgar Anstey *p* John Taylor *d* Margaret Thomson (*ph* Alex Strasser *m* Ernst Meyer *comm s* Roy Hay)
9 mins MOMA NFA

HOMEFRONT – NFS, ARP, etc

Go to blazes
Will Hay demonstrates the right and wrong way to tackle incendiaries
Reviews DNL III 70, MFB IX 65
MoI *pc* Ealing Studios *p* Michael Balcon *d* Walter Forde *sc* Diana Morgan, Angus MacPhail *ph* Ernest Palmer *cast* Will Hay
5 mins

Hook ladder drill
Instructional film on the use of hook ladders. For use by authorized Fire Officers only for showing to National Fire Service personnel
MoI & National Fire Service *pc* London Fire Brigade
21 mins

A new fire bomb
An instructional film on how Fire Guards must tackle the new type of explosive incendiary bomb, showing particularly how what were once right ways of tackling fire bombs are now wrong and dangerous
Reviews DNL III 125, MFB IX 120
MoI & Min of Home Security *pc* Shell *p* Edgar Anstey *d* J B Napier-Bell *ph* Stanley Rodwell
9 mins IWM LC NFA

HOMEFRONT – Wartime social services

Ask CAB
A Citizens' Advice Bureau exists in every town to help people with their war-time problems and difficulties
Review MFB IX 136
MoI *pc* Verity *d* Henry Cass *p* Sydney Box, Maxwell Munden
8 mins IWM

CEMA
The aim of the Council for the Encouragement of Music and the Arts is 'to bring the best to as many people as possible to cheer them on to better times'. In this film a harp trio plays Vaughan Williams' arrangement of 'Greensleeves' in a village church, an industrial town sees its first exhibition of paintings by living artists, the Old Vic Company presents 'Merry Wives of Windsor' in a provincial theatre, and the Jacques Symphony Orchestra plays the first movement of Tchaikowsky's Piano Concerto in a factory canteen
Reviews DNL III 125, MFB XII 142
MoI & Board of Educ *pc* Strand *p* Alexander Shaw *d* John Banting, Dylan Thomas, Charles de Lautour, Alan Osbiston, Peter Graham Scott, Desmond Dickinson *ph* Charles Marlborough
16 mins LC NFA

Dinner at school
Large numbers of children are now given good midday meals at schools at a charge or, where necessary, for nothing. The progress so far made should be increased until dinner at school is a normal feature of school life for all children
MoI & Board of Educ & Min of Food *pc* Seven League *d* Hans Nieter
10 mins LC

Eating at work
Rationing, overtime, night shifts and housewives at work make it more difficult for workers to get proper meals. Good factory canteens where people can also relax are the obvious and sound solution
Review DNL II 189
sp British Commercial Gas Assoc *pc* Strand *assoc p* Edgar Anstey *d* Ralph Bond *ph* Gerald Gibbs
12 mins LC NFA

For children only
An appeal to mothers to take full advantage of the schemes for providing children with fruit juices and cod-liver oil containing vitamins essential to healthy growth
Reviews DNL III 55, KYB 1943
MoI & Min of Food *pc* Strand *p* Alexan-

der Shaw *d* John Eldridge *ph* Charles Marlborough
7 mins LC

FIGHTING SERVICES & CAMPAIGNS

According to plan
pc British Movietonews *p* Gerald Sanger
8 mins

Air operations
A short account of the preparation, execution and return from a Wellington raid on Germany; consisting of scenes from *Target for tonight*
MoI & Air Min *pc* Crown *p* Ian Dalrymple *d* Harry Watt
20 mins CFL IWM LC

The army lays the rails
Wherever the Army fights it must have rapid and efficient communications. This film shows the work of the Royal Engineers in laying and running railways
Review MFB IX 23
MoI & War Office *pc* Army Film Unit *d* Tennyson d'Eyncourt, Gerald Keen *m* Hans May
7 mins IWM LC

Balloon site 568
Looking after a barrage balloon is a tough and uninviting job. But it is an important job and WAAFs are now doing it and enjoying it
Reviews DNL III 100, MFB IX 64
MoI & Air Min *pc* Strand *p* Alexander Shaw *d* Ivan Moffat *ph* Jo Jago *sc* Dylan Thomas, Ivan Moffat
8 mins IWM LC NFA

Battle for freedom
The New Nations of the British Commonwealth fight side by side with Britain, Russia, America and China to win freedom for all men everywhere. The film reviews the strategic situation in the Atlantic, Russia and the Middle East, the Pacific and the Far East and shows the particular part played on each of these war fronts by each of the United Nations
MoI *pc* Strand *p* Basil Wright *d* Alan Osbiston
15 mins IWM NFA

Coastal Command
(The work of Coastal Command)
Reviews DNL III 152, MFB IX 125
pc Crown *p* Ian Dalrymple *d* J B Holmes *assoc d* Ralph Elton, Jack Lee, Richard McNaughton *m* R Vaughan Williams *m d* Muir Mathieson
73 mins IWM NFA

Commissioning a battleship
(The preparation of HMS Howe for her first voyage)
MoI *pc* GB News
11 mins IWM

Find, fix and strike
(Documentary record of the training of the Fleet Air Arm)
Review MFB IX 111
pc Ealing Studios *p* Michael Balcon, Cavalcanti *d* Compton Bennett *asst p* Charles Crichton
33 mins NFA

Free house
(Sailors from Allied forces talk informally)
Review MFB IX 104
MoI *pc* Verity *d* Henry Cass *p* Sydney Box, Maxwell Munden
5 mins

His Majesty's jollies
(The Royal Marines training)
Reviews DNL III 125, MFB IX 120
MoI *pc* British Paramount News *p & d* G T Cummins
26 mins

HM motor launches
Naval launches of a new type are now being produced by mass-production methods. The film shows how the various

parts are made in different places to standard specifications and brought together in the final assembly yard. It ends with scenes of tests and of a flotilla of launches on active service
Review MFB XII 10
MoI & Admiralty *pc* GB News
10 mins IWM LC NFA

HMS King George V
A tour of the battleship HMS King George V at sea on active service. The film shows the workshops, kitchens and mess rooms, chapel, gun turrets with the crews practising, operating theatre and sick bay, and the Admiral and his staff at work
Review DNL III 25
MoI & Admiralty *pc* Laurence and Elton *compiler* L Laurence *ph* Raymond Elton
16 mins IWM

Lift your head, comrade
The story of the men who form one of the fifteen alien companies of the Pioneer Corps–German and Austrian anti-fascists who between them served 125 years in gaols and concentration camps before escaping to England. Today they are on the right side of the barbed wire training to fight anywhere. (*Into battle* series no 1)
Reviews DNL IV 165, MFB IX 162
MoI *pc* Spectator *p* Basil Wright *d* Michael Hankinson *sc* Arthur Koestler
15 mins IWM LC NFA

Men of Timor
(Australian troops, cut off on the island of Timor, operate as a guerilla unit against the Japanese garrison)
8 mins IWM (incomplete)

Middle-East
(Strategy in the Middle East)
Reviews DNL III 70, MFB IX 51
MoI *pc* Shell *p* Edgar Anstey *d* Grahame Tharp *anim* Francis Rodker
5 mins NFA

Paratroops
A picture of the physical training and training in jumping from stages, captive balloons and aircraft given to paratroops
MoI *pc* Celluloid Despatch *p & compiler* Sylvia Cummins
10 mins IWM

The right man
An account of tests and methods used by the Army Directorate for Selection of Personnel to see that the right men are put into the right jobs
Reviews DNL III 100, MFB IX 92
MoI & War Office *pc* Army Film Unit *d* Alex Bryce *ed* F Clare
8 mins IWM LC NFA

The siege of Tobruk
The history of the siege of Tobruk from March to December 9, 1941, when the garrison fought its way out to meet the Eighth Army
MoI & War Office *pc* Army Film Unit *p* Alex Bryce *m* Richard Addinsell
17 mins CFL IWM

Street fighting
A realistic demonstration by Coldstream Guards of street-fighting tactics
Reviews DNL III 151
MoI & War Office *pc* Army Film Unit *d* Hugh Stewart, Gerald Keen *ed* F Clarke
14 mins IWM LC NFA

Tank battle
(What happens on the battlefield in a battle between two opposing tank forces)
Reviews DNL IV 165, MFB IX 162
MoI *pc* Army Film Unit *d* Gerald Keen *comm s* Raymond Glendenning *ed* Edward Carrick
12 mins

They serve abroad
MoI *pc* Army Film Unit *d* Roy Boulting *ed* J Durst
7 mins

Tobruk
MoI *pc* Army Film Unit *p* Alex Bryce *ed* R Verrall *m* Richard Addinsell

Troopship
A record of life on board a troopship bound for somewhere out East; featuring Addinsell's *Hold your hats on.*
Reviews DNL III 100, MFB IX 92
MoI & War Office *pc* Army Film Unit *d* Hugh Stewart, Tennyson d'Eyncourt *m* Richard Addinsell *ed* A Best
8 mins IWM

Wavell's 30,000
(Wavell's advance into Libya)
Reviews DNL III 37, MFB IX 14
pc Army Film Unit & Crown *p* Ian Dalrymple *d* John Monck *m* John Greenwood
50 mins IWM NFA

DOMINIONS & COLONIES – General

Building for victory
A newsreel compilation showing guns, tanks, shells aircraft and ships being built in the arsenals of the Empire
MoI *pc* Pathé
10 mins IWM

Empire aid
Reviews KYB 1943, MFB IX 104
MoI *pc* British Movietonews *p* Gerald Sanger
5 mins

HM Navies go to sea
A newsreel compilation showing the warships from Canada, Australia and South Africa that side by side with the ships of the Royal Navy guard the Empire's sea communications
MoI *pc* British Movietonews *p* Gerald Sanger
10 mins IWM

RAF action
A newsreel compilation showing the fighters and bombers flown by airmen from all parts of the Empire
Review DNL III 138
MoI *pc* British Movietonews
10 mins IWM LC NARS NFA

DOMINIONS & COLONIES – Africa

War came to Kenya
An account of Kenya's contribution to the war up to the advance of the British and South African forces into Abyssinia
Review MFB IX 92
Kenya Information Office *pc* African Films *d* G Johnson
18 mins IWM

With our African troops – early training
pc Colonial Film Unit
7 mins

With our African troops – on active service
pc Colonial Film Unit
7 mins

DOMINIONS & COLONIES – Canada

The battle for oil
In America, the Caucasus and the Middle East lie the oilfields which produce the greatest part of the world's supply of oil. Without oil in vast quantities armies, air forces and navies cannot move. To prevent the Axis powers from seizing any of the great oilfields or cutting supplies from them to the United Nations is a primary consideration of strategy. The film shows how this battle for oil affects both strategy and tactics. It also shows the steps being taken in Canada to conserve oil supplies and, by new drilling, to increase supplies from Canada's oilfields
pc National Film Board of Canada
15 mins NFA

Heroes of the Atlantic
To Halifax, Nova Scotia, come merchant ships and warships of all kinds, from all parts of the Empire and from America, for repair and refueling and to take on cargoes for Britain. The film shows this great Canadian port at work and the training of Canadian sailors. Guarded by Canadian destroyers and aircraft, a convoy sets out across the Atlantic. (*Canada carries on* series)
pc National Film Board of Canada *d* J Davidson
15 mins IWM NFA

Motor cycle training
Methods of training and tests for motorcyclists in the Canadian Army
Reviews DNL III 151, MFB IX 137
MoI & National Film Board of Canada *pc* Canadian Army *d* J McDougall
8 mins IWM LC

North-west frontier
North of the Mackenzie River lie 100,000 square miles of Canada inhabited by Eskimos and Indians, the mineral resources of which are only now being fully prospected. Exploration since 1920 has revealed oil, pitchblende for radium, lignite, lead, zinc and gold. The opening-up of the territory presents social problems for the future of the native inhabitants: for them the Government must provide new means of livelihood and modern schools and hospitals
pc National Film Board of Canada *p* James Beveridge *ed* Stanley Hawes, James Beveridge *nar* Terence O'Dell
32 mins NFA

Prairie gold
This film of the Canadian wheat industry was made from the pre-war film *The kinsman*. It shows the preparation of the soil and sowing, the work of agricultural research stations in improving harvests, harvesting, marketing and transport through the Great Lakes to Montreal to be shipped to Britain
Review MFB IX 108
Canadian Govt Wheat Board *d* G Sparling *re-ed* H Shepherd
20 mins NFA

The strategy of metals
A review of Canada's great mineral resources, which are now being fully prospected and mined to meet the needs of the United Nations. The film ends with a visit to Ford's of Canada, where thousands of army trucks are now being produced. (*Canada carries on* series)
pc National Film Board of Canada
20 mins IWM

Wood for war
Lumberjacks of the Canadian Army, using their special skill and knowledge, fell timber on the hillsides of Scotland
Reviews DNL III 37, MFB IX 78
MoI & National Film Board of Canada *pc* Canadian Army *d* J McDougall *ph* George Noble
9 mins IWM

DOMINIONS & COLONIES – India

The changing face of India
A picture of contrasts between rural life in the villages and the India of the cities. The film shows a typical village, its school, doctor, and entertainments. In contrast it shows modern blocks of flats and hotels in Bombay. But more important than these for the future of India are the research laboratories for agriculture, medicine and industry
sp Films Advisory Board of India *pc* Indian Film Unit *p* Alexander Shaw *d* Ezra Mir, Bhaskar Rao
11 mins

Defenders of India
A tribute to the Indian soldiers who fought in East Africa and Libya; with a foreword by General Auchinleck
Reviews DNL III 9, KYB 1943
sp Films Advisory Board of India *pc*

Bombay Talkies
9 mins IWM

Made in India
India is a land of villages and peasants. But today India also ranks among the great industrial powers. The traditional handicrafts and the new industries are both essential to India's development and the well-being of her people
sp Films Advisory Board of India *pc* Indian Film Unit *p* Alexander Shaw *d* Ezra Mir, Sherraz Farrukhi *sc* Minco Masini, based on his book *Our India*
12 mins

Men of India
Men of India, of many races and religions, whose fathers sold lamps in bazaars and knew nothing more mechanical than an ox-wagon, work together in a factory making armoured trucks
Reviews DNL III 70, MFB IX 65
MoI & Films Advisory Board of India *pc* Indian Film Unit & Strand *p* Alexander Shaw *English comm s* Edmund Willard *d* Ezra Mir *ed* Jinaraja Bodhye
8 mins

Our Indian soldiers
This was compiled from material from *A day with the Indian Army*
pc Colonial Film Unit
6 mins

Tins for India
The manufacture in an Indian factory of the kerosene tins which, after they have fulfilled the purpose for which they are made, are used by villagers to carry water and roof houses
Review MFB IX 139
Petroleum Films Bureau *pc* Shell (India) *d & ph* Bimal Roy
8 mins NFA

Women of India
In India today women are working in offices and in the professions for a better future for all the women of India
Films Advisory Board of India *pc* Indian Film Unit *p* Alexander Shaw *d* Bhaskar Rao
10 mins

ALLIES – General

Battle of supplies
A review of the supply problems which the United Nations must overcome in order to win the war. The film shows the overwhelming resources in munitions production and manpower available from the countries of the British Commonwealth and America. But to be effective in Russia, the Middle East and Far East these men and munitions must be transported by long sea routes open to attack by Axis submarines and aircraft. More ships and the use of every possible ship for essential war purposes must be the first concern of the United Nations
Review DNL III 156
MoI *pc* Strand *supervising ed* Alan Osbiston *ed* H A Oswald *diagrams* J F Horrabin *m* Victor Hely Hutchinson *m d* Muir Mathieson *p* Basil Wright
18 mins WM NFA

ALLIES – Czechoslovakia

Fighting allies
The story of the Czechs in Britain, in the fighting forces, working on the land and producing munitions of war
MoI *pc* British Movietonews *d* Louise Birt
9 mins IWM

ALLIES – France

Free French Navy
The story of the men who escaped to join the Fighting French and man the warships which escaped to continue the

fight under General de Gaulle
MoI *pc* Spectator *p* Michael Hankinson *d* Robin Carruthers *cast* Guy Guy-Maas
7 mins IWM

ALLIES – Norway

Men of Norway
The story of Norway's resistance to Nazis and quislings and of the Norwegians who have escaped to fight for their country's liberty; manning Norwegian freighters and tankers and training in Norwegian fighting units in Britain and Canada. (*March of Time* 7th year no 6, British series)
Review DNL II 229
pc March of Time
20 mins IWM

ALLIES – Poland

Diary of a Polish airman
The story of a Polish airman who escaped from Poland and fought in France, escaped to Britain and was killed in a fighter sweep
Reviews DNL III 54, MFB IX 37
MoI & Polish MoI *pc* Concanen *p* Derrick de Marney *d* Eugene Cekalski
8 mins IWM LC NFA PAC

Poland's new front
With the signing of the alliance between Poland and the USSR Polish armies are re-formed and equipped in Russia to fight for their country's liberation
Polish MoI *pc* Polish Film Unit *comp* Eugene Cekalski
8 mins IWM

The Poles weigh anchor
Life on a destroyer manned by Polish men and officers on convoy duty with the Royal Navy
Review MFB IX 37
Polish MoI *pc* Concanen *p* Derrick de Marney *d* Eugene Cekalski
12 mins

A Polish sailor
(A Polish seaman recalls his escape to England and experiences in a Murmansk convoy. Distribution arrangements unclear)
pc Concanen *p* Derrick de Marney *d & ed* Eugene Cekalski
11 mins IWM

ALLIES – USA

America moves her Japs
On the outbreak of war it became necessary for America to transfer thousands of Japanese Americans from her Pacific coast. The film is a record of the operation as it was carried out by the US Army and the War Relocation Authority. (US title *Japanese relocation*)
Review MFB IX 149
sp US Govt *pc* US Office of War Information *cast* Milton S Eisenhower
9 mins IWM (as *Japanese relocation*)

Bomber
America builds two-engined bombers for the United Nations
sp US Govt *pc* US Office of Emergency Management *sc* Carl Sandburgh
10 mins

A child went forth
A visit to an American school for under-fives held in a camp on a farm where the children can learn while they play in natural and free surroundings
sp New York University *p* Joseph Losey, John Ferno
20 mins CFL

The city
Film essay on the need for town-planning in order to solve the problems created by lack of planning in the nineteenth century and to build decent and healthy homes for today and tomorrow. The

film is closely based on Lewis Mumford's book *The Culture of Cities*. (Film made in 1939)
Review DNL I Dec 15
sp American Institute of Planners *pc* Civic Films *d & ph* Ralph Steiner, Willard van Dyke *m* Aaron Copland
55 mins BFI NFA (extract)

Defence for America
A review of America's industrial capacity for munitions production; made before America's entry into the war
sp National Assoc of Manufacturers *pc* Paramount *d* L Rousch
10 mins

From ships of the air
Paratroops of the American Marine Corps in training
sp US Marine Corps *pc* US Marine Corps Film Unit
7 mins IWM

Harvests for tomorrow
A story of the growth, decline and rebirth of the soil, seen in the houses and barns, cattle and crops, the town and people of New England
Review MFB XII 102
sp US Govt *pc* US Dept of Ag *d* P Burnford
28 mins NFA

Henry Browne, farmer
One-tenth of the population of the United States are negroes. Many negroes are small farmers. This film tells the story of one of them, Henry Browne, from Tuskegee, Alabama, who with his wife and two children farms a small holding, while their son is being trained to be a US army pilot
Review MFB XIII 39
sp US Office of War Information *pc* US Dept of Ag *d* Roger Barlow
11 mins

Home on the range
The States of Montana, Wyoming, Dakota and Nebraska form the chief cattle-raising area of the United States. This film, made in Montana, gives a picture of life in this area
Review MFB XII 102
sp US Office of War Information *pc* US Dept of Ag *d* Tom Hogan
11 mins

The home place
A survey of the outstanding types of American rural domestic architecture, showing how they followed traditions brought from Europe but also conformed to the local needs and materials discovered by settlers as they pushed westward across the continent
sp US Govt *pc* US Dept of Ag *d* R Evans
30 mins

Lake carrier
Across the Great Lakes during eight months of the year are carried supplies of iron ore to maintain production throughout the whole year in the steel furnaces of Detroit and Chicago
Review KYB 1943
sp US Govt *pc* US Office for Emergency Management *comm s* Frederic March
10 mins

Minnesota document
sp University of Minnesota *pc* Visual Educ Service *d* R Kisack
50 mins NFA

Power and the land
Since 1935, electricity for light and power has been brought to hundreds of thousands of American farms which until then had only kerosene for light and no power but that of the people and animals who worked on the farms. In telling this story the film presents a picture of the ordinary small farms and farming communities which are the foundation of American agriculture
US Govt *pc* US Dept of Ag & US Rural Electrification Administration *d* Joris Ivens *ed* Helen Van Dongen *ph* Floyd Crosby, Arthur Ornitz *sc* Edwin Locke

m Douglas Moore
38 mins

Tanks
America builds tanks for the United Nations
US Govt *pc* US Office for Emergency Management *comm s* Orson Welles
10 mins

What so proudly we hail
A day in the life of Sidney Case, motor engineer, his wife and two children, ordinary Americans working hard, living simply, confident in the future for themselves and their neighbours
General Motors *pc* Sound Masters
18 mins IWM

ALLIES – USSR

Defeat of the Germans near Moscow
This film, from material shot on the field of battle by Soviet cameramen, gives a concentrated picture of the war in Russia, showing how men, women and children rallied to the defence of Moscow, and representing the campaign as being not merely the means of stopping Hitler, but the beginning of the work of wiping out his troops. Close-up studies show the nature of the task and uncover the evidence of German atrocities and vandalism as the enemy are driven back to Mozhaisk and beyond. (Russian title *Razgrom nemetzkikh voisk pod Moskvoi*)
Review MFB IX 77
sp Soviet Film Agency *pc* Central Newsreel Studio *English comm s* Wilfred Pickles *supervision* D Varlamov, J Kapalin *ed* Paul Capon
57 mins CFL NFA

The five men of Velish
A story of Nazi brutality in Russia (shown by photographs taken by a Nazi) and of the spirit to resist that inspires the Soviet people
Reviews KYB 1943, MFB IX 79
MoI *pc* Soviet Film Agency
8 mins IWM LC

The half of a nation
(Women in Russia)
pc Soviet War News Film Agency
5 mins

A house in London
On a blitzed house in Finsbury M Maisky, the Soviet Ambassador, unveils for the London County Council a plaque recording that Lenin lived there. The film shows the ceremony and records the speech made by M Maisky. The film is an exact English version of the film produced for Russia, one of the fifty-three countries to which films are sent by the MoI
Review DNL III 151
MoI *pc* British Paramount News *p* G T Cummins
9 mins NFA

Inside fighting Russia
(An explanation of how Soviet strategy disrupted Hitler's timetable and so changed the course of the war. Shows Red Army troops in action, women cultivating the fields and workers in industry. *World in action* series. International release title *Our Russian ally*)
Reviews DNL IV 181, MFB IX 162
pc National Film Board of Canada *p* John Grierson
22 mins

Leningrad fights
The city is besieged. Winter brings almost intolerable hardships. Food supplies dwindle; the water system freezes. But the road and railway across the ice of Lake Ladoga remain as the lifeline, and the resistance of the population never breaks. The spring of 1942 brings some relief, but not the final raising of the siege. (Original title *Leningrad v borbe*)
sp Soviet Film Agency *pc* Lenfilm Newsreel Studios, Leningrad *English comm w* John Gordon (Editor of *Sunday Express*) *English comm s* Ed Murrow (European

Director, CBS)
60 mins CFL

100 million women
Soviet women in industry and on the land, in the civil defence services and with the Red Army
Review MFB IX 25
MoI *pc* Soviet Film Agency
9 mins IWM LC

The other RAF
The men of the Red Air Force
pc Soviet Film Agency
8 mins IWM

Soviet school child
Soviet education from nursery schools to technical institutes and universities, showing the subjects taught and the methods of teaching at each type of school. The schools shown are situated in many different parts of the USSR
MoI & Soviet Film Agency *pc* Central Studio, Moscow
23 mins LC NFA

Strong point 42
The story of how a German strong point was located and destroyed. Dialogue in English
Review MFB IX 52
Soviet Film Agency *pc* Mosfilm
18 mins IWM

Via Persia
Along the route for supplies for Russia, from the Persian Gulf by rail and road to the Caspian Sea, operated by British Army railway engineers and Red Army truck drivers
Review MFB IX 137
MoI & War Office *pc* Army Film Unit
library compilation Jack Chambers
8 mins IWM LC

OVERSEAS DISTRIBUTION

ABCD of health

According to plan

All those in favour

America moves her Japs

Arms from scrap

Ask CAB

Atlantic charter

Balloon site 568

Barbados day at Portsmouth
Review DNL III 139
pc Colonial Film Unit
6 mins

Battle for freedom

Battles of supplies

Birth of a tank

Blood transfusion

Border weave
(The story of how tweed cloth is made)
Reviews DNL III 21, FoB 1942-3, MFB IX 148
sp British Council *pc* Turner *p* George E Turner *ph* Jack Cardiff
15 mins colour NFA

Bren gun carriers
Review DNL III 139
pc Colonial Film Unit
8 mins

Builders

Building for victory

Cally House

CEMA

Chacun son lieu
(French and Arabic versions only)
MoI *pc* Strand *d* Ralph Keene *assoc p* Basil Wright
12 mins

Chiang Kai-Shek in India

Coastal Command

Coastal village
Human Geography series. Newlyn Bay is a Cornish fishing village sheltered by headlands, and geographically an ideal place for a fishing community. From here fishermen go to sea in all weathers. Scenes of deep-sea herring fishing in early autumn are included
Reviews FoB 1942-3, MFB XIV 123
sp British Council *pc* GB Instructional *d* Stanley Irving
11 mins NFA

Commachio
MoI
NFA

The countrywoman

Cultivation

The day that saved the world

Dig for victory

Dinner at school

Ditching

Dockers

Dover
MoI
NARS

Empire aid

Essential jobs

Fighting allies

Filling the gap

Fireguard
(Overseas distribution)
Review DNL III 21
MoI *pc* Shell *p* Edgar Anstey *d* Geoffrey Bell *ph* Sidney Beadle
25 mins NARS NFA

For children only

Free French Navy

The great harvest

Greetings to Soviet schoolchildren
(Not shown in Britain)
MoI *pc* British Movietonews *p* Gerald Sanger

Heavier than air
This film was not seen in Britain. (Instructional film for civilians on gas warfare)
MoI *pc* GB Screen Services *p* Eric Dane *d* Francis Searle
8 mins IWM LC

Hedging

A house in London

How to thatch

HMS King George V

India arms for victory
pc Indian Films Advisory Board *d* S V Kriparan

Indians in action
(Overseas distribution only)
MoI *pc* Celluloid Dispatch *ed* Sylvia Cummins
9 mins IWM

Jane Brown changes her job

Knights of St John

Land girl

A letter from home
(Not shown in Britain)
MoI *pc* 20th Century-Fox *p* Edward Black *d* Carol Reed *cast* Celia Johnson
14 mins NFA

Life begins again

Lift your head, comrade

Listen to Britain

London, autumn 1941
(This film was not released in Britain)
MoI *pc* Films of GB *p* Andrew Buchanan *comm s* Sir Gilbert Scott
8 mins NFA

London scrapbook
(The changes which the war has brought to London and Londoners. Intended for American audiences)
Review DNL III 70
MoI *pc* Spectator *p* Basil Wright *d* Derrick de Marney, Eugene Cekalski *ph* A H Luff *cast* Bessie Love, Basil Radford, Leslie Mitchell
11 mins NFA

Malta GC

Men of tomorrow

Middle-East

Mobile engineers

Motor cycle training

A new fire bomb

New towns for old

Newfoundlanders at war
(Overseas distribution only)
MoI *pc* Pathé
10 mins IWM

Newspaper train

Night shift

No accidents

The nose has it

100 million women

Ordinary people
(How some Londoners spend their day during the blitz—shopping, cab driving, in court and helping bombed-out neighbours. Film made in 1941. Overseas distribution only)
MoI *pc* Crown *d* J B Holmes, Jack Lee (*ph* Jonah Jones)
24 mins IWM NFA PAC

Paratroops

Partners in crime

Proof positive

RAF action

RAF rescue boats
pc Colonial Film Unit
7 mins

Raid on France
(This was an adaptation of Dickinson's *Next of kin* and was not shown in Britain. Sent to Russia)
pc Ealing Studios *p* Michael Balcon *d* Thorold Dickinson

Report from Britain
(Not shown in Britain)
MoI *pc* British Movietonews *p* Gerald Sanger

Rush hour

Russian lesson
(Not shown in Britain)
MoI *pc* Strand *p* Alexander Shaw *d* Ivan Moffat
12 mins NFA

Self-help in food
pc Colonial Film Unit
13 mins

Shock troops
(British troops train and prepare for offensive warfare. Not shown in Britain)
MoI *pc* Spectator
11 mins IWM LC

Soldier's comforts from Uganda
Review DNL III 139
pc Colonial Film Unit
8 mins

Song of the Clyde
(The Clyde from source to sea)
Reviews DNL III 21, FoB 1942-3, MFB IX 24
British Council *pc* Merton Park *d & p* James Rogers
11 mins LC NFA

Speaking from America
(Short-wave radio reception. Film made 1938-39)
Review FoB 1940
pc GPO *p* Cavalcanti *d* Humphrey Jennings
10 mins NFA

Speed up on Stirlings

Spring on the farm

Street fighting

The sword of the spirit
(Involvement of Britain's Catholics in the war effort. Overseas only)
Review MPH 12.12.42
MoI *pc* Verity *p* Sydney Box, James Carr *d* Henry Cass *comm w & s* Robert Speight
15 mins LC NFA

Take cover
pc Colonial Film Unit
31 mins silent

A tale of two cities

Tank battle

Teeth of steel
(Modern excavators at work)
Reviews DNL III 54, FoB 1942-3, MFB IX 149
British Council *pc* Technique *p* James Carr *d* Ronald Riley *sc* Maxwell Munden *ph* Geoffrey Unsworth
10 mins colour NFA

These are ATS and WRNS
pc Colonial Film Unit

These are British soldiers
pc Colonial Film Unit

These are mobile canteens
pc Colonial Film Unit

They met in London

This is a fireman
pc Colonial Film Unit
12 mins

Troopship

Twenty-one miles

UBX
MoI & Directorate of Army Kinematography
NARS

Uganda police
(The training and work of the African police in Uganda)
Review DNL III 139
pc Colonial Film Unit
8 mins silent

United nations
(Overseas distribution only. A record of the first United Nations Day in Great Britain on 14 June 1942)
Reviews DNL III 113, MFB IX 121
MoI *pc* Crown *p* Ian Dalrymple
11 mins colour IWM

Via Persia

Victory over darkness

Water

Water cycle
The water cycle of evaporation (from the sea, from fresh water, and from vegetation) and precipitation on to the earth and the sea; a process without which life would not be possible. (Film made in 1933)
Reviews FoB 1942-3, MFB I 27
ICI *pc* GB Instructional *d* Mary Field *ph* Jack Parker, F Percy Smith
11 mins NFA

Water service
The engineering and scientific methods used in the collection, storage, purification and distribution of water supplies
Reviews FoB 1942-3, MFB XIV 90
British Council *pc* Selwyn
11 mins NFA

Wavell's 30,000

We speak to India
(The part played by Indians in the war effort in the services and in civilian life. Overseas distribution only)
Review DNL III 130
MoI *pc* Everyman *assoc p* Alexander Shaw *d* Richard Massingham *ph* Alex Strasser *comm* Z A Bakhari
5 mins

Western Isles

Women away from home

WVS

Young farmers

Youth takes a hand

NEWSREEL TRAILERS

ATS
sp War Office
2 mins

Be prepared
MoI & Min of War Transport *pc* Spectator
d Gilbert Gunn

Care of clothes
MoI & Board of Trade *pc* Rotha Productions

Cease fire

Chicken feed
Review DNL IV 182

MoI & Min of Supply *pc* Spectator *d* B Luff

Child road safety
MoI & Min of War Transport *pc* Spectator *d* Jack Ellitt

Collapsible metal tubes
MoI & Min of Supply *pc* Realist *d* Len Lye
NFA

Cooks
MoI *pc* Verity *d* Kenneth Annakin

Correct addressing
MoI & GPO *pc* Pathé *d* L Behr

Diphtheria 1 & 2
Review DNL IV 182
MoI & Min of Health *pc* Rotha *d* Jack Chambers

Eyes on the target
MoI & Min of Fuel & Power *pc* Film Traders *d* George Hollering

Five-inch bather
(Economic use of water in the bath)
Review DNL IV 182
MoI & Min of Fuel & Power *pc* Public Relationship *d* Richard Massingham

Fuel economy (cooking)
Dept of Mines *pc* Films of GB
1 min

Fuel economy (hot water)
Dept of Mines *pc* Films of GB
1 min

Hogsnorton
MoI & Min of Fuel & Power *pc* Strand *d* Donald Taylor *cast* Gillie Potter

Is your journey really necessary?
MoI & Min of War Transport *pc* Spectator *d* Gilbert Gunn

Just in case you are bombed

Kitchen waste for pigs
MoI & Min of Food *pc* McDougal & McKendrick

Little Annie's rag-book
(Salvage)
MoI & Min of Supply *pc* Rotha Productions *d* L Bradshaw
NFA

The magician
MoI & Min of Fuel & Power *pc* Rotha Productions *d* Budge Cooper

Metal salvage
MoI & Min of Supply *pc* Films of GB

Milk
MoI & Min of Food *pc* Publicity

NAAFI
(Recruiting film to persuade women that working in the Naafi is worthwhile and fun)
MoI & Min of Labour *pc* Rotha Productions *d* S Eisler
2 mins NFA

Paper salvage
MoI & Min of Supply *pc* Films of GB

Postman always rings at Christmas
MoI & GPO *pc* Nettlefolds *d* G Shurley

Potatoes

Rags for salvage

Railings
MoI & Min of Works & Buildings *pc* Publicity *d* A Hopkins

Recuiting women

Rout the rats
MoI & Min of Food *pc* Strand

Rubber salvage
Review DNL IV 182
MoI & Min of Supply *pc* Films of GB *cast* Basil Radford

Sabotage!
(Care of clothes to save materials. Also known as *Care of clothes*)
MoI & Board of Trade *pc* Rotha Productions
1 min NFA

Save the toothpaste tubes

Save water

Save your bacon
Review DNL IV 182
MoI

Scrap metal

Sensible buying
MoI & Board of Trade *pc* Rotha Productions *d* Peter Hennessey
2 mins NFA

Service women
MoI *pc* Publicity *d* A Hopkins

Sneezing
MoI & Min of Health *pc* Strand *cast* Cyril Fletcher

Sorting salvage
Review DNL IV 182
MoI & Min of Supply *pc* Spectator *d* Jack Ellitt

Water pipes
MoI & Min of Health *pc* Film Traders *d* George Hollering

Water saving
MoI & Min of Health *pc* Film Traders *d* George Hollering

The way to his heart
Review DNL IV 182
MoI & Min of Food *pc* Strand *d* Donald Taylor
2 mins IWM

1943

HOMEFRONT – General

ABCA
The Army Bureau of Current Affairs was set up by the War Office in 1941 to teach the soldiers the alphabet of world affairs and the progress of the war. The basis of the scheme is one hour's discussion every week as part of every unit's time-table with an officer acting as chairman. The film shows how the scheme has developed and argues that ABCA is giving the soldier a new weapon which is helping to win the war and will help him in building the peace
Review MFB XI 110
MoI & War Office *pc* Army Film Unit *p & d* Ronald Riley *ph* Charles Marlborough *m* William Alwyn *comm s* Geoffrey Sumner *sc* Jack Saward
15 mins IWM NFA

Believe it or not
The scope and variety of the work done by the Red Cross and St John War Organisation, as seen by Ripley the cartoonist
sp Red Cross & St John *pc* Public Relationship *p* Lewis Grant Wallace *d* Richard Massingham
15 mins IWM

The biter bit
(How Germany is now feeling the weight of Allied bombing)
Review MFB X 105
pc Coombe *p* Alexander Korda
15 mins IWM (incomplete) MOMA NFA

Breathing space
A picture of some of the ways in which people in Britain spend their time off, singing, dancing and listening to music. (Overseas version lasting 30 minutes with same title)
Review DNL IV 215
MoI *pc* Strand *p* Alexander Shaw *d* Charles de Lautour *ph* Charles Marlborough *ed* Alan Osbiston
10 mins IWM

The crown of the year
The grain harvest is the crown of the farming year for the 500,000 farmers of whom George Hodge, an East Norfolk farmer is one. After the grain the bulk of the root crops are lifted. With Harvest Festival the ploughs are out on the stubble fields. The farmers make their cropping plans for the new year and the yearly round begins again
Reviews DNL IV 215, MFB X 83
MoI & Min of Ag *pc* Green Park *assoc p* Edgar Anstey *d* Ralph Keene *ph* Raymond Elton, Erwin Hillier, Reginald Wyer *m* William Alwyn
19 mins NFA

Dustbin parade
An urgent call to everyone, in cartoon form, to salvage and save every possible bit of paper, cloth, metal, bone and rubber
Review MFB IX 137
MoI & Min of Supply *pc* Realist *p* John Taylor *anim* John Halas, Joy Batchelor *assoc p* Edgar Anstey
6 mins IWM NFA

Dustbin parade. *A bone, a tin can, a wooden spinning top and a rag report for service in war industry.*

Fires were started
(Dramatisation of the work of the National Fire Service during the blitz of winter and spring 1940-41. Also shown as *I was a fireman*)
Reviews DNL IV 200, MFB X 37
MoI *pc* Crown *p* Ian Dalrymple *d* Humphrey Jennings *ph* C Pennington-Richards *settings* Edward Carrick *m* William Alwyn *m d* Muir Mathieson
63 mins IWM NFA

First aid on the spot
MoI *pc* GB Screen Services *d* Francis Searle
12 mins

Food flashes
(Series of short message films with themes such as 'Eat potatoes not bread' etc)
MoI and Min of Food
2-5 mins each B&W and colour NFA

The harvest shall come
The story of neglect and decay, relieved only during 1914-18 and again today under the stress of war, is factual; it is set in Suffolk. Tom Grimwood, a character created by H W Freeman and played by John Slater, is typical of farm workers and of all workers, who expect that in the new world they are now fighting for all men everywhere shall have food and a job
Reviews DNL III 68, MFB XIX 141
sp ICI *pc* Realist *p* Basil Wright *d* Max Anderson *ph* A E Jeakins *sc* H W Freeman *m* William Alwyn *comm s* Edmund Willard, Bruce Belfrage *cast* John Slater, Eileen Beldon, Richard George
38 mins NFA

In enemy hands
The story of the organisation maintained by the Red Cross and St John War Organisation and the International Red Cross Society to trace prisoners-of-war so as to enable next-of-kin to keep in touch with them
sp Red Cross & St John War Organisation *pc* GB News
22 mins

It's just the way it is
(The parents of an airman who died returning from an air raid on Germany

meet their son's Wing Commander who explains that the accident was one of the chances of war)
Review MFB X 68
MoI *pc* Two Cities *d* Leslie Fenton
15 mins NFA

Men from the sea
Crews from four merchant ships sunk in the North Atlantic are brought into a Scottish port. At the Merchant Navy Club they get clothes, money, ration cards and rail warrants to take them to their homes for a rest before joining new ships. At the Admiralty in London the enquiry into the sinking of the *Arctic Star* reveals a story of endurance and heroism typical of the men of the merchant navy in war and peace. (*Into battle* series no 9)
Review MFB X 93
MoI & Admiralty *pc* Spectator *d* Gilbert Gunn
16 mins IWM

Our film
The story of the formation of a Joint Production Committee of workers and management to discover and remove obstacles to maximum war production. The film was made and financed by the workers and technicians of Denham Film Studios
Reviews DNL III 63, MFB IX 77
pc Denham Film Studios *cast* John Slater
15 mins NFA

Radio in battle
The tactics of every battlefield depend on a radio network between infantry and tanks, advancing units and headquarters, the Army and the Air Force. The film shows this network in action. Workers in radio factories are supplying to every front equipment essential to success
MoI & Min of Supply *pc* Shell *p* Edgar Anstey *d* J B Napier-Bell
12 mins IWM

Sea Scouts
(How the Sea Scouts are trained to carry on Britain's seafaring tradition)
Reviews FoB 1941, MFB IX 51
pc Technique *d* Julian Wintle
11 mins

Seeds and science
For good crops farmers must have good seeds. Plant breeding research by agricultural botanists leads to new and improved varieties of seeds. The film shows the kind of work carried on by Dr Hunter, the breeder of Spratt-Archer barley, Maurice Buck (wheats), Dr Bell (winter barleys) and Dr Carson (oats)
Review MFB XIV 133
MoI & Min of Ag *pc* Strand *p* Donald Taylor *assoc p* Edgar Anstey *d* Alan Osbiston
13 mins NFA

Sky giant – the story of the Avro-Lancaster
A picture of Lancasters in production and in action, of the men and women who make them and of crews who flew them in one of the 1,000 bomber raids
MoI & Min of Aircraft Production *pc* British Movietonews *p* Gerald Sanger
10 mins IWM LC NFA

These are the men
(An exposé of the Nazi leaders. *Into battle* series no 4)
Reviews DNL IV 195, MFB X 32
MoI *pc* Strand *p* Donald Taylor *devised & comp* Alan Osbiston, Dylan Thomas *idea* Robert Neumann *comm s* James McKechnie, Bryan Herbert *sd* Ken Cameron
15 mins IWM LC NARS NFA

Tyneside story
For years before the war shipyards with a long line of well-built ships to their credit lay derelict. The skilled men who knew how to build ships had found other jobs or been unemployed. Now they have been directed back into the yards. Women, too, have been trained to

work in the yards. Today as the ships are launched the men ask what use will be found for their skill when the war ends
Review MFB XI 34
MoI & Min of Labour *pc* Spectator *p* Michael Hankinson *d* Gilbert Gunn *story* Jack Common *cast* People's Theatre Co, Newcastle upon Tyne
15 mins IWM LC

Underground front
(Importance of coal mining in wartime. Report of how steps were taken to increase pit output since the winter of 1942-43)
pc Movietone
IWM

Vegetable harvest
MoI *pc* Rotha Productions *p* Paul Rotha *assoc p* Edgar Anstey *d* John Page
8 mins

We sail at midnight
(The operation of the Lease-Lend arrangement in terms of the supply of essential tools to a British tank factory)
Reviews DNL III 151, MFB IX 149
MoI *pc* Crown *p* Ian Dalrymple *d* Julian Spiro *ph* H E Fowle *m* Richard Addinsell
27 mins

Winter work in the garden

Workers' week end
The men and women in the North-West of England set themselves the task of building a Wellington bomber in the record time of 30 hours. They did the job in 24¾ hours and the cameras recorded them doing it. The job was done in the workers' own time and they gave their bonus to Red Cross Aid to Russia Fund
Reviews DNL IV 227, MFB X 116
MoI *pc* Crown *p* John Monck *d* Raymond Elton
14 mins IWM NFA

World of plenty
A film about food, how it is grown and harvested, marketed and eaten. The people quoted and interviewed include farmers and a housewife; President Roosevelt, Vice-President Wallace and Mr Claude Wickard, US Secretary of Agriculture; Mr Wellington Koo; Sir John Orr; Lord Woolton; Lord Horder; Sir John Russell and Mr L F Easterbrook
Reviews DNL IV 217, MFB X 88
MoI *pc* Rotha Productions *p & d* Paul Rotha *assoc d* Yvonne Fletcher *sc* Paul Rotha, Eric Knight, Miles Malleson *m* William Alwyn
46 mins BFI MOMA

HOMEFRONT – Scotland & Wales

Power for the highlands
The mountains and glens of the Highlands look beautiful to the casual visitor. But there are few people living there. Bracken has wasted the hillsides, land that might produce crops and support sheep and cattle is unfarmed, and water from the mountains, a great potential source of power, rushes down uncontrolled turning valleys into bogs. The North of Scotland Hydro-Electricity Board has now been set up by Parliament to convert this water into power and to promote developments in the Highlands. Two soldiers of the 51st (Highland) Division, an engineer, and a ghillie, discuss how the scheme can benefit the people of the Highlands, and two American soldiers explain what has been achieved by similar schemes under the Tennessee Valley Authority. The film was taken in Glen Affric, Strathfarrar, Duckie and Galloway
Reviews DNL V 5, MFB XI 7, MFB XI 137
MoI & Scottish Office *pc* Rotha Productions *p* Paul Rotha *d* Jack Chambers *sc* Roger McDougall *ph* Wolfgang Suschitzky *m* Ian Whyte
31 mins LC NFA

Wales – green mountain, black mountain
Wales is a country of great contrasts. On the green hills are the farms; in the valleys the black mining villages. Before the war, in many parts of Wales, young men waited in vain for work; now all who can work are working hard, digging coal out of the rich mountains, rearing sheep on mountain slopes which new-sown grasses have made good pasture again. In town and village, in the mines, foundries and shipyards and on the farms, life throbs with work for all. Never again must there be young men with no work in derelict towns. (Made in Welsh and English. Film made in 1942)
Reviews DNL III 152, MFB XII 42
MoI *pc* Strand *p* Donald Taylor *d* John Eldridge *ph* Jo Jago *sc & comm w* Dylan Thomas *m* William Alwyn
12 mins WM (English)

Wales, green mountain, black mountain. *Miners come from the pits after work.*

HOMEFRONT – Instructional

Feeding your hens in wartime
Instructional film on preparing kitchen waste and how to use it with the ration of balanced meal
MoI & Min of Ag *pc* Films of GB *d* Andrew Buchanan *assoc p* Edgar Anstey
11 mins NFA

Keeping rabbits for extra meat
Advice for domestic keepers on selecting breeds and healthy does, care of young, types of hutches, feeding and the use of kitchen waste with the official bran ration. It is only available to Rabbit Clubs
Review DNL III 37
MoI & Min of Ag *pc* Strand *assoc p* Edgar Anstey *d* Ralph Bond *ph* Charles Marlborough *comm s* Wilfred Pickles
9 mins LC

More eggs from your hens
Advice for domestic keepers on how to choose good hens and how to look after and feed half-a-dozen of them
Review DNL III 21
MoI & Min of Ag *pc* Merton Park *assoc p* Edgar Anstey *p* Terence Bishop *ph* James Rogers *ed* Cath Miller *d* James Rogers
10 mins MOMA NARS NFA

Tuberculosis
Tuberculosis is on the increase. The film shows how it is contracted and may be avoided, and the importance of early examination and treatment by a doctor. Immediate and proper treatment can lead to complete recovery
MoI & Min of Health *pc* Seven League
11 mins

Twelve days
Farmers must give twelve days' notice of their intention to sell livestock. The film explains the reason for this by revealing the complex organisation necessary to ensure that everyone gets his meat ration
Review DNL III 113
MoI & Min of Food *pc* Merton Park *d* Cecil Musk *ph* Alan Dinsdale *sc* Mary Benedetta *sound* Charles Tasto *ed* Cath Miller
12 mins IWM

HOMEFRONT – Specialised instructional

Clamping potatoes
An instructional film for commercial growers on the Lincolnshire method of clamping potato crops
Reviews DNL III 125, MFB XIV 104
MoI & Min of Ag *pc* Realist *p* John Taylor *d* Max Anderson *ph* John Taylor
8 mins NFA

Silage
(Two methods of making silage)
Review DNL IV 226
MoI *pc* Realist *d* Margaret Thomson *ph* A E Jeakins
LC

HOMEFRONT – ARP, CD, NFS, etc

City fire, December 29, 1940
Film record, with commentary, of the City Fire of December 29, 1940, edited by Pathé Pictures from material photographed by the Film Unit of the London Fire Brigade. For loan to authorized Fire Officers for showing to National Fire Service personnel
Review KYB 1943
MoI & Min of Home Security *pc* London Fire Brigade
13 mins IWM (mute version entitled *London fire raids 29-30 December 1940*)

Civil defence ambulance
Instructional film on daily routine at an Ambulance Station and proper methods of ambulance service in a raid. Available only for the training of Civil Defence workers
MoI & Min of Home Security *pc* GB Screen Services *d* Francis Searle
20 mins IWM LC

Control room
The Civil Defence Control Room is the nerve centre of a town's organisation for fighting a blitz. Everything that happens during a raid is reported to the Control Room, where a picture is built up of the damage done and of the steps being taken to deal with it. This film was made with the help of the Civil Defence Services of Bristol. The incidents are imaginary
Reviews DNL III 156, KYB 1943
MoI & Min of Home Security *pc* Shell *p* Edgar Anstey *d* Geoffrey Bell *ph* Sidney Beadle *anim* Francis Rodker *asst d* Lionel Cole
25 mins IWM LC NFA

Debris tunnelling
(How to get people from under the debris of bombed buildings by means of a tunnel)
Review DNL IV 202
MoI *pc* Shell *p* Edgar Anstey *d* Kay Mander *ph* Wolfgang Suschitzky
19 mins IWM LC NFA

Decontamination of streets
Instructional film on the proper method of decontaminating a street in which a liquid-gas bomb has fallen. Available only for the training of civil defence workers
MoI & Min of Home Security *pc* Verity *p* Sydney Box, James Carr *d* Louise Birt
15 mins IWM LC NARS NFA

Factory fireguard
MoI *pc* Verity *p* Sydney Box *d* Louise Birt
28 mins LC NARS NFA

First-aid post
Instructional film on routine management of a First-Aid Post and proper methods of receiving and dealing with casualties in a raid. Available only for the training of civil defence workers
MoI for Min of Home Security *pc* GB Screen Services *d* Francis Searle
14 mins IWM LC

London blitz, May 10-11, 1941
This film is available to authorized Fire Officers only for showing to National Fire Service personnel
MoI & Min of Home Security *pc* London Fire Brigade
8 mins

Mobilising procedure
Instructional film on National Fire Service mobilising procedure as it should operate in a typical situation shown from stage to stage until appliances have been mobilised from all sources including adjoining Regions
Review DNL III 125
MoI & National Fire Service *pc* Shell *p* Edgar Anstey *d* Kay Mander
21 mins IWM NARS

Model procedure for water relaying
Instructional film on the theory and practice of water relaying illustrated by exact procedure for a number of typical situations
MoI & National Fire Service *pc* Shell *p* Edgar Anstey *d* Kay Mander
33 mins IWM LC NARS

Pembroke docks oil fire
Available only to authorized Fire Officers for showing to National Fire Service personnel
MoI & Min of Home Security *ph* London Fire Brigade
6 mins

Surrey commercial docks fire September 1940
MoI & Min of Home Security *ph* London Fire Brigade
16 mins

Thameshaven oil fire
(For National Fire Service training.) Available only to authorised Fire Officers for showing to National Fire Service personnel
MoI & Min of Home Security *ph* London Fire Brigade
10 mins

HOMEFRONT – Wartime social services

Back to normal
Mrs Foster, a housewife with two children, who lost a leg in a blitz, and Mr Philips, who lost an arm at Sidi Rezegh, show how they and others have been enabled, with good artificial limbs and training at Roehampton Hospital, to return to normal life with restored capacity and confidence
Review MFB XI 22
MoI & Min of Pensions *pc* Merlin *d* Roger McDougall *p* Michael Hankinson
15 mins

Catering
A film for the staffs of canteens in factories, offices, British restaurants and the fighting forces. The film deals with the training of cooks and provision of suitable equipment, scientific planning of meals, and waste of food and of vitamins in food by bad cooking and bad serving
MoI, Min of Food, War Office & Air Min *pc* Spectator *p* Michael Hankinson *d* Gilbert Gunn
18 mins

Double thread
Good nursery schools and teachers are as important as good homes and parents to young children if they are to learn for themselves how to live and not to be forced to live at adult pace. The film shows how a nursery school enables children to play, eat, rest, look after themselves and indulge their curiosity at their own pace during a typical day
Reviews FoB 1946, MFB XI 35
sp Nursery School Assoc *pc* GB Instructional *d* Mary Field
33 mins NFA

FIGHTING SERVICES & CAMPAIGNS

Africa freed
(A full account of the Tunisian campaign, 1942-43. A British follow-up to *Desert victory* which was not released due to the American view that there was too much emphasis on British troops. Followed by *Tunisian victory*)
MoI *pc* Crown & Services Film Units
70 mins IWM

Cameramen at war
A tribute to the cameramen of the Services and the newsreel companies who sent back from the battlefronts front-line reports such as those collected here by Len Lye
Reviews DNL V 8, MFB XI 7
MoI *pc* Realist *p* John Taylor *d* Len Lye *comm s* Raymond Glendenning *m* Ernst Meyer
15 mins IWM LC NFA

Cameramen at war. *News cameras lined up for front line filming.*

Close quarters
(A routine submarine patrol by a British submarine in the North Sea off the coast of Norway. Short non-theatric version made entitled *Up periscope!*)
Reviews DNL IV 215, MFB X 73
MoI *pc* Crown *d* Jack Lee *ph* Jonah Jones *p* Ian Dalrymple
75 mins IWM NFA

Camermen at war. *RAF cameraman filming from an aircraft.*

Desert victory
The film begins in the days when Generals Alexander and Montgomery took command, after General Auchinleck had fallen back and established a firm forty-mile front, sixty miles from Alexandria. The disposition of the opposed forces and the strategy of both sides is explained by means of diagrams. After the opening barrage and break-through at El Alamein the cameras follow the advance through Mersa Matruh, Halfaya Pass, Sollum, Tobruk, Benghazi and El Agheila, to the victory parade in Tripoli. (Adult audiences only)
Reviews DNL IV 189, MFB X 25
MoI *pc* British Service Film Units *p* David Macdonald *d* Roy Boulting *comm s* James Lansdal Hodson *m* William Alwyn *ed* A Best, F Clarke
60 mins CFL IWM MOMA NARS NFA

In the drink
Bombers are equipped with collapsible rubber dinghies in which the crew can float until picked up by the Air Sea Rescue Service. The film shows the equipment for all emergencies which is packed into the dinghies and what happens from the time the bomber hits the sea
MoI & Air Min *pc* New Realm *p* E Roy *d* Howard Hughes
16 mins IWM

Desert victory. *Action during the battle of El Alamein.*

Invincible?
(A captured enemy newsreel, issued by the Germans in French for circulation in North Africa, turned into a propaganda film for Britain. *Into battle* series no 2)
Reviews DNL IV 181, MFB X 19
English version: US Army Signal Corps, MoI & British Movietonews *comm s* Leslie Mitchell
15 mins IWM NFA

Kill or be killed
From somewhere in a wood 800 yards away a German sniper is trying to pick off the men in a British post. Rifleman Smith goes out to get him. The film shows how stalker and sniper manoeuvre for position, the mistakes both make and why the stalker succeeds. (Not suitable for children. Film made in 1942)
Reviews DNL IV 165, KYB 1943
MoI & War Office *pc* Realist *p* John Taylor *d* Len Lye *ph* A E Jeakins *comm s* Marius Goring
18 mins IWM NFA

Desert victory. *Tanks in the victory parade in Tripoli.*

Desert victory. *Stretcher bearers at El Alamein.*

Madagascar
(The Madagascar operation)
pc British Movietonews

Kill or be killed. *British soldier lies in wait for a German sniper.*

Operational height
(The story of the crew of a barrage balloon guarding the sea approaches to Britain. Short version entitled *The last hazard*)
Reviews DNL IV 191, MFB X 3
MoI *pc* RAF Film Unit
32 mins IWM NFA

Kill or be killed. *The dead German sniper.*

Tunisian victory

This film continues the story of the North Africa campaign, begun in *Desert victory*, which it overlaps in time. Beginning with the American-British landings in North Africa (November 8th, 1942) the film shows how the Eighth Army's victories were now seen to be part of a master plan, sealed on February 6th, 1943, by the appointment of General Eisenhower to the United Command. The strategy of the final phase of the campaign is explained and its working out is shown, beginning with General Montgomery's attack on the Mareth Line and ending with the final capitulation of the enemy forces in May 1943

Reviews DNL V 20, MFB XI 28

MoI & US Office of War Information *pc* British & American Service Film Units *p* Hugh Stewart, Roy Boulting, Frank Capra *comm s* Bernard Miles, Burgess Meredith *m* William Alwyn

79 mins CFL IWM

The volunteer

(An engineer and a pilot in the Fleet Air Arm–their training and experiences on the job)

Review MFB X 122

MoI *pc* Archers *p & d & sc* Michael Powell, Emeric Pressburger *cast* Ralph Richardson, Pat McGrath

44 mins IWM NFA

War in the Pacific

A survey of the war in the Pacific from Pearl Harbour to the recapture of Guadalcanal by the Americans and the defeat of the Japanese in New Guinea by the Australians. The film discusses the bearing of these defensive campaigns on the strategy and tactics for the offensive against Japan

Review MFB X 68

MoI *pc* Shell *p* Edgar Anstey *d* Grahame Tharp *anim* Francis Rodker

16 mins IWM NFA

War review no 1

(The great surrender at Stalingrad; hazards of the Mediterranean supply line; US carrier beats sea blitz)

MoI *pc* British Movietonews *p* Gerald Sanger

9 mins IWM

War review no 2

(Axis leave Africa)

MoI *pc* British Movietonews *p* Gerald Sanger

9 mins IWM

DOMINIONS & COLONIES – General

The freedom of Aberfeldy

(An Australian soldier, a New Zealand pilot and a Canadian sailor are welcomed by the villagers of Aberfeldy)

Review DNL IV 181

MoI *pc* Alan Harper *p* Alan Harper *ph* Henry Cooper

10 mins LC

Greek testament

(A record of Greece under occupation)

Review MFB X 49

pc Ealing Studios *p* Michael Balcon *d* C Hasse

45 mins NFA

DOMINIONS & COLONIES – Canada

Battle is our business
The story of battle training for the infantry men of Canada's citizens' army. (*Into battle* series no 3)
Review MFB X 19
MoI & National Film Board of Canada
14 mins IWM

High over the borders
Defying distance and national frontiers thousands of birds fly south every year from Alaska and Canada, over land and across the sea, to the United States and the countries of South America, and later return. The film shows the nesting and feeding habits and flight of many varieties of birds and explains the methods of banding, observing and indexing through which the United States Government is building up a complete picture of the phenomenon of migration
pc National Film Board of Canada *d* Irving Jacob *ed* John Ferno
23 mins

DOMINIONS & COLONIES – India

Our heritage no 1
Architecture and sculpture of South India, 7th to 17th centuries AD. The rock temples of Ajanta; the Buddhist, Jain and Hindu shrines at Ellora; the sculptored monolithic shrines at Mahabhalipuram; two temples at Tanjore; the shrine of Jaganath at Orissa; Bhuvaneswar, the temple city of Shiva; the Black Pagoda of Konarak; Rameshiwaram; mosques and tombs of Bijapur; the temples and sculpture of Madura
Review MFB XII 159
pc Information Films of India
17 mins

DOMINIONS & COLONIES – Malta

Malta GC
Vital link in Mediterranean strategy, Malta withstood more than 3,000 raids until the tide turned and Malta became an offensive base. This film, made as a tribute to the endurance of the people of Malta, shows actual raids and the consequent devastation and how the Maltese carried on their life and work during their ordeal. Music specially composed by Sir Arnold Bax, Master of the King's Music
Reviews DNL IV 171, MFB X 8
MoI *pc* Army Film Unit, RAF Film Unit & Crown Film Unit *p* Ian Dalrymple *assoc p* John Monck *comm s* Laurence Olivier *m* Arnold Bax *ed* A Best
19 mins IWM LC NFA

DOMINIONS & COLONIES – South Africa

South Africa
South Africa is a land of plains and high mountains with a 3,000 mile coastline on the Atlantic and Indian Oceans. It is a land of many peoples—English, Afrikaner, Indian, Bantu, Zulu, Swazi and Hottentot. It is a land of farming, mines and factories. On September 6th, 1939, after two days debate, South Africa decided, in full responsibility as a free and sovereign dominion, to declare war. Since then the peoples of South Africa have sent their men and their country's resources to many parts of the world, because they know that wherever free men are threatened they are threatened also
Review MFB XI 62
MoI & South African Bureau of Information *pc* Crown
15 mins LC

ALLIES – General

Common cause
An American and a Chinese pilot fighting together in China, a Russian and a British sailor at Murmansk, discover behind the surface differences of national character and custom a common outlook and a great common purpose
Reviews DNL IV 181, MFB XIII 26
MoI *pc* Verity *p* Maxwell Munden, Derrick de Marney *d* Henry Cass *ph* Eric Cross *ed* Peter Tanner
12 mins IWM NFA

Nations within a nation
In Britain, when Europe was overrun by the Nazis, men and women from many countries found refuge and the opportunity to renew together the fight for their countries' freedom. The film shows units of the Netherlands Navy and their Maritime Court in London; the Belgian fishing fleet and Belgians cutting diamonds; Czech students at Oxford and Czechs making Bren guns; ships of the Norwegian merchant navy (the second largest in Europe) and a Norwegian school; a French rehabilitation centre open to men of all the United Nations, soldiers, sailors and airmen of Poland, Greece and Jugo-Slavia
MoI *pc* British Paramount News *p* G T Cummins
16 mins IWM LC

ALLIES – China

China
Since the invasion of Manchuria in 1931 China has been withstanding Japanese aggression. The film shows something of how this fight has been maintained and of the new China which has been born under Chiang Kai-shek
Review DNL IV 191
MoI *pc* Rotha Productions *p* Donald Alexander *d* Budge Cooper
16 mins IWM NFA

Report from China
An account of some of the things seen by the Parliamentary Mission, headed by Lord Ailwyn, which visited China in 1942
Review MFB XI 137
MoI *pc* British Movietonews *p* Gerald Sanger
9 mins IWM

ALLIES – Czechoslovakia

The silent village
The story of the men of Lidice who lit in fascist darkness a lamp that shall never be put out. Lidice in Czechoslovakia was a village of miners. This film, in their honour, was made in a similar Welsh mining community–the village of Cwmgiedd. It was made with the cooperation of the Czechoslovakian Ministry of Foregin Affairs, the South Wales Miners Federation and the people of the Swansea and Dulais valleys
Reviews DNL IV 216, MFB X 61
MoI *pc* Crown *p & d* Humphrey Jennings *ph* H E Fowle *ed* S McAllister
36 mins CFL MOMA

ALLIES – Norway

Before the raid
(The looting of a Norwegian fishing village by the Germans; resistance by the Norwegians; German reprisals and the escape of some Norwegians to Britain)
Reviews DNL IV 227, MFB X 93
MoI *pc* Crown *p* Ian Dalrymple *d* Jiri Weiss *ph* E Catford
35 mins IWM NFA

ALLIES – Poland

Calling Mr Smith
(Polish propaganda denunciation of German 'kultur'. Distribution arrangements unclear)

pc Polish Film Unit *p* Eugene Cekalski
9 mins Dufaycolor IWM NFA

The Polonaise – hymn of freedom
(Poland before war came. Distribution arrangements unclear)
17 mins IWM

ALLIES – USA

Cowboy
The cowboys and Indians of the Wild West are dead. Cowboys today are no less tough and resourceful, but their job is the vital one of raising cattle by modern methods of scientific breeding and management. (*The American scene* no 2)
Review MFB XIII 39
sp US Office of War Information *pc* United Films
18 mins

Democracy in action
A survey of the vast agricultural resources of the United States, showing how farmers are working with the Agricultural Adjustment Administration to produce more of the foods needed for the United States war effort
sp US Office of War Information *pc* United Films
11 mins IWM

A letter from Ulster
(American servicemen in Ireland)
Review MFB X 8
MoI *pc* Crown *p* Ian Dalrymple *d* Brian Hurst
44 mins NFA

On the farm
pc Harmon Foundation
20 mins

Swedes in America
Ingrid Bergman visits some of America's two million Swedes to find out what they have given and are giving to the development of their adopted country while still retaining their own language and customs. (Alternative title *Ingrid Bergman answers*)
Review MFB XI 55
US Office of War Information *pc* United Films
18 mins IWM

OVERSEAS DISTRIBUTION

Before the raid

Blind people
(How blind people can learn to do manual work well enough to earn a living)
pc Colonial Film Unit
15 mins silent

Breathing space

Britain beats the clock
(Not shown in Britain. British wartime munitions production)
MoI *pc* British Paramount News *p* G T Cummins
16 mins NFA

The British and current affairs
MoI
NARS

Browned off

China

Citizens of tomorrow
(Latin American distribution)
MoI *pc* Realist
18 mins

Civil defence ambulance

Clamping potatoes

Close quarters

Colonial centre
pc Colonial Film Unit
3 mins

Come again
(Not shown in Britain. How an Australian pilot, a Canadian sailor and a New Zealand engineer spend their leave in Britain)
pc Crown *d* Ralph Elton
15 mins NFA

The coming of age and accession to the throne by the Kabaka of Uganda, Edward Mutesa II, November 19th & 20th 1942
(A record of this event in Kampala)
pc Colonial Film Unit
10 mins colour silent NFA

Control room

The crown of the year

Danger area

Debris tunnelling

The development of the rabbit

Distillation
(The distillation of crude oil)
Reviews DNL I July 6, FoB 1942-3
pc Shell *p* Arthur Elton *d* Peter Baylis *anim* Francis Rodker
15 mins NFA

Doing without
(Not shown in Britain)
MoI *pc* Spectator *p* Michael Hankinson *d* Gilbert Gunn
12 mins

Dustbin parade

Empress Stadium
(Russian distribution only)
MoI *pc* British Paramount News

Factory fireguard

Feeding the army
pc Colonial Film Unit
7 mins

Feeding your hens in wartime

Fires were started

First aid on the spot

First-aid post

Fishermen of England
(Not shown in Britain)
sp British Council *pc* Spectator *p & d* Ivan Scott
8 mins

The freedom of Aberfeldy

Good value
(Not shown in Britain. Skill and care in British industry)
Reviews FoB 1942-3, MFB IX 104
sp British Council *pc* Realist *p* John Taylor *d* Hans Nieter
8 mins NFA

Heroic Malta
pc Colonial Film Unit
4 mins

In which we live

Invincible?

It's just the way it is

Kill or be killed

A letter from Ulster

The life cycle of maize
Biology series. The camera speeds up the growth of maize, the universal corn, from seed to harvest. Stomata, magnified, are shown in action in fine and wet weather; germination is described; experiments show which mineral salts are needed in the soil
Review FoB 1942-3
sp British Council *pc* GB Instructional *d* Mary Field *ph* F Percy Smith
10 mins NFA

The life cycle of pin mould
Biology series. Pin Mould is seen growing rapidly on an apple and on porridge. The camera speeds up its growth. Spores germinate rapidly on moist substances. A single spore is observed branching out under the microscope, and heads containing new spores are seen coming into being and ripening
Review FoB 1942-3
sp British Council *pc* GB Instructional *d* Mary Field *ph* F Percy Smith
10 mins NFA

The life cycle of the newt
Biology series. Growth of the smooth newt from the egg, through the tadpole stage, to full development, and return of the three-year-old newt to the pond in spring to breed. Crested newts, axolotls, and salamanders have a similar life history
Reviews FoB 1942-3, MFB XIV 56
sp British Council *pc* GB Instructional *d* Mary Field *ph* F Percy Smith
11 mins NFA

London 1942

Looking through glass
Britain has attained a leading position in glass manufacture. This film includes scenes of sand purification, furnaces, bubbling molten glass, grinding, polishing, and cutting. Scientific instruments using glass, and perfectly balanced lenses are made in Britain today
Reviews FoB 1942-3, MFB XII 89
sp British Council *pc* Merton Park *d* Cecil Musk *ph* Alan Dinsdale *ed* Cath Miller *sound* Al Rhind *m* Leslie Bridgewater
17 mins NFA

Lowland village
Human Geography series. Lavenham, in Suffolk, is a typical lowland village, once a centre of the wool industry. It is both mediaeval and modern. It lies amid fertile arable lowlands and its life depends on farming
Review FoB 1942-3
sp British Council *pc* GB Instructional *d* D Catling *ph* Jack Parker
10 mins NFA

Make fruitful the land
(Agriculture and the rotation of crops)
Reviews DNL VI 8, FoB 1942-3, MFB XVI 89
sp British Council *pc* Green Park *diagrams* W Larkins
17 mins colour NFA

Maltese land girl
MoI *pc* British Movietonews
8 mins

Mechanical vultures
(This film was not shown in Britain. Arabic version)
MoI *pc* Films of GB *p* Andrew Buchanan *d* Henry Cooper, Charles Francis
6 mins

Middle East cartoons
No 1: Abu's dungeon; no 2: Abu's poisoned well; no 3: Abu's harvest; no 4: Abu builds a dam. Series of cartoons directing anti-Nazi propaganda to the peoples of the Middle East during the war
MoI *pc* Halas & Batchelor
10 mins each

1943
OVERSEAS DISTRIBUTION

Milk production in Britain
MoI *pc* Films of GB *d* Andrew Buchanan *assoc p* Edgar Anstey
pc Spectator
10 mins NFA

Mobile library
pc Colonial Film Unit

Model procedures for water relaying

Moving forts
MoI *pc* Films of GB *p* Andrew Buchanan *d* Henry Cooper *ph* Charles Francis

Nations within a nation

New Zealand home front
MoI *pc* Films of GB *p* Andrew Buchanan *d* Henry Cooper *ph* Charles Francis

Next of kin

North Sea

Nurse Ademola
(An African nurse is seen in various phases of training at one of the great London hospitals)
pc Colonial Film Unit
8 mins silent

Order of Lenin
(Not shown in Britain)
MoI *pc* Spectator *p* Michael Hankinson *d* Gilbert Gunn
8 mins NFA

Plastic surgery in wartime

P/O Peter Thomas
pc Colonial Film Unit
4 mins

Power to order
The development of the railway system and the construction of a modern locomotive
Review FoB 1942-3

Radio in battle

Radio report
(Not shown in Britain)
pc British Movietonews *p* Gerald Sanger *diagrams* W Larkins

Raid report
(Overseas only)
pc Movietone

Report from China

Return of the Emperor
pc Colonial Film Unit
9 mins LC

St Paul's Cathedral
(History of the cathedral)
Reviews FoB 1942-3, MFB IX 94
pc Merton Park *p & d* James Rogers
14 mins NFA

Salute to the Red Army
(Not shown in Britain. Britain honours Red Army Day, February 23, 1943)
pc Newsreel Assoc *ed* Raymond Perrin
11 mins IWM

Seeds and science

The silent village

Sky giant

South Africa

Steel dhows
(Not shown in Britain)
MoI *pc* Films of GB *p* Andrew Buchanan *d* Henry Cooper *ph* Charles Francis

Summer on the farm

These are British sailors
pc Colonial Film Unit
IWM

These are the men

They fight by night
The war effort is carried on round the clock. (Intended for overseas distribution)
MoI *pc* British Movietonews *p* Gerald Sanger
10 mins IWM

Timbermen from Honduras
pc Colonial Film Unit
5 mins

Turkish ambassador's visit
(Not shown in Britain)
MoI *pc* British Movietonews *p* Gerald Sanger
4 mins

Turkish honoured guests
(Not shown in Britain)
MoI *pc* British Movietonews *p* Gerald Sanger
4 mins

Turkish production mission
(Not shown in Britain)
MoI *pc* British Movietonews *p* Gerald Sanger
8 mins

Twelve days

Tyneside story

Until the morning
MoI *pc* Spectator
12 mins

Vegetable harvest

The volunteer

War in the Pacific

We sail at midnight

We want rubber
pc Colonial Film Unit
5 mins

Welcome to Britain
(A guide to British behaviour for American soldiers. Overseas distribution only)
Review DNL V 29
MoI *pc* Strand *p* Arthur Elton *assoc p* St John Legh Clowes *d* Anthony Asquith *ph* Jo Jago *cast* Burgess Meredith, Carla Lehmann, Beatrice Lillie, Bob Hope, Felix Aylmer
60 mins BFI MOMA NFA

Winter work in the garden

Women of Britain
(The many jobs being carried by women in the Land Army Auxiliary forces, railways etc)
Review MPH 11.9.43
MoI *pc* Spectator
11 mins

Workers' weekend

World of plenty

Youth
(Overseas distribution. Russia)
MoI *pc* Verity

NEWSREEL TRAILERS

All lines engaged

Anti-personnel bomb
MoI & Min of Home Security *pc* Verity

Any questions
MoI *d* Miss Davies

1943
NEWSREEL TRAILERS

Be a good guy

Bicycle made for two
MoI & Min of Supply *pc* Byron *d* J Raymond *cast* Harry Tate Junior

Black diamonds
MoI & Min of Fuel & Power *pc* Verity *d* Kenneth Annakin

Blackout sense
Review DNL IV 182
MoI & Min of War Transport *pc* Rotha Productions
2 mins

Blitz pacts
MoI & Min of Home Security *pc* Spectator

Blood will out
MoI & Min of Health *pc* Film Traders *d* G Hollering

Bones
MoI & Min of Supply *pc* Strand *d* Alan Harper

Brains Trust
MoI & Min of Home Security *pc* Spectator *d* Michael Hankinson *with* Stanley Holloway, Douglas Young, Gavin Gordon, Edward Cooper

Censorship of prisoners' mail
sp Postal & Telephone Censorship *pc* Byron *d* J Raymond

Compost heap
MoI & Min of Ag *pc* Realist *comm s* Roy Hay
5 mins NFA

Contraries
Semi-animated cartoon
sp Min of Supply *pc* McDougall & MacKendrick
1½ mins NFA

Dig for victory
MoI *pc* Spectator *assoc p* Edgar Anstey

Diphtheria III
MoI & Min of Health *pc* Larkins *d* W M Larkins

Diphtheria IV
MoI & Min of Health *pc* Larkins *d* W M Larkins

Don't travel in the rush hours
MoI & Min of War Transport *pc* Rotha Productions *d* R Loew
2 mins NFA

Early digging
Animated cartoon
MoI & Min of Ag *pc* Halas & Batchelor

Firewatch dog
sp Fire Offices Ctte *pc* Spectator *d* Gilbert Gunn

Garden pests
MoI & Min of Ag *pc* GB Instructional

Get the coke habit
MoI & Min of Fuel & Power *pc* Crown

Guy Fawkes
(Recruiting for Women's Services)
MoI & Min of Fuel & Power *pc* Nettlefold *d* Harry Hughes

Harriet and the matches
Fire Offices Ctte *pc* Nettlefold *d* Bladon Peake

Harry Tate junior

Here we go gathering spuds
sp Dept of Ag for Scotland *pc* Spectator *d* A H Luff

How to use your doctor
MoI & Min of Health *pc* Strand *d* Peter Price

I stopped, I looked . . .
Animated cartoon
MoI & Min of War Transport *pc* Halas & Batchelor *song by* Michael Carr

Master builders
sp Dept of Educ for Scotland *pc* Scottish Films

A matter of interest
sp National Savings Ctte for Scotland *pc* Nettlefold *d* Harry Hughes

Model sorter
sp Min of Supply *pc* Halas & Batchelor *comm s* Cyril Ritchard

Nero
MoI & Min of Fuel & Power *pc* McDougall & MacKendrick

Nightingales
Min of Labour *pc* Pathé *d* Derrick de Marney
1 min NFA

No fire without smoke
(Chemical warfare and firefighting)
sp Fire Offices Ctte *pc* Nettlefold *d* Bladon Peake

Old logs
MoI & Min of Health & Min of Fuel & Power *pc* Film Traders *d* George Hollering

Paper chase
MoI & Min of Supply *pc* Byron *d* J Raymond
1 min NFA

Peak load
Cartoon by Strausfeld
MoI & Min of Fuel & Power *pc* Film Traders *d* George Hollering

Planned crops
Review DNL IV 182
MoI & Min of Ag *pc* Realist *d* Len Lye *cast* Ted Ray

Pre-blitz precautions
MoI & Min of Home Security *pc* Spectator

Random harvest
Scottish Office *pc* Public Relationship *d* Richard Massingham
2 mins

The sacred flame
MoI & Min of Fuel & Power *pc* Spectator *d* Gilbert Gunn

Salvage of succubi

Salvage of tin tubes
Review DNL IV 182
MoI *pc* Realist

Salvage saves shipping
Cartoon
MoI & Min of Supply *pc* Film Traders *d* George Hollering

Scottish savings (1)
Scottish Office *pc* Byron *d* J Raymond
2 mins NFA

Scottish savings (2)
Scottish Savings Ctte *pc* Gainsborough *d* L Arliss *cast* Will Fyffe

Shorter trunks
GPO *pc* Argyle British Productions *d* J Argyle

Skeleton in the cupboard
MoI & Min of Supply *pc* Film Traders *d* George Hollering

Splinters of 1943

1943
NEWSREEL TRAILERS

Sternutation
MoI & Min of Health *pc* Spectator *d* Michael Hankinson

Tell me, where is fancy bread?
MoI & Min of Food *pc* Crown *d* Peter Bolton

War bonds

Women's industrial recruiting
Review DNL IV 182
MoI *pc* Films of GB

1944

HOMEFRONT – General

Atlantic trawler
Life aboard a West Coast trawler, under arduous and dangerous war-time conditions. The film shows not only the daily life at sea–with fishing day and night and hauling every three or four hours–but also the men's relations with the shore and their homes
Reviews DNL V 29, MFB IX 122
MoI *pc* Realist *p* John Taylor *d* Frank Sainsbury *ph* A E Jeakins, H E Fowle, Cyril Phillips *sc* Frank Sainsbury *comm s* W Bland
22 mins IWM

Browned off
Review MFB XI 20
MoI *pc* Strand *p* Donald Taylor *cast* Jenny Laird, John Martin
37 mins

Conquest of a germ
A tribute, in dramatised form, to the research workers and doctors who discovered the sulphonamide drugs which have revolutionised the treatment of pneumonia, child-birth fever, meningitis and other diseases, and saved the lives of thousands of men on the battlefields
Review MFB XI 93
MoI *pc* Gryphon *p* Donald Taylor *d* John Eldridge *ph* Jo Jago, Gerald Gibbs
16 mins NFA

Danger area
The story of a hazardous job in a Royal Ordnance shell-filling factory. Working 23 hours on end with an explosive they have never handled before, 30 men produce a batch of special shells in time to protect an important convoy. The film was made with the men of a Royal Ordnance Factory
Reviews DNL V 28, MFB XI 34
MoI & Min of Supply *pc* Verity *p* Sydney Box *d* Henry Cass *sc* Inez Holden *ph* Raymond Elton
20 mins IWM NFA

A date with a tank
The story of the 17-pounder gun–design, test, mass-production in the factories–that smashed the new Tiger tanks when they were thrown against the Eighth Army positions in the Mareth Line
Review MFB XI 93
MoI & War Office *pc* Army Film Unit *d* Donald Bull
15 mins IWM

Flax
Farmers in Britain are now for the first time growing flax, not for linen, but for airplane fabric, parachute harnesses and fire hoses. The film shows flax harvesting, processing and weaving the fibre
MoI & Min of Supply *pc* Strand *p & d* Donald Taylor
10 mins NFA

Food flashes
(Series of short message films with themes such as 'Eat potatoes not bread', etc)
MoI & Min of Food
2-5 mins each B&W and colour NFA

For this our heritage
The story of pre-Service training for girls of fourteen to twenty with the Rangers, showing how a wide range of activities is related to the work which girls are doing in wartime
sp Girl Guides Assoc *pc* Tanar *p* R Calvert *comm s* Freddie Grisewood
16 mins Kodachrome IWM

The great circle
Through the use of great circle air-routes, which shorten distances of aeroplane travel to their minimum, there is no part of the world farther than three days' travel from another. These routes have served us in war, and can serve us as well in peace
Review MFB XI 93
MoI *pc* Shell *p* Edgar Anstey *d* J B Napier Bell
14 mins NFA

Heirs of tomorrow
(Residential nursery schools for children under five)
Review MFB XII 114
pc Movietonews *d* Raymond Perrin
11 mins

In which we live
The autobiography of a man's suit and ingeniously presented for the benefit of every woman. (Also known as *The story of a suit*)
MoI & Board of Trade *pc* Public Relationship *p* Lewis Grant Wallace *d* Richard Massingham
12 mins NFA

Manpower
Seven men and women must work as civilians to make the weapons and equipment for one fighting man. By planning the use of manpower, Britain has achieved the highest output per person of any nation in the world. In peacetime this power can be used to create a better world to live in
MoI & Min of Labour *pc* Strand *p* Alexander Shaw
9 mins IWM

Men of tomorrow
While they still carry on their normal training Boy Scouts find new jobs to do now and new tasks ahead of them
Review MPH 6.7.46
MoI *pc* Verity *p* Sydney Box, James Carr *d* A Travers
10 mins IWM

Of one blood
Through the Army Blood Transfusion Service, working with the Emergency Blood Transfusion Service of the Ministry of Health and the Scottish National Blood Transfusion Service, supplies of blood are provided by civilians for the British Army and the armies of the United Nations wherever they are fighting. The film shows how the blood is collected from donors in villages and

factories and how it is tested, grouped and prepared for despatch
MoI & Army Blood Transfusion Service *pc* Seven League *d* Hans Nieter *assoc p* Paul Rotha
15 mins IWM

Our country
A panorama of Britain seen through the eyes of a merchant seaman returning after two years at sea. He visits the blitzed streets of London, the harvest fields of Kent, the mining valleys of South Wales, the steel foundries and factories of the Midlands, and the lumber camps of Scotland, and for a moment shares the life of the people he meets. The treatment of the film is poetic and impressionistic
Reviews DNL V 46, MFB XII 84
MoI *pc* Strand *p* Alexander Shaw *d* John Eldridge, *ph* Jo Jago, *comm w* Dylan Thomas *m* William Alwyn
45 mins NFA

Paving the way
A picture of the opportunities for education and recreation that can be found in Youth Centres
Review MFB XI 64
Board of Educ *pc* GB Instructional
12 mins

The story of DDT
Dichlor-diphenyl-trichlorethane was discovered seventy years ago by Othmar Zeider, a German chemistry student, but its uses as an insecticide were not proved and realised until World War II. Typhus, trench fever, malaria, typhoid and dysentery follow in the trail of war, and devastate armies and civilians. These diseases are carried by insects. Experiments carried out by the British Army on insects, animals and volunteers from the RAMC, proved that DDT was the deadliest killer of lice, flies, bed-bugs, mosquitoes and their larvae, and that it did not harm human beings. DDT mass-produced in special factories and made up in various forms protected the armies in Europe and the Far East against disease. In Naples in January-February 1944, for the first time in medical history, a typhus epidemic was effectively checked by DDT. Out of war has come a new weapon for the battle against disease
Reviews DNL V 102, MFB XIII 39
War Office *pc* Army Kinematograph Services
23 mins CFL IWM NFA

Transatlantic airport
The airport at Prestwick, Scotland, and how it became a meeting-point of world air-routes during the war
Reviews DNL V 53, MFB XII 9, MFB XIV 90
MoI *pc* Crown *p* Arthur Elton *d* Michael Gordon *ph* Fred Gamage *sound* Ken Cameron
15 mins IWM NFA

Two fathers
(Dramatised playlet about the war)
Review MFB XII 9
pc Crown *p* Arthur Elton *d* Anthony Asquith
13 mins NFA

Two good fairies
(Life in England after implementation of the Beveridge plan)
Review DNL V 5
CWS *pc* Crown *d* Germain Burger *ph* Jack Rose *sc* C E M Joad
17 mins

Willing hands
The WVS undertook much new work in 1944
MoI & Min of Home Security *pc* World Wide *p* James Carr *d* Mary Francis
11 mins IWM LC

Words and actions
The word 'democracy' means rule by the people. Parliament and local councils are means by which laws are made and administered by the people for the people. But democratic government is only sustained and developed by ordinary men

and women taking a lively interest in their own affairs. They must decide what they want, find out if there are laws to give it, and if there are not act together to get laws passed
Reviews DNL IV 226, MFB XI 84
British Commercial Gas Assoc *pc* Realist *p* John Taylor *d* Max Anderson *ph* A E Jeakins *sc* Frank Sainsbury, John Taylor
15 mins BFI IWM NFA

HOMEFRONT – Scotland & Wales

The children's story
The care and education of children in Scotland. (Film made in 1938)
Review MFB XII 41
sp Films of Scotland Ctte *pc* Strand *p* Stuart Legg *d* Alexander Shaw
14 mins MOMA NFA

Clydebuilt
To the world 'Clydebuilt' is a guarantee; to the men of the Clyde it is a working standard–good materials and sound craftsmanship resulting in a lasting job. As the film follows the construction of a ship it explains the difference between riveting and welding and shows how pre-fabrication on American lines is practised on the Clyde today within the limits of space, plant and skilled welders available
Review DNL V 8
MoI & Admiralty *pc* Spectator *p* Michael Hankinson *d* Robin Carruthers *ph* A H Luff
23 mins IWM LC

Coalminer
At the outbreak of war Charlie Jones, a Rhondda miner, returned to the coalface at the age of 56 after thirteen years out of work. In a talk with Arthur Horner, President of the South Wales Miners' Federation, he discusses the miners' life, changed conditions in the pits and the part that Pit Production Committees can play in increasing output
MoI & Min of Fuel and Power *pc* Strand *p* Basil Wright *d* Charles de Lautour
15 mins IWM

Good health to Scotland
The film shows child welfare clinics and schools, medical examinations in factories and special hospitals for industrial workers, inspection by Port Medical Authorities of incoming ships, and achievements and plans for good houses which are the foundation of a people's health
MoI & Dept of Health for Scotland *pc* Scottish Films *d* S Russell
19 mins

Highland doctor
Thirty years ago there were few doctors for the Highlands and Islands of Scotland. They could visit few patients because of the long distances and bad roads to be covered on foot, horse and by boat; and their fees were inevitably high. Dr McWilliam recalls those days as he waits for the air ambulance which is to take a crofter's wife to a Glasgow hospital for a special operation. Today there are more doctors and nurses and they have cars; the roads have been improved; the hospitals serving the district have been enlarged to receive patients brought in by ambulances; and the services are available at fees which people can afford. All this could only be achieved because the Government initiated and subsidised the Highlands and Islands Medical Service. The film was taken in the islands of Lewis and Harris and North Uist, and at Ullapool, Inverness and Dingwall
Review DNL V 5
MoI & Dept of Health for Scotland *pc* Rotha Productions *p* Paul Rotha *d* Kay Mander *ph* E Catford
21 mins MOMA NFA

HOMEFRONT – Instructional

Action
Games provide training and exercise in the discipline, strength, self-assurance and alertness demanded of everyone in wartime
MoI & Board of Educ *pc* Technique-Verity *p* Sydney Box, James Carr *d* Muriel Baker *comm s* John Snagge
9 mins LC

Defeat tuberculosis
Tuberculosis is on the increase. The film shows how it is contracted and may be avoided, and the importance of early examination and treatment by a doctor. Immediate and proper treatment can lead to complete recovery
Review MFB X 109
MoI & Min of Health *pc* Seven League *assoc p* Paul Rotha *d* Hans Nieter
11 mins IWM NFA

Eggs and milk
How to make good use of dried eggs and dried milk, two of the food discoveries of the war
MoI & Min of Food *pc* Films of GB *p* Andrew Buchanan *d* Henry Cooper *ph* Charles Francis
6 mins

The eye and the ear
MoI
10 mins NFA

Garden friends and foes
How to distinguish and deal with insects that destroy vegetables–wireworm on potatoes, carrots and tomatoes; millipede on peas, beans, carrots; leatherjackets on lettuce and spinach; blackfly on beans; slugs and cabbage butterflies; and potato eelworm
Review DNL IV 181
MoI & Min of Ag *pc* GB Instructional *d* D Catling *comm s* E V Emmett *assoc p* Edgar Anstey
10 mins CFL NFA

Garden tools
The choice, proper use and care of ten essential tools–spade, fork, rake, draw hoe, Dutch hoe, onion hoe, trowel, dibber, watering can and line
MoI & Min of Ag *pc* Realist *p* John Taylor *d* Margaret Thomson *assoc p* Edgar Anstey *ph* Jack Harding, A E Jeakins
12 mins CFL NFA

Growing good potatoes
An instructional film for small and commercial growers on planting, cultivation, and disease prevention
sp Plant Protection *pc* Strand *p* Donald Taylor *d* Ralph Bond
10 mins

How to make chutney and sauces
MoI & Min of Food *pc* Films of GB *p* Andrew Buchanan *d* Henry Cooper *ph* Charles Francis
10 mins colour

Lifting
Thousands of men and women injure themselves in lifting or moving heavy weights. This film shows the right way to tackle a number of jobs so as to avoid accidents and strains and to make the jobs themselves easier
MoI & Min of Labour *pc* CWS Film Unit *d* George Wynn
9 mins CFL NFA

Oven bottling
A demonstration of the simplest method of bottling fruit, the oven method
MoI & Min of Food *pc* Pathé
5 mins NFA

A ride with Uncle Joe
On a ride in a lorry four children see for themselves how people should behave on the roads and learn the good sense of the rule 'Look right–look left–and then, if nothing is coming, cross'
Review MFB XI 75
MoI & Min of War Transport *pc* Verity

p Maxwell Munden *d* Kenneth Annakin
10 mins NFA

Rugmaking
(Types of rugs and how the craft is taught in Women's Institutes)
Reviews DNL I Apr 6, MFB VII 137
National Federation of Women's Institutes *pc* GB Instructional *d* Mary Field *comm* Peter Herbert
14 mins silent

Saving your own seeds
A film for gardeners and allotment holders on how to produce seeds for peas and beans, tomatoes, marrows, shallots, leeks and onions
Review DNL IV 181
MoI & Min of Ag *pc* Realist *p* John Taylor *d* Margaret Thomson *ph* A E Jeakins *comm s* Roy Hay *m* Ernst Meyer *assoc p* Edgar Anstey
17 mins NFA

Simple fruit pruning
A film for gardeners on pruning apples, plums, black currant and raspberry, gooseberry and red currant
MoI & Min of Ag *pc* Realist *p* John Taylor *d* Rosanne Hunter *assoc p* Edgar Anstey *ph* A E Jeakins *comm s* A G Street
20 mins CFL NFA

Subject for discussion
A discussion of the symptoms and effects of venereal disease and methods of treatment
Reviews DNL IV 191, MFB X 45
Central Council for Health Educ & MoI *pc* Seven League *d* Hans Nieter *ph* Wolfgang Suschitzky *assoc p* Basil Wright
15 mins IWM LC

Winter work in the garden
A film for gardeners on work which must be done to ensure good crops, including liming and ridging the ground, use of compost, setting out seed potatoes, parsnips, cabbages and sprouts
Review DNL V 16
MoI & Min of Ag *pc* Realist *p* John Taylor *assoc p* Edgar Anstey *d* Albert Pearl *ph* Cyril Phillips
10 mins CFL

HOMEFRONT – Specialised instructional

Boiler house practice
A film on fuel economy for boiler plant managers, engineers and stokers
MoI for Min of Fuel & Power *pc* CWS Film Unit *d* George Wynn
26 mins NFA

Cereal seed disinfection
A film for farmers on the prevention of seedborne diseases like bunt, smut and stripe that cause heavy crop losses. The film shows how seed can be dressed with organo-mercury dusts in manufactured or home-made dressing machines
Review MFB XIV 104
MoI & Min of Ag *pc* Films of GB *p* Andrew Buchanan *d* Henry Cooper *ph* Charles Francis *assoc p* Edgar Anstey
12 mins NFA

Clean milk
Cleanliness at every stage of milk production is vital to the nation's health. The film deals with care of the cows, construction and cleansing of byres and dairy sculleries, and the sterilisation of equipment and containers
Review DNL IV 181
MoI & Dept of Ag *pc* Realist *p* Frank Sainsbury *d* Margaret Thomson *ph* A E Jeakins *comm s* Finlay Currie *assoc p* Edgar Anstey
15 mins IWM

Food from straw
Instructional film on the preparation of straw pulp for feeding cattle and its food value compared with cereals and roots
Review MFB XIV 132

sp ICI *pc* GB Instructional *d* Stanley Irving
6 mins NFA

Fruit spraying
An instructional film on the equipment, chemicals and methods used by commercial fruit growers
Review DNL III 90
sp Technical Products *pc* Shell *p* Edgar Anstey *d* Kay Mander *ph* Sidney Beadle
23 mins NFA

Fuel and the tractor
A film for farmers on how to look after tractors and to organise their work so as to economise in the use of tractor fuel
sp Ford Motors *pc* Verity
17 mins

Grass and clover seed production
A film for farmers on increasing the production of good seeds, showing methods of sowing, fertilising, cutting and threshing. The grasses dealt with are Red and Wild White Clovers, Leafy Perennial Rye Grass and Cocksfoot. Reference is made to the experimental work done at the Welsh Plant Breeding Station
Review MFB XIV 133
MoI & Min of Ag *pc* Strand *assoc p* Edgar Anstey (*d* L E Cook, J L Fyle)
15 mins NFA

Harness your horse-power
There is a right and a wrong way to treat a farm tractor. The film shows both ways and the results
sp Ford Motor Company *pc* Verity *p* Sydney Box, James Carr *d* Clifford Hornby
15 mins

Making good hay
A film for farmers on methods of cutting, drying, gathering, stacking and baling
Review MFB XVI 51
MoI & Min of Ag *pc* Realist *assoc p* Edgar Anstey *p* John Taylor *d* Margaret Thomson *ph* A E Jeakins *m* Ernst Meyer *comm s* Roy Hay
10 mins NFA

Making grass silage
A film for farmers on methods of making good silage in pits, clamps or built silos
MoI & Min of Ag *pc* Realist *assoc p* Edgar Anstey *p* John Taylor *d* Margaret Thomson *ph* A E Jeakins *m* Ernst Meyer
10 mins NFA

Neuro-psychiatry
An account of the organisation and methods of one of the seven hospitals established under the Emergency Medical Services for the treatment and rehabilitation of service and civilian patients suffering from neurosis . . . The film ends with talks between Dr Maclay, the director of the hospital, and an Army officer and a Ministry of Labour official about the future of a number of patients about to leave the hospital. The loan of this film is limited to specialist audiences. Applications must state the exact audience to which the film would be shown. (American release title *Psychiatry in action*)
Review FoB 1944-5
MoI & Min of Health *pc* Spectator *p* Basil Wright *d* Michael Hankinson
68 mins NFA

Plastic surgery in wartime
The film deals with the work done both for civilian and military casualties at one of the Ministry of Health's special plastic and facio-maxillary centres. The commentary is spoken by Sir Harold Gillies, Consultant Adviser in the Ministry of Health's Emergency Medical Service
MoI for Min of Health *pc* Realist *p* John Taylor *d* Frank Sainsbury *ph* Jack Cardiff *comm s* Sir Harold Gillies
26 mins colour NFA

Potato Blight
A film for farmers on growing and storing potato crops free from blight. The

film explains how the fungus lives and spreads on the haulm and the tubers, and shows various methods of spraying and dusting
MoI & Min of Ag *pc* Realist *p* John Taylor *d* Rosanne Hunter *assoc p* Edgar Anstey *ph* Cyril Phillips
20 mins NFA

Reseeding for better grass
A film for farmers on how to turn coarse pasturelands into good grazing by ploughing up and reseeding the land without a cereal nursecrop or first putting it through a rotation
MoI & Min of Ag *pc* Realist *p* John Taylor *assoc p* Edgar Anstey *d* Margaret Thomson *ph* J Edwell *m* Ernst Meyer *comm s* Roy Hay
10 mins NFA

Scabies
An exposition for doctors, health visitors, sanitary inspectors, nurses and medical orderlies of the modern methods used in the diagnosis and treatment of scabies . . . The film is only available for showing to audiences indicated above
Review DNL VI 105
MoI & Min of Health *pc* Spectator *p* Michael Hankinson *d* Robin Carruthers
36 mins NFA

Scabies mite
Instructional film for specialists and students showing in detail, by means of photomicrography and diagrams, the life cycle of the Sarcoptes. (Short version of *Scabies*)
Review MFB XI 65
MoI & Min of Health *pc* Byron and Science
7 mins CFL

Steam
A film for managers and engineers on efficient use of steam to save fuel in the boiler house. Lagging, stopping leaks, conserving room heat, increasing heat output, recovering flash steam, making use of the heat in the condensate, are among the methods of increasing efficiency shown
MoI for Min of Fuel and Power *pc* CWS Film Unit
21 mins

Stooking and stacking
A film for farmers on the 'three men, six rows' method of stooking and the siting and building of rectangular and round stacks
Review DNL IV 202
MoI & Min of Ag *pc* Realist *p* John Taylor *d* Rosanne Hunter *ph* A E Jeakins *comm s* Finlay Currie
13 mins NFA

Surgery in chest diseases
A detailed study of a case of cancer of the left lung (a squamous-celled carcinoma), showing all stages, including diagnosis by radiography, the operation for total removal of the lung and the rehabilitation of the patient. Brief glances at other cases help to fill out the general picture of the civilian Chest Surgery Centre at which the film was made. (Only for specialised medical and scientific audiences)
Reviews DNL IV 226, FoB 1944-5
British Council *pc* GB Instructional *d* A R Dobson *ph* Frank North *sc* Mary Cathcart Borer *diagrams* H L Stringer
40 mins

Tuberculosis
Fourth film in *Health of dairy cattle* series. Effects of tuberculosis, its detection by tuberculin-testing, and prevention by clean farming methods
Reviews FoB 1946, MFB XIV 121
ICI *pc* GB Screen Services
9 mins NFA

Vegetable seed growing
A film for farmers on commercial production of vegetable seeds: swedes, carrots, onions, leeks, mangold and sugar beet, cabbage, broccoli and sprouts

MoI & Min of Ag *pc* Strand *p* Alexander Shaw *d* Peter Graham Scott *assoc p* Edgar Anstey
13 mins NFA

Wartime shipment of packed petroleum
Instructional film in two parts, each about 20 minutes in length and each of which can be shown separately. Part 1: *Handling and stowage* shows how risk of danger to the cans, with consequent loss of petrol and danger of disastrous fire, during loading and in transport in a rolling or pitching ship, can be minimised. Part 2: *Fire prevention and fire fighting* shows the precautions to be taken during loading and unloading and the methods of fighting fires if they occur
MoI & Min of War Transport *pc* Shell *p* Edgar Anstey *d* J B Napier Bell
40 mins NFA

We'll finish the job
Instructional film, for aircraft workers only, on importance of good finish and precise assembly
40 mins IWM

Welding helps the farmer
A film for farmers on the repair of farm machines and implements by blacksmiths trained in welding, one of the developments being encouraged by the Rural Industries Bureau
MoI & Min of Ag *pc* Films of GB *p* Andrew Buchanan *d* Henry Cooper *ph* Charles Francis
9 mins

HOMEFRONT – CD, NFS, etc.

Damage control – chemistry of fire
US Navy training film made available through the Admiralty for NFS and selected CD personnel only through Film Officers at MoI Regional HQ
44 mins

Rescue reconnaissance
Demonstration by a Rescue Party of a Civil Defence Reserve Unit of methods of reconnaissance before work of clearance or tunnelling begins
Review DNL V 29
MoI & Min of Home Security *pc* Shell *p* Edgar Anstey *d* Grahame Tharp *ph* Sidney Beadle *asst d* Lionel Cole
36 mins IWM

Respirator, cape and cleansing drill
Air Ministry training film available for NFS only through Film Officers at MoI Regional HQ. (Chemical warfare and firefighting)
33 mins

FIGHTING SERVICES & CAMPAIGNS

By sea and land
A Royal Marine patrol at work in Normandy in the period following D-Day. While ashore they maintain contact with the warships, which act as their supporting artillery
Review MFB XI 109
MoI & Admiralty *pc* Crown *p* J B Holmes *d* Jack Lee
13 mins IWM (Spanish titles, English soundtrack) NFA

Eve of battle
A survey of the vast preparations in Britain, by the Allied fighting services and an army of civilian workers, for the liberation of Europe
Review MFB XI 73
MoI & US Govt *pc* Army Film Unit *p* David Macdonald
19 mins IWM

Failure of a strategy
(Propaganda compilation to show why the Axis failed to achieve their Middle East objectives)
MoI *ed* Peter Tanner
20 mins IWM NFA

A harbour goes to France
The story of Mulberry, the harbour larger than Dover Harbour, designed, tested and built in Britain, towed across the Channel and set down in the sea at Arromanches. This unprecedented engineering achievement ensured for the Allied Armies the constant supplies essential in the first stages of the liberation of Europe
Review MFB XI 134
MoI & Admiralty *pc* Admiralty & Army Film Units *p* David Macdonald *m* Christian Daunton *ed* R Lloyd, A Best
15 mins CFL IWM

Hitler listens
(Careless talk story. Intended for servicemen. Probably only released within the armed services)
MoI & War Office
6 mins IWM

The last hazard
A dramatised story of the RAF men who maintained the seaborne balloon barrage in the Thames estuary, adapted from the film *Operational height*
MoI & Air Min *pc* RAF Film Unit
20 mins IWM

Left of the line
A short pictorial record of the British and Canadian liberation armies fighting from the beaches to Brussels, liberated September 3rd, 1944. The film does not attempt to depict the campaign as a whole
Review DNL V 45
MoI *pc* British & Canadian Army Film Units *p* David Macdonald *m* Hubert Clifford *ed* A Best, J Durst
26 mins CFL IWM

Malta convoy
An eye-witness account by Commander Anthony Kimmins of the supply convoy which fought its way through from Gibraltar to Malta in August, 1942, protected by ships of the Mediterranean fleet and aircraft of the Fleet Air Arm and, in the last stages, by fighter aircraft from Malta
Review MFB XI 125
MoI *pc* British Movietonews *p* Gerald Sanger
13 mins CFL IWM NFA

Man wounded
Thousands of men who would have died of their wounds in the last war recover in this to become healthy, active citizens again. The development of blood transfusion techniques, the use of the sulphonamide drugs and other discoveries of modern medicine and surgery are part of the story. But as important is the organisation of the Royal Army Medical Corps in providing prompt and efficient treatment on the field of battle and rapid evacuation of casualties to base hospitals. Back in England the men are treated in hospitals and trained at rehabilitation centres either for return to the Army or to new jobs
MoI & War Office *pc* Army Film Unit *d* Donald Bull *ed* Edward Carrick
18 mins IWM LC

Memphis Belle
A daylight bombing expedition over the Continent of Europe by American Flying Fortresses from a base in England. The film shows preparations, briefing, the flight out, the general plan of attack (by diagrams), defence against enemy fighters and flak, bombing of targets, the return home, attention to wounded, and visits to the bomber base by distinguished personages. The combat scenes were shot in action over enemy territory
Reviews DNL V 51, MFB XI 70
sp US Office of War Information *pc* US 8th Air Force & AAF First Motion Picture Unit *d* Lt Col William Wyler
40 mins colour IWM NFA

Minefield!
The Royal Engineers clear a gap for attack
Reviews DNL V 29, MFB XI 48
MoI & War Office *pc* Army Film Unit

ed J Durst *p* Roy Boulting
16 mins IWM

Naples is a battlefield
The capture of Naples, the first great European city to be liberated, revealed the magnitude of the tasks involved in re-creating the means of livelihood and the machinery of government in a devastated, starving and disease-ridden city
Reviews DNL V 16, MFB XI 21
MoI *pc* RAF & Army Film Units *ed* Peter Baylis, R Verrall
15 mins CFL IWM

Prelude to service
An outline of the activities of the Army Cadet Force
War Office *pc* Warners
9 mins

She serves abroad
Women from many parts of the Empire are on active service in the Middle East with the ATS, WRNS, and WAAF and Queen Alexandra's Nursing Service
MoI & War Office *pc* Army Film Unit
8 mins IWM LC

There's a future in it
(A tribute to British bomber crews)
Review MFB XI 14
pc Strand *p & d* Leslie Fenton *cast* Ann Dvorak, Barry Morse, Len & Bill Lowe
43 mins NFA

Towards the offensive
The Air Forces of the United Nations are preparing the way for the final offensive against Hitler's Fortress of Europe. The film shows a dawn raid on a port by Bostons escorted by Spitfires flown by French pilots, a daylight raid by American Fortresses assisted by RAF fighters, and a night raid by British heavy bombers on Italy
Air Min & MoI *pc* RAF Film Unit
17 mins IWM

The true story of Lili Marlene
(The history of the song and its use by troops of both sides during the war)
Review MFB XI 73
pc Crown *p* J B Holmes *d* Humphrey Jennings *cast* Marius Goring, Lucie Mannheim
29 mins NFA

Up periscope!
Made from the feature film *Close quarters*, this film tells of the successful action at the end of a routine patrol by a British submarine in the North Sea, off the coast of Norway; made with officers and men of the Royal Navy
MoI & Admiralty *pc* Crown *d* Jack Lee *ph* Jonah Jones *p* Ian Dalrymple
20 mins IWM NFA

Western approaches
(Sea war drama. Twenty-four merchant seamen from a torpedoed ship are sailing a lifeboat out in the Atlantic. Drama between a lone merchantman which comes to their rescue and a U-boat which is finally sunk. Film made in 1944)
Review MFB XI 140
pc Crown *p* Ian Dalrymple *d* Pat Jackson *ph* Jack Cardiff *m* Clifton Parker
83 mins colour IWM NFA

With the marines at Tarawa
The assault on and capture of this Pacific Island which was an important Japanese air base, by US Marines
US Office of War Information *pc* US Marine Corps
19 mins

DOMINIONS & COLONIES – India

The conquest of the dry lands
The Punjab is the Land of the Five Rivers. The land between the rivers was waterless and barren. The irrigation and hydro-electric system imposed on the

rivers has given fertility to the waste lands and provided power for new industries
Review MFB XIV 147
pc Information Films of India *p* Ezra Mir *adap* Sylvia Cummins
10 mins IWM (mute)

Covering with affection
The production of hand-made woollen blankets in the villages and towns of India
Review DNL IV 202
sp Films Advisory Board of India *p* Shanataram *d* Bhaskar Rao
10 mins

Grand Trunk Road
The Grand Trunk Road in India runs 1,500 miles from Calcutta to the North-West Frontier, serving the military, industrial, cultural and religious needs of India
sp Films Advisory Board of India *pc* Shell (India)
11 mins NFA

DOMINIONS & COLONIES – New Zealand

New Zealand
The two islands of New Zealand are the home of two peoples—the Maoris, who discovered them in the tenth century, and the English, who first settled there in the nineteenth century. Today they live in unity. It is to defend this heritage that the full productive strength of New Zealand's mountains, forests, fields, mines and factories has been turned to war needs and that two-thirds of the men of military age volunteered for service
Review MFB XII 115
MoI & Govt of New Zealand *pc* Crown
15 mins LC

DOMINIONS & COLONIES – West Indies

Hello West Indies
From the chain of islands which bridges the Caribbean Sea, from the Bahamas to Trinidad, hundreds of West Indians have come of their own accord to England to help win the war. Learie Constantine, now a Welfare Officer with the Ministry of Labour, introduces skilled men working in factories side by side with English men and women and others being trained to work the latest types of machinery. Flying Officer Ulric Cross, RAF bomber-pilot, introduces men and women in all the Services. Carlton Fairweather introduces the lumbermen of Honduras. (Theatrical version entitled *West Indies calling*)
Review MFB XIII 27 (under theatrical title)
MoI *pc* Rotha Productions *p* Paul Rotha *d* John Page
14 mins NFA

The modern spirit
The story of petroleum production in Trinidad, from drilling a new well to the export of oil to Britain. (Film made in 1937)
pc GB Instructional *d* Frank Bundy
16 mins

West Indies calling
(The contribution of the West Indians to the war effort both in the forces and in civilian life. This title is used in the DNL for the 15-minute version. The non-theatrical title is *Hello West Indies*)
Review MFB XIII 27
MoI *pc* Rotha Productions *d* John Page *p* Paul Rotha
14 mins IWM NFA

ALLIES – China

Chinese in Britain
As seamen, doctors, engineers and

students, Chinese living in Britain fought for China's liberation and prepared for their work there after the war
Review DNL VI 9
pc Strand *p* Donald Taylor *d* C Heck
11 mins IWM LC

ALLIES – France

Le journal de la résistance
The full-length film of the liberation of Paris (shot by FFI cameramen), extracts from which appeared in the newsreels. Front-line type of material shows, at close quarters, the building of barricades, the street fighting in which both men and women took part, the taking of prisoners and collaborators and the final jubilation at the entry of General de Gaulle
Review DNL V 45
pc Liberation Ctte of the French Cinema *English comm s* Noel Coward *French comm s* Pierre Blanchard
35 mins IWM (English version)

ALLIES – Middle East

Cairo
(Tourist 'sights')
MoI (Middle East) *p* Charles Martin *d & ph* Frank Hurley
12 mins IWM

Scenes from a day in the life of a King
(A typical day for the 9-year old Feisal II of Iraq and his uncle Amir Abdul-Illah, the Regent)
MoI (Middle East) *p* Charles Martin *d & ph* Frank Hartley
10 mins IWM

ALLIES – Netherlands

The Dutch tradition
Windmills, dykes, tulips, wooden shoes are traditional symbols of Holland. But Holland with its population of 8 millions is also the centre of an Empire with a population of 70 millions marked by traditions of enterprise, courage and freedom. In 1940 Holland was overwhelmed by the Nazis and in 1941 Sumatra, Java and all the islands forming the Netherlands East Indies were overrun by the Japanese. Today Dutch forces fight from new bases in Britain, Australia and North America; and Surinam and the islands of the Netherlands West Indies in the Caribbean Sea provide essential bauxite and petroleum
sp Netherlands Information Bureau & National Film Board of Canada *pc* John Ferno
28 mins

New earth
This film tells the story of the reclamation of the Zuiderzee between 1922 and 1932, one of the world's great engineering achievements, by which Holland won in peace and for the uses of peace half a million acres of new earth. The film shows how the first dyke, 19 miles long, was built in the sea between North Holland and Friesland, how behind this further dykes and canals were made until the sea bed was laid bare to be drained and prepared for cultivation, and how homes were built and crops grown. (Original title *Nieuwe Gronden*, made in 1934)
sp Netherlands Information Bureau *pc* Joris Ivens
23 mins BFI IWM NFA (section)

ALLIES – Poland

Strangers
The story of the Poles who came to Scotland and, as they trained to fight again for the deliverance of their country, learnt to know Scots men and women and ceased to be strangers
Review MFB XI 109
Polish MoI *pc* Polish Film Unit *ed* Stefan

Osiecki *sc* Bruce Graeme *comm s* James McKechnie
11 mins IWM NFA

Tale of a city
(The war history of Warsaw, including 'clandestine' film. Distribution arrangements unclear)
pc Polish Film Unit
10 mins IWM

Unfinished journey
The story of General Sikorski's leadership of the Poles as Commander-in-Chief of the Polish forces and Premier of the Polish Government in England
Reviews DNL V 16, MFB XI 94
Polish MoI *pc* Concanen *p* Derrick de Marney *d* Eugene Cekalski
10 mins IWM NFA

ALLIES – USA

Autobiography of a jeep
The Jeep can drive over the roughest country, cross rivers, pack into a transport aircraft, launch a glider, pull and mount a gun. Wherever the US Army fights–in the Pacific, Alaska and Europe–you will see the Jeep. (G for general, P for purpose)
Reviews KW 13.1.44, MFB XI 7
sp US Office of War Information *pc* United Films *p* Joseph Krumgold *d* Irving Lerner *ph* Roger Barlow *nar* Robert Sloane
10 mins

Crops for combat
Flax, cotton seed, peanuts and soya beans are crops for combat grown by American farmers to provide concentrated foods, meal for cattle and oils and fats for munitions
sp US Office of War Information *pc* US Dept of Ag *d* Tom Hogan
9 mins IWM

New England's eight million Yankees
In New England today, in towns like Exeter, New Hampshire, the descendants of the colonists of 300 years ago take up again the fight to preserve the freedom which their ancestors sought and established
pc March of Time
20 mins

Oswego
Oswego is an ordinary small town on Lake Ontario. The film shows what life is like and how the people brought men from many of the United Nations to live there for a week so that they could get to know them better and talk about the war and the peace that they must win together. (*American scene series* no 3)
Review MFB XI 63
US Office of War Information *pc* United Films
15 mins IWM

Pipeline
Transporting petroleum by pipeline leaves boats, railroads and trucks free for other important traffic. This film shows how a 59-mile pipeline was laid from Fall River to Boston, New England, through rock and marsh, under 28 railroads and 97 highways. The story is told by a Texan who worked on the line
Review MFB XI 109
Petroleum Films Bureau *pc* Documentary Film
13 mins

ALLIES – USSR

Road to Russia
In 1942 Paiforce (Persia and Iraq Force) was created to guard the oil routes and carry supplies to Russia. The film is the story of the vast enterprise, civilian and military, by means of which thousands of tons a month of British and American war material were sent, by rail and road, from the Persian Gulf to the Russo-

Persian frontier
Review MFB XII 54
pc MoI (Middle east)
19 mins LC NFA

A Soviet village
The liberation of Boutovka, a village near Moscow, by the Red Army, and its rebuilding and rehabilitation, after occupation by the enemy, participation in partisan warfare, and devastation by the retreating Germans. (Compiled from Soviet newsreels)
MoI *pc* Rotha Productions *p* Paul Rotha *ed* Bunch Lee
9 mins IWM

The story of Stalingrad
The failure of the German attempt to conquer Stalingrad, the key city on the Volga, during the campaign beginning in summer 1942 . . . Nazi atrocities revealed as the Germans are driven back. The encirclement is completed and Field-Marshal Von Paulus finally surrenders with his remaining forces on 2nd Feb, 1943
Review MFB X 57
Soviet Film Agency *pc* Central Newsreel Studio, Moscow *comp* L Varlamov, A Kuznetsov *ph* Red Army cameramen *military advisor* Col S Chabrov
63 mins CFL IWM NFA

USSR at war
A two-reel film made by March of Time from the feature length Soviet film, *Day of war,* showing the fight in the front line and in the factories, at sea and in the air, in all parts of the Soviet Union
Review MFB XI 137
March of Time *pc* Central Newsreel Studio, Moscow
23 mins IWM

OVERSEAS DISTRIBUTION

Africa's fighting men
pc Colonial Film Unit
12 mins

Anti-personnel obstacles, elementary
MoI
NARS

Bailey bridge

Camouflage
MoI
NARS

Campo 63
(The life of Italian prisoners of war in a typical British camp. Intended for screening in liberated Italy)
IWM

Canteen command
(NAAFI activities and organisations. Overseas distribution only)
MoI *pc* Spectator *p* Michael Hankinson *d* Gilbert Gunn
11 mins IWM LC

Charlie the rascal
pc Colonial Film Unit
2 mins

Checkmate!
(Overseas distribution only. Latin America)
MoI *pc* Merton Park
14 mins IWM (incomplete)

Chinese mission to Britain
(Not shown in Britain)
MoI *pc* British Movietonews *p* Gerald Sanger
8 mins

Churchill in the Middle East
(Overseas distribution)
MoI
4 mins NFA (Arabic commentary)

Cine-sports magazine
(Series, numbers 1-20. Not shown in Britain)

MoI *pc* GB Screen Services
10 mins each

Clean milk

Coalminer

Cossack horseman
(Listed in DNL 1944. No further information)
pc Colonial Film Unit
3 mins

Defeat tuberculosis

Don't neglect your bicycle
pc Colonial Film Unit
4 mins

Farming in Russia
pc Colonial Film Unit

Floating men
(Not shown in Britain. Arabic version)
MoI *pc* Films of GB *p* Andrew Buchanan
d Henry Cooper *ph* Charles Francis
7 mins

Freed prisoners of war return to South Africa
pc Colonial Film Unit

Germans in Norway
pc Colonial Film Unit
6 mins

Highland doctor

The house fly
MoI
NARS

A hundred years old
MoI *pc* GB Instructional *d* B Salt

Katsina tank
MoI *pc* Colonial Film Unit
8 mins

The King and his people
(Not shown in Britain)
MoI *pc* British Movietonews *p* Gerald Sanger
9 mins IWM

Latin Americans in England
(Not shown in Britain)
MoI *pc* British Paramount News

Machi Gaba
(Made to encourage Nigerian tribal chiefs to take a closer interest in their people's welfare. Demonstrates simple measures for safeguarding health)
pc Colonial Film Unit
14 mins silent

Making good hay

Making grass silage

Malta convoy

Margarine
pc Colonial Film Unit
11 mins

Memphis Belle

Mr Wise and Mr Foolish go to town
(The obvious effects of neglected venereal disease)
pc Colonial Film Unit
23 mins silent

Motive power
(Not shown in Britain)
MoI *pc* Films of GB *p* Andrew Buchanan
d Henry Cooper *ph* Charles Francis

Of one blood

Our heritage no 2
Architecture and sculpture of North and Central India, 12th to 18th centuries AD. The marble temples of Delwara at Mount Abu: the fortress of Gwalior; the Kutb

Minar and Shah Jehan's fort at Delhi; the Taj Mahal at Agra; Fatehpur Sikri; the tomb of Emperor Jehangir; the Badshahi Mosque and the mausoleum of Ranjit Singh at Lahore; Jaipur; and the Golden Temple at Amritsar
Review MFB XIII 10
pc Information Films of India
16 mins

Rationing in Britain
(Not shown in Britain. An American woman commentator looks at the effects of rationing on the English people)
MoI *pc* World Wide *p* Ralph Bond *d* Graham Cutts
11 mins IWM

Reseeding for better grass

A ride with Uncle Joe

Road to victory
(Overseas only)
Govt of South Africa *pc* African Film Productions
5 mins IWM

Sam the cyclist
pc Colonial Film Unit

Saving your own seeds

Scabies

Ship against plane
(Not shown in Britain. Air-sea combat in the Pacific theatre)
MoI *pc* British Movietonews *p* Gerald Sanger
11 mins IWM

Simple fruit pruning

Sport
(Overseas distribution)
pc Strand *d* Ralph Bond

Springtime in an English village
(The election and crowning of the May Queen in an English village, the May Queen is an African child)
pc Colonial Film Unit
8 mins

Steel
(Manufacture of steel)
Reviews DNL VI 8, FoB 1944-5, MFB XII 94
British Council *pc* Technique *p & d* Ronald Riley *ph* Jack Cardiff
20 mins colour NFA

Stooking and stacking

There's a future in it

They live again
Principles of surgical treatment and rehabilitation methods as practised at a miners' hospital in the Midlands. (Shortened version of *Accident service*)
Reviews FoB 1944-5, MFB XII 125
sp British Council *pc* GB Instructional *d* A R Dobson
18 mins NFA

V1
(The flying bombs. Overseas distribution only)
pc Crown *p* Humphrey Jennings
9 mins IWM NFA PAC

Vegetable seed growing

Wartime shipment of packed petroleum

Welding helps the farmer

West African editors
pc Colonial Film Unit
9 mins

West Indies join the RAF
pc Colonial Film Unit
8 mins

Yaws
(Treatment of yaws in a scattered population by mobile Medical Units)
pc Colonial Film Unit
10 mins silent

Your people in Britain
pc Colonial Film Unit

NEWSREEL TRAILERS

AGAG
MoI & Min of War Transport *pc* Publicity Pictures

The Behemoth

Blitz on bugs
Cartoon
MoI & Min of Ag *pc* Halas Batchelor

Blood transfusion
MoI & Min of Health *pc* Concanen *d* Derrick de Marney

Bones, bones, bones
MoI & Min of Supply *pc* Elwis

Books for the brave
MoI & Min of Supply *pc* Concanen *d* Derrick de Marney

Bristles and brushes
MoI & Min of Supply *pc* Elwis

Burning results
Chemical warfare and firefighting
sp Fire Offices Ctte *pc* Strand *d* Gilbert Gunn

Butterfly bomb
(Newsreel trailer telling civilians how to recognise and deal with small anti-personnel bombs)
MoI *pc* Verity *d* Louise Birt
2 mins IWM LC NFA

Careless talk
sp Security Services *pc* Strand *d* Gilbert Gunn

Children's vitamins
MoI & Min of Food *pc* Merton Park *d* R Curtis

Christmas wishes
Cartoon
sp GPO *pc* Halas & Batchelor

Clear the roads
MoI & Min of Supply *pc* Concanen *d* Derrick de Marney

Coals of fire
MoI & Min of Fuel and Power *pc* Concanen *d* Derrick de Marney

Cold comfort
Cartoon
MoI & Min of Fuel and Power *pc* Halas & Batchelor

Come on, girls
MoI & War Office *pc* Merton Park *d* W McQuitty

Compost heap
MoI & Min of Ag *pc* Halas & Batchelor

The conjurer
MoI & Min of Fuel and Power *pc* Merton Park *d* A C Hammond

Diphtheria V
MoI & Min of Health *pc* Strand *d* R McDougall

Diphtheria VI
MoI & Min of Health *pc* Concanen *d* Derrick de Marney

Do moths make good mothers?
MoI & Board of Trade *pc* Publicity

Domestic workers
MoI & Min of Labour *pc* Merton Park *d* R Curtis

Early April
MoI & Min of Ag *pc* Merton Park *d* R Curtis

Eat more green vegetables
MoI & Min of Food

Fifteen bob
sp National Savings Ctte *pc* Rotha Productions

From rags to stitches
MoI & Min of Supply *pc* Halas & Batchelor

Grain harvest
(Harvesting on a Scottish lowland farm)
sp Scottish Office *pc* Campbell Harper
5 mins

Harvest uplift
sp Min of Ag *pc* Verity *d* W McQuitty

Here we go gathering spuds
sp Scottish Office *sp* Spectator

How to use your doctor
sp Min of Health *pc* Strand *d* Peter Price

It makes you think
sp Fire Offices Ctte *pc* Elwis

John Bull's workers
sp Min of Labour *pc* Concanen *d* Derrick de Marney

Kitchen nuts
MoI & Min of Fuel and Power *pc* Crown *d* Gerald Bryant

Little drops of water
MoI & Min of Health *pc* Concanen *d* Derrick de Marney

Old logs
MoI & Min of Fuel *pc* Film Traders *d* G Hollering

One pair of nostrils
Cartoon
MoI & Min of Health

Pay as you earn
MoI & Treasury *pc* Strand *d* Roger McDougall

Proceed according to plan
MoI & Min of Ag *pc* Crown *d* Gerald Bryant

Rags to stitches

Save fuel for battle
MoI
NFA

Spending money

Thank you, housewives
MoI & Min of Supply *pc* Crown *d* Michael Gordon

That's the stuff to give 'em!
MoI & Min of Supply *pc* Crown *d* Michael Gordon

A ticket's dream
MoI & Min of Supply *pc* Elwis

Tim marches back
GPO *pc* Film Traders *d* George Hollering

Tom Johnstone's appeal
sp Scottish Office *pc* Merton Park *d* Cecil Musk

Tyre economy
MoI & Min of Supply *pc* Film Traders *d* George Hollering

Walk short journeys

1944
NEWSREEL TRAILERS

Write to the forces
MoI & War Office *pc* Army Film Unit

You can't keep an old blade down
MoI & Min of Supply *pc* Strand *d* Roger McDougall

Your perishing rubber
MoI & Min of Supply *pc* Crown *d* Gerald Bryant

1945

HOMEFRONT – General

Bailey bridge
Mr D C (now Sir Donald) Bailey demonstrates the principles of the design worked out at the Experimental Bridging Establishment of the Ministry of Supply, and the Bridge is shown being erected and in use in different forms in a number of situations
Review DNL V 94
MoI & War Office & Min of Supply *pc* Merlin *p* Michael Hankinson *d* Arthur Barnes
11 mins IWM NFA

Channel Islands 1940-1945
An account of the German invasion of the Channel Islands in 1940, of life and resistance under the occupation, of growing hopes and diminishing supplies after D-Day, and of the end of the war and final liberation. Incidents of the occupation period are re-enacted by islanders
Review DNL VI 24
MoI *pc* Crown *p* Basil Wright *d* Gerald Bryant *ph* Jonah Jones
16 mins IWM NFA

A city reborn
A soldier on leave and two 'directed' workers, sent to devastated Coventry, find the city full of plans for rebuilding. The City Architect's model for the central section of the city is seen, and the idea of grouping shops, schools, industry and entertainment according to a rational and harmonious plan is expounded. There is much discussion in the film, including a defence, in popular style, of prefabricated houses such as the city's own factories could produce
MoI *pc* Gryphon & Verity *p* Donald Taylor *d* John Eldridge
23 mins NFA

Cornish valley
Third in *Pattern of Britain* series . . . The farms of Coombe Valley near the border of north Cornwall and Devon are fairly typical of the south-west peninsula, a

country of open windswept uplands and deep sheltered valleys, of steep slopes and small fields. Frank Allin, the eldest of three brothers, farms Stowe Barton and breeds sheep; Fred at Lee breeds pedigree Red Devon cattle; Ernest dairy-farms at Burridge, and his son-in-law farms 120 acres at Sanctuary. Wives and daughters, as well as sons, have their customary jobs on these family farms and little labour is employed
Reviews DNL V 72, MFB XIV 121
MoI & Min of Ag *pc* Green Park *assoc p* Edgar Anstey *d* Ralph Keene *ph* Peter Hennessy
17 mins NFA

Cotswold club
Assisted by the County Organiser for Village Produce Associations, a Cotswold village forms a local association to buy seeds, plants and fertilisers and to market surplus produce for its members
Reviews DNL V 28, MFB XIII 159
MoI & Min of Ag *pc* Strand *assoc p* Edgar Anstey, Donald Taylor *d* Charles de Lautour *ph* Cyril Arapoff
12 mins NFA

The crofters
Second in *Pattern of Britain* series . . . Achriesgill is a crofting community in Sutherlandshire in the extreme north-west of the Scottish Highlands
Reviews DNL V 64, MFB XIII 129
MoI & Min of Ag *pc* Green Park *assoc p* Edgar Anstey *d* Ralph Keene *ph* Peter Hennessy *m* Dennis Blood
24 mins NFA

A farm is reclaimed
How, with the aid and advice of the local Agricultural Executive Committee, the assistance of government grants, and his own good farming sense, a Scottish farmer put a derelict farm of 250 acres into good heart in one year
Reviews DNL V 45, KYB 1945, MFB XIV 12
MoI & the Dept of Ag *pc* Campbell Harper *d* Alan Harper
16 mins NFA

Fenlands
Fourth in *Pattern of Britain* series . . . Life in East Anglia, where three hundred years of draining and water control have converted fen into rich farming country. Once given over to wild-fowling and sedge-cutting, the land now produces grain, vegetables, apples, strawberries, and sugar beet, which have brought a quiet prosperity to the small Fenland towns. Constant vigilance is needed to preserve, against flood and erosion, the gains made
Reviews DNL VI 8, MFB XIII 76
MoI & Min of Ag *pc* Green Park *d* Kenneth Annakin *ph* Peter Hennessy
19 mins NFA

Food flashes
(Series of short message films with themes such as 'Eat potatoes not bread', etc.)
MoI and Min of Food
2-5 mins each B&W and colour NFA

Fuel for battle
The work of Pit Production Committees in maintaining coal production
MoI & Min of Fuel and Power *pc* Strand *p* Donald Taylor *d* John Eldridge
21 mins NFA

The grassy shires
First in a series of films on *The pattern of Britain* . . . The rich grasslands of Leicestershire (and other Midland counties) are especially suitable for dairy and stock farming. The growing of corn and root crops during the war suggests that the land, by means of ley farming, could continue to produce these as well as rich milk, fat cheese and prime English beef. Made in the Vale of Belvoir and Welland Valley
Reviews DNL V 23, MFB XIII 116
MoI & Min of Ag *pc* Green Park *p* Edgar Anstey *d* Ralph Keene *ph* Peter Hennessy

m William Alwyn
16 mins NFA

Jigsaw
Anti-gossip film, produced from an Admiralty training film
pc Verity *d* Henry Cass *p* Sydney Box
20 mins IWM

Lessons from the air
BBC school broadcasts help to extend the experience of schoolchildren, whether in town or country, beyond their own immediate locality. The development of a talk to schools is traced from its general conception at a meeting of the Central Council for School Broadcasting to its actual delivery, and various typical broadcasts, on music, history, and so on, are shown taking place
Review DNL VI 24
sp British Council *pc* Merton Park
19 mins NFA

Myra Hess
Dame Myra Hess playing the first movement of Beethoven's 'Sonata Appassionata' for pianoforte. (Uses material shot for *Diary for Timothy*)
Reviews DNL VI 24, MFB XIII 130, MFB XIII 153
MoI *pc* Crown
11 mins NFA

Necessary journey
A typical story of the work of the railways in wartime
MoI & Min of War Transport *pc* Seven League *d* Hans Nieter
15 mins IWM

New builders
Far more builders than we have got are needed for post-war work. In the film we see a school of a secondary type which trains boys of 13 and 14 as builders. A general education is given as well as courses in bricklaying, plastering, mason's work, carpentry, plumbing and building construction. Apprenticeship is the final stage
Review DNL V 45
MoI *pc* Rotha Productions *p* Paul Rotha *d* Kay Mander *ph* Wolfgang Suschitzky
20 mins IWM NFA

The new crop
A picture of the forester's craft and an account of how the Forestry Commission is raising new crops of timber, under reafforestation schemes which will renew Britain's resources, depleted twice in 25 years
Review DNL V 28
MoI *pc* Green Park *assoc p* Edgar Anstey *d* Kenneth Annakin *ph* Geoffrey Williams
19 mins NFA

The new mine
A modern Scottish colliery, at Comrie, is situated in unspoilt country, has symmetrical surface buildings, up-to-date machinery, ventilation and safety devices, and new methods in mining practice
Reviews DNL VI 58, FoB 1944-5, MFB XII 24
sp British Council *pc* GB Instructional *d* Irene Wilson
17 mins NFA

Other men's lives
(Careless talk film.) Intended for munitions workers
MoI *pc* Verity *p* Sydney Box *d* Henry Cass
10 mins IWM

Our enemy – Japan
(Possibly not released due to Japanese surrender)
pc World Wide
25 mins NFA

Penicillin
The story of the discovery of penicillin by Professor (later Sir Alexander) Fleming in 1928 and of its great development during the war for wide antiseptic purposes. The various stages of experiment are shown, and the problems of production in large quantities are touched on.

While penicillin will not act against all diseases (as for example consumption and influenza) it is very effective against VD, child-birth fever, and many others, and was invaluable for dealing with wounded soldiers during the war. Work on penicillin continues
Reviews DNL V 77, MFB XII 88
ICI *pc* Realist *p* John Taylor *d* Alexander Shaw, Kay Mander
20 mins NFA (incomplete)

The plan and the people
The LCC plan for London . . . as it affects the lives of a particular local community in one borough. The question is raised of which are most necessary—flats, houses, or open spaces; and the public's responsibility in determining the issues is emphasised
Review DNL VI 8
MoI *pc* Realist *p* John Taylor *d* Frank Sainsbury *ph* A E Jeakins *cast* Alfred Bass, Neville Mapp
19 mins

Proud city
The LCC project for the re-planning and rebuilding of London explained by the two architects responsible for the plan, Sir Patrick Abercrombie and Mr J H Forshaw (the latter Chief Architect to the LCC), with comments by Lord Latham, under whose chairmanship the LCC commissioned the plan
Reviews DNL VI 8, MFB XII 140, MFB XIII 72
MoI *pc* Green Park *p* Edgar Anstey *d* Ralph Keene
26 mins NFA

Public opinion
An ABCA film on the individual's responsibility in the shaping of public opinion. The film illustrates the great power of the printed word for both good and evil, and adds illustrations of the power of the radio and the cinema. The part played by the individual in the growth and expression of mass opinions as an influence on public policy is indicated, with the formation of bodies such as the NSPCC, and the Trade Unions as examples of what can be achieved, through energy and organisation, from small beginnings
Reviews DNL VI 24, MFB XIII 129
War Office & Army Bureau of Current Affairs *pc* Verity
15 mins IWM

Shop to let
Post-war jobs series *What's the next job?* Conditions and prospects in the retail trade: from the one-man business to the large-scale organisations such as departmental stores, chain stores, and the Co-operative Movement. The film stresses the planning and organisation which go to the making of even a small business; and the parts played by various jobs in the complex organisation of a departmental store are outlined in considerable detail
Review MFB XII 143
War Office, Board of Trade & Min of Labour *pc* British Movietonews
22 mins IWM

A soldier comes home
(The psychological readjustment necessary for wives and husbands after wartime separation)
Review DNL VI 8
MoI *pc* Gryphon *p* Donald Taylor *d* John Eldridge
5 mins

Teaching
Post-war jobs. The proposals of the Education Act, 1944, require a greatly increased number of teachers. Special training colleges are being established for men and women wishing to become teachers
Reviews MFB XII 125, MFB XII 142, MFB XIII 91
MoI & Min of Educ *pc* Merlin *p* Michael Hankinson *d* Roger McDougall
25 mins IWM

This was Japan
A marshalling of evidence for the indictment of Japan's militaristic and aggressive policy which led to war
Review MFB XII 113
MoI *pc* Crown *p* Basil Wright *ed* Alan Osbiston, Terry Trench
13 mins IWM NFA

This was Japan. *The Samurai warrior tradition seen as one of the roots of the new militarism.*

Time and tide
A characteristic job of the Admiralty Salvage Department–raising and removing a sunken ship from one of the many harbours which were blocked or obstructed by such wreckage
Review DNL V 94
MoI & Admiralty *pc* Rotha Productions *p* Paul Rotha *d* Jack Eldridge *ed* Jack Ellitt
15 mins LC NFA

Total war in Britain
The story of the total mobilisation of Britain's manpower, womanpower and industrial resources for war in the four years from Dunkirk to the invasion of Western Europe. Based on an official British Government report
Review DNL VI 24
MoI *pc* Films of Fact *p & ed* Paul Rotha, Michael Orrom *sc* Miles Tomalin, Ritchie Calder *comm s* John Mills *diagrams* Isotype *m* William Alwyn
21 mins CFL IWM NFA

What's the next job?
First in a series of films produced for the Ministry of Labour to help men and women in choosing new civilian jobs. Each film aims at giving the facts rather than persuading anyone to take up a particular job. The pros and cons of each trade or profession are stated in terms of qualifications needed, training schemes available, pay, working conditions, prospects of secure employment and advancement. This introductory film shows how the Employment Exchanges and other services of the Ministry of Labour can help to find the right job, and provide special training if necessary
Review MFB XII 125
War Office & Min of Labour *pc* Army Kinematograph Services
23 mins IWM

HOMEFRONT – Scotland & Northern Ireland

Children of the city
Study of juvenile delinquency in Scotland
Reviews DNL V 28, MFB XIII 178
MoI & Scottish Educ & Home Depts *pc* Rotha Productions *p* Paul Rotha *d* Budge Cooper *ph* Wolfgang Suschitzky
32 mins CFL NFA

Housing in Scotland
Scotland's housing plans are being framed to meet opinions obtained by the Scottish Housing Advisory Committee from men and women in the Services and in the factories. Permanent and temporary houses, cottages, flats, tenements, and duplex houses which can later be transformed into single dwellings, all figure in the plans, and the film shows the first examples
MoI & Scottish Dept of Health *pc* Merlin *d* Gilbert Gunn
14 mins NFA

Things seen in Northern Ireland
Views of the north coastline, the Giants

Causeway and inland valleys, Belfast and its shipyards. Rural scenery
Review MFB X 11
12 mins

HOMEFRONT – Instructional

The burning question
Humorous exposition, by Gillie Potter, of how to cut down the consumption of raw coal in the home and avoid waste in the use of gas and electricity, the latter again meaning an economy in coal, which is the source of nearly all our heat and light
Reviews DNL V 102, MFB XV 148
MoI & Min of Fuel and Power *pc* World Wide *p* Ralph Bond *d* Ken Hughes *ph* Geoffrey Williams *cast* Gillie Potter, Marianne Stone
11 mins

Deep pan bottling
A way of preserving fruit without sugar. Suitable also for tomatoes
Review BFY 368
MoI & Min of Food *pc* Films of GB *p* Andrew Buchanan *d* Henry Cooper *ph* Charles Francis
9 mins NFA

Defeat diphtheria
(Re-edited version of the 1941 film)
pc New Realm *ed* Sylvia Cummins

How to bake
MoI & Min of Food in association with Board of Educ *pc* Films of GB *p* Andrew Buchanan *d* Henry Cooper *ph* Charles Francis
6 mins

How to boil
sp MoI & Min of Food in association with Board of Educ *pc* Films of GB *p* Andrew Buchanan *d* Henry Cooper *ph* Charles Francis
7 mins

How to cook green vegetables
MoI & Min of Food in association with Board of Educ *pc* Films of GB *p* Andrew Buchanan *d* Henry Cooper *ph* Charles Francis
10 mins NFA

How to fry
MoI & Min of Food in association with Board of Educ *pc* Films of GB *p* Andrew Buchanan *d* Henry Cooper *ph* Charles Francis
6 mins

How to make short pastry
sp MoI for Min of Food in association with Board of Educ *pc* Films of GB *p* Andrew Buchanan *d* Henry Cooper *ph* Charles Francis
10 mins

Patching and darning
Instructional film made for the make-do-and-mend campaign
MoI & Board of Trade *pc* Films of GB *p* Andrew Buchanan *d* Henry Cooper *ph* Charles Francis
11 mins

Round figures
The importance for health of good posture. Humorous treatment, using as examples a man in the street, a housewife, and a factory worker
Reviews MFB XII 11, MFB XIII 69
Central Council for Health Educ *pc* Coombe Productions
8 mins CFL NFA

Subject discussed
The causes, symptoms, effects and treatment of syphilis and gonorrhoea are explained by a woman Industrial Medical Officer and a county Director of VD Services in answer to questions put by Commander Campbell
MoI & Min of Health & Central Council for Health Educ *pc* Gryphon *p* Donald Taylor *d* Charles de Lautour
15 mins CFL NFA

Your children's eyes
The structure of the eyes is explained by means of models and diagrams. The film shows why and how common defects, diseases and injuries should be treated: long- and short-sightedness, astigmatism and squint; blepharitis, conjunctivitis and styes; grit and dirt. It is important that the eyes are not strained in reading or by close needlework, and above all that the children are kept happy and in good general health
Review DNL V 92
MoI & Depts of Health & Council for Health Educ *pc* Realist *p* John Taylor *d & ph* Alex Strasser *m* William Alwyn *comm s* Carlton Hobbs
19 mins CFL NFA PAC

HOMEFRONT – Specialised instructional

The movement of the tongue in speech
(Movement of the human tongue and lips during speech as seen in a male patient with part of his right cheek removed by a surgical operation)
Review DNL V 93
sp ICI *pc* Realist *p* John Taylor *ph* Cyril Knowles *adviser* D B Fry
13 mins NFA

The technique of anaesthesia series
No 1 The signs and stages of anaesthesia
No 2 Open drop ether
No 3 Nitrous oxide-oxygen-ether anaesthesia
No 4 The carbon-dioxide absorption technique
No 5 Endotracheal anaesthesia
No 6 Intravenous anaesthesia, part I
No 7 Intravenous anaesthesia, part II
No 8 Spinal anaesthesia
No 9 Respiratory and cardiac arrest
No 10 Operative shock
No 11 Handling and care of the patient
Review DNL VI 31
ICI *pc* Realist *p* John Taylor *ph* A E Jeakins
25 mins each NFA

Technique of instruction in the army
Made for the training of Army instructors. Shows the basic methods–lesson, lecture, discussion; use of visual aids etc. Emphasises the need for preparation, and illustrates both good and bad techniques. The film is in three parts: (1) Foundations, (2) Framework, (3) Method
War Office *pc* Army Kinematograph Services
61 mins IWM NARS

Training in mechanised mining
A detailed account of the six months' course for mineworkers at the Mines Mechanisation Training Centre, Sheffield, claimed as the first of its kind in the world
Review DNL VI 25
MoI & Mins of Fuel, Labour *pc* Films of GB *p & d* Andrew Buchanan
26 mins

FIGHTING SERVICES & CAMPAIGNS

The air plan
(Foreword: 'This film is intended to show the part played by the RAF, the Dominion and Allied Air Forces flying with them in the invasion of NW Europe. This story cannot be told without references to the equally great part played by the USAF but justice cannot be done to their work within the scope of this short film')
Review MFB XII 102
pc RAF Film Unit
28 mins IWM

Air transport support
This film is made in 3 parts–*The army goes by air, Tactical loading* and *Strategic loading*
sp Army Kinematograph Corp *pc* World Wide *p* Hindle Edgar *d* Graham Cutts, Clifford Dyment *ph* Geoffrey Williams, Ronald Anscombe

The big pack
(The work of the maintenance command of the RAF in organising supplies necessary for a major overseas operation)
Reviews DNL V 53, MFB XI 99
MoI *pc* RAF Film Unit *m* Gordon Jacob
35 mins IWM

The broad fourteens
(The first posting and eventual first action of a newly trained Motor Torpedo Boat crew)
pc Crown *p* J B Holmes *d* Richard McNaughton
35 mins IWM LC

Broken dykes
In autumn 1944 the Allies were compelled to bomb the dykes of Walcheren in order to flood the Germans out of that heavily fortified island. The film shows the ensuing destruction, the efforts made by Allies and Dutch to rescue the population, and the subsequent wrecked state of Walcheren, left four-fifths under the sea
Reviews DNL V 94, MFB XII 102
MoI from material supplied by Netherlands Govt *d* John Ferno
14 mins NFA

Burma victory
(A record of the Burma campaign)
Review MFB XII 129
pc Army Film Unit *p* David Macdonald *d* Roy Boulting
62 mins IWM

Central front, Burma
(The campaign in Burma, from the Japanese 'March on Delhi' to the Allied capture of Mandalay and Rangoon)
MoI *pc* Gryphon *p* Donald Taylor
10 mins IWM

The eighty days
A picture of the intensive V-1 attack on Southern England of June 1944, of the destruction of the flying bombs by the combined efforts of AA, Balloon and Fighter Commands, and of the damage done
MoI *pc* Crown *p & d* Humphrey Jennings *comm s* Ed Murrow
14 mins CFL IWM NFA

Failure of the dictators
(The war against Germany 1941-43. Prelude to the *From Italy to D-Day* series)
MoI *ed* Peter Tanner
30 mins IWM NFA

From D-Day to Paris
(The liberation of France and concurrent actions elsewhere in the war in Europe. Follows *From Italy to D-Day* and precedes *From Paris to the Rhine*)
MoI *pc* British Movietonews *ed* Raymond Perrin
50 mins IWM NFA

From Paris to the Rhine
(The course of the war in Europe in the last months of 1944. Follows *From D-Day to Paris* and precedes *From the Rhine to victory*)
MoI *pc* British Movietonews *ed* Raymond Perrin
50 mins IWM NFA

Front line air force
Allied Air Forces supporting the ground troops in the attack on the Salerno beaches
MoI *pc* RAF Film Unit
9 mins IWM

In defence of Britain
(The story of the V1 campaign)
pc RAF Film Unit
7 mins IWM

MAC ship
Conversion of an oil-tanker into a merchant aircraft carrier. These ships could still carry large cargoes of oil
pc Shell *d* Rex Baxter
13 mins NFA

The eighty days. *A body is extracted from the ruins after a V-1 has struck.*

Memphis Belle

Night flight
Shows how map-reading is the fundamental aid to aircraft navigation
MoI & Air Min *pc* RAF Film Unit
22 mins IWM

Pacific thrust
A diagrammatic exposition of the strategy of war in the Pacific, January 1945. Supplementary film to *War in the Pacific*, March 1945
Review MFB XII 24
MoI *pc* Verity *d* Kenneth Annakin
15 mins IWM

REME
The work of the Royal Electrical and Mechanical Engineers, who service and repair guns, tanks, vehicles and equipment from the moment of unloading right up to the battlefront
MoI & War Office *pc* Army Film Unit *ed* R Verrall
10 mins IWM

Report from Burma
Major Frank Owen, editor of the 14th Army's own newspaper SEAC, reveals in this picture the nature of the war in Burma—a war of jungle and mountain, mist, mud and monsoon rain. (*Know the Commonwealth series* no 4)
Review MFB XII 64
MoI & War Office *pc* New Realm *comp* Sylvia Cummins
14 mins IWM

Round pegs
The principles and practice of personnel selection as applied to recruits in the British Army. (Short version of *Personnel selection in the British Army 1944—recruits*)
MoI *pc* Shell *p & ed* Sylvia Cummins
15 mins

Salvage hits back
The Army in the Middle East sets an example
MoI & War Office *pc* Army Kine Service
12 mins IWM

Soldier-sailor
(Life on the defensively equipped merchant ships with naval gunners and Royal Artillery Maritime Regiment men)
Review MFB XII 59
MoI *pc* Realist *p* John Taylor *d* Alexander Shaw *ph* A E Jeakins, Raymond Elton *sc* Frank Launder *m* William Alwyn *cast* Rosamund John, Jean Kent, Charles Victor, Jean Cadell
61 mins IWM NFA

The eighty days. *Girls keep watch for V-1's approaching the coastline.*

The true glory. *Normandy landings.*

Stricken peninsula
The problems of reconstruction were revealed in the tasks which faced the Allied Armies in Southern Italy, the first part of Europe to be freed. Food was short and land uncultivated. Bridges, railways, roads, engines and trucks had been wrecked. There was little fuel or power for transport and industry; water supplies had been wrecked. Epidemics broke out and hospitals were closed. There were no schools for the children. Free political parties, trade unions and Press had long been suppressed
Reviews DNL V 77, MFB XII 88, MFB XIII 40
MoI *pc* Army Film Unit & Seven League *d* Paul Fletcher *m* R Vaughan Williams *supervising ed* Hans Nieter
15 mins LC NFA

Target Germany
(The way in which RAF Bomber Command carried out its assigned task of smashing Germany's war industries)
MoI *pc* Seven League *p* Hans Nieter
22 mins IWM

Three cadets
Three boys, belonging respectively to the Army Cadet Force, Air Training Corps, and Sea Cadets, meet at a summer camp for combined operations practice and compare notes. The film illustrates each boy's description of his training
MoI & Service Depts *pc* Green Park *p* Ralph Keene *d* Kenneth Annakin
22 mins NFA

The true glory. *One soldier supports a wounded friend—Normandy.*

The true glory. *Montgomery, Eisenhower, and Bradly study a map—Normandy campaign.*

The true glory. *Allied DUKW's in flooded Holland.*

The true glory
A joint Anglo-American film which surveys the entire final campaign on the Western Front, from the period just before D-Day to the final victory . . . The film is based on material photographed by combat cameramen of the USA, Canada, France, Poland, Belgium, Netherlands, Czechoslovakia, Norway and Great Britain, and is introduced by General Eisenhower
Review MFB XII 94
Govts of GB & USA *pc* Army Film Unit & American Army Film Unit *d* Carol Reed, Garson Kanin *m* William Alwyn
87 mins CFL IWM MOMA NARS

DOMINIONS & COLONIES – Africa

The eighth plague
Fighting the locust plague in a desert part of East Africa, one of the locusts' breeding grounds. The struggle against this destructive insect, which ravages crops over half the globe, has now become international
Review MFB XIII 178
sp MoI & Colonial Office *pc* Crown *ph* R Kingston-Davies *m* Arnold van Wyk
11 mins MOMA NFA

The true glory. *Two British soldiers during fighting in a German town.*

The true glory. *Young German soldiers run forward to surrender during the Allied advance into Germany.*

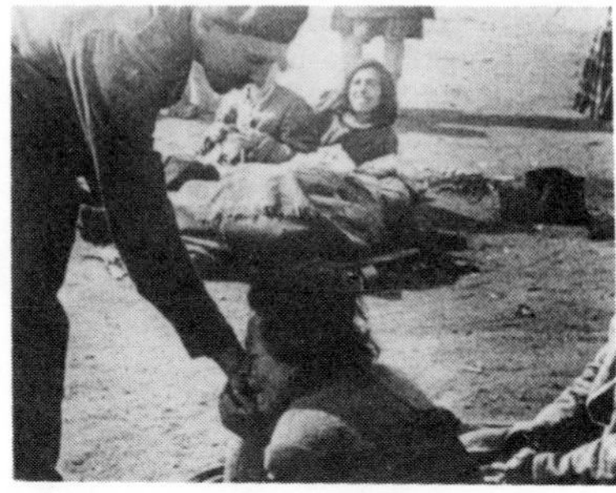

The true glory. *A woman survivor in Belsen kisses the hand of one of the British soldiers who liberated the camp.*

Prelude to war. *Montage photo identifying the three dictators who have destroyed world peace.*

A Mamprusi village
Life in the Northern Territories of the Gold Coast, with emphasis on the system of Indirect Rule, under which the native administration is responsible for taxation and for public expenditure on roads, police, courts of justice, etc
Reviews DNL V 92, MFB XIII 144
MoI & Colonial Office *pc* Exploitation *d* John Page
19 mins IWM NFA

Partners
The principle of partnership between the native and European peoples as the basis of Colonial administration in East Africa. White settlers have brought trade and commerce to this region, but they cannot ignore the human problems of the original inhabitants—problems of food, of health, of education, and of social values in general. Above all looms the problem of how to bring modern civilisation to tribal culture without destroying what was good in the old. (*Know the Commonwealth series* no 4)
Review MFB XIII 177
MoI & Colonial Office *pc* Crown *comm w & s* Dr Julian Huxley
16 mins

Sisal
Cultivation and treatment of sisal in Tanganyika, where this raw material for rope-making is one of the most important products
Review MFB XIII 144
MoI & Colonial Office *pc* Crown *d* Kingston Davies
10 mins NFA

Zanzibar
The native quarter, bazaars, transport. Palaces of the Sultan, etc. The clove and coconut industries; sport; scenery
20 mins

DOMINIONS & COLONIES – Canada

Birds and beasts of Canada
10 mins silent

Canada's north-west
The needs of the Japanese war, which brought about the creation of the Alaska Highway, gave a new impetus to the development of the North-Western region of Canada, which, though sub-Arctic, is rich in resources and calls for a national development plan
Reviews KYB 1946, MFB XII 88
pc National Film Board of Canada
10 mins

Quebec
10 mins

War pictorial news. *Scene after the liberation of the Channel Islands taken from a British government newsreel.*

DOMINIONS & COLONIES – Ceylon

Fortress Ceylon
Ceylon as a defensive fortress, a training ground for the jungle troops of the United Nations and a springboard for attack against Japan
sp Public Relations, India Command *pc* Army Film Centre
9 mins IWM

DOMINIONS & COLONIES – Fiji

Fiji return
Many native soldiers of the Fiji Islands were in the Pacific War. This film contains a record of their fighting on Bougainville. On their return home they were greeted by the British Governor and welcomed with native ceremonies and dancing
MoI *pc* New Realm *p* Sylvia Cummins
13 mins

DOMINIONS & COLONIES – India

Johnny Gurkha
A picture of the Gurkhas and Nepal, their native province, including farming, ceremonial dancing, and the life of the small town with its bazaars and tradesmen. The latter part of the film concentrates on the recruitment of Gurkha soldiers and their training under British and native officers
MoI *pc* Crown
10 mins IWM

DOMINIONS & COLONIES – New Zealand

Maximum effort
On operations with New Zealanders in a Lancaster aircrew. With Royal New Zealand Air Force
MoI *pc* Merlin *d* Michael Hankinson
20 mins IWM

New Zealand was there
(A record of the part played by the RNZAF within the RAF in the war over Europe)
MoI *pc* British Movietonews *ed* Raymond Perrin *comm s* Leslie Mitchell
11 mins IWM

ALLIES Czechoslovakia

Night and day
A Czecho-Slovak squadron on operations with RAF Coastal Command
pc Czecho-Slovak Film Unit & Gryphon
p Donald Taylor *d* Jiri Weiss
17 mins IWM NFA

ALLIES – France

French town
Life returns to a town in France while the German retreat is still only three miles away, and the urgent problems of reconstruction–transport, food and housing–are tackled at once
Review MFB XII 24
MoI & Office of War Information *pc* Realist *p* John Taylor *d* Alexander Shaw *ph* A E Jeakins *m* William Alwyn *comm s* Cedric Hardwicke
12 mins IWM NFA

ALLIES – Egypt

Today and tomorrow
The story of the organisation of food supplies, during the war, by the Middle East Supply Centre, set up by the British authorities in Cairo. Eighteen nations cooperated in the task, which was not only to supply the armies, but to prevent famine among the six million people of

the Middle East. The film points to the future problems of world food organisation
Reviews DNL VI 54, MFB XII 147
MoI *pc* World Wide *p* Ralph Bond *asst p* Arthur Elton *d* Robin Carruthers *comm w* Arthur Calder-Marshall *comm s* Valentine Dyall, Colin Wills *m* William Alwyn *m d* Muir Mathieson
42 mins BFI NFA

ALLIES – Poland

Z Ziemi Włoskiej do Polskiej
(The repatriation of Polish soldiers who had been serving in Italy at the end of the war. Distribution arrangements unclear)
14 mins IWM (in Polish)

ALLIES – USA

Some like it rough
Which is tougher–American football or British rugger? A light essay on national characteristics
Review MFB XIV 123
MoI *pc* Public Relationship *d* Richard Massingham *comm w* Nicholas Bentley *comm s* Jack Buchanan *cast* John Sweet
14 mins NFA

ALLIES – Yugoslavia

The nine hundred
A story of the National Liberation Army of Yugoslavia. In summer 1944, a Yugoslav Army Corps was cut off and surrounded, and aircraft from Balkan Air Force HQ went in, in daylight, to evacuate 900 persons. Photographed by Combat Camera Units of the Mediterranean Allied Air Forces, RAF and British Army Film Units
Reviews DNL V 83, MFB XII 64
MoI *pc* RAF & Army Film Units *ph* Francis Burgess *d* Capt Jerrold Krimsky
19 mins IWM NFA

The star and the sand
In January 1944, 30,000 Yugoslavs were evacuated to UNRRA camps in the Sinai desert in Egypt. The film follows the evolution of the camps into self-governing communities with their own industries, schools, medical services, Press and entertainments. Made in collaboration with UNRRA and the Yugoslav Camp Committee
Review DNL V 102
MoI *pc* Merlin *d* Gilbert Gunn *ph* Cyril Bristow *sc* Arthur Calder-Marshall *m* Ivor Walsworth
20 mins IWM

OVERSEAS DISTRIBUTION

African timber
pc Colonial Film Unit
20 mins

Africans study social work in Britain
pc Colonial Film Unit
11 mins

Bomb repair speed up
(Overseas distribution. Special effort to repair 750,000 homes damaged by the V1s between September 1944 and March 1945)
MoI *pc* British Paramount News *p* G T Cummins
15 mins IWM

Boy Scouts
pc Colonial Film Unit
33 mins

Boy Scouts in Uganda
pc Colonial Film Unit

British Empire at war, nos 1-39
MoI *pc* Colonial Film Unit

British family in peace and war
pc Colonial Film Unit
18 mins

Cambridge
(The University of Cambridge, including a lecture by Sir Lawrence Bragg)
Reviews DNL V 29, FoB 1944-5, MFB XII 23 104
sp British Council *pc* Everyman *p* Lewis Grant Wallace *d* Richard Massingham *ph* Alex Strasser
25 mins CFL NFA

Catholics in Britain
(Not shown in Britain)
MoI *pc* Verity *p* Sydney Box *d* Henry Cass
14 mins

District Officer
The career and duties of a native District Magistrate in Bengal. Starting as a Sub-Divisional Officer, he rises to Additional District Magistrate, and finally, as District Magistrate, has charge of a three-million population in an area the size of Switzerland
Review MFB XIV 134
pc Information Films of India *p* Ezra Mir *d* Kenneth Villiers *ph* Kustom Master *ed* S G Desai
12 mins NFA

English village

Far East war magaine no 1
(Overseas distribution. Logistical problems in Burma)
6 mins IWM

Girl Guides in Uganda
pc Colonial Film Unit

Home Guard stand down
pc Colonial Film Unit
10 mins NFA

Hospital school
The Lord Mayor Treloar Cripples' Hospital and College at Alton is now the biggest hospital-school of the kind in the country. The children are not only given the medical and surgical treatment which they require, but their educational training, secondary as well as primary, is continued throughout their stay, and much of it is given out of doors
Reviews FoB 1944-5, MFB XIII 178
sp British Council *pc* Spectator *d* A Barnes *ph* E N Edwell *sound* W S Bland *comm s* Frederick Allen *m* Jack Beaver
11 mins NFA

HRH Duke of Gloucester
(Overseas only)
MoI *pc* British Movietonews *p* Gerald Sanger

Jigsaw

Jonathan builds a dam
pc Colonial Film Unit

Julius Caesar
(An excerpt from the play by Shakespeare, with the speeches of Brutus and Mark Anthony after Caesar's murder)
Reviews FoB 1944-5, MFB XII 88
sp British Council *pc* Verity *p* Sydney Box *d* Henry Cass *cast* Felix Aylmer, Leo Genn
19 mins NFA

Kenya daisies
(Harvesting of pyrethrum flowers in Kenya and preparation of insecticide)
pc Colonial Film Unit
10 mins silent

Learie Constantine
(Learie Constantine at work looking after the interests of West Indians in London for the Ministry of Labour. He is also seen playing cricket)
pc Colonial Film Unit
9 mins NFA

London children celebrate victory
pc Colonial Film Unit
9 mins

Macbeth
An extract from the play by Shakespeare
Review FoB 1944-5
sp British Council *pc* Verity *p* Sydney Box *d* Henry Cass *cast* Wilfred Lawson, Cathleen Nesbitt
15 mins NFA

Maximum effort

Neuro-psychiatry

The new mine

Patients are in
(Intended for overseas use only)
MoI *pc* Crown *p* Basil Wright *d* Peter Bolton
10 mins

Portuguese ambassador's tour
MoI *pc* Film Traders *d* George Hollering
10 mins

Resident Minister in British West Africa
MoI *pc* Taurus *p & d* John Page
11 mins

Secondary modern school
pc Colonial Film Unit
40 mins

Slim Rhyder
pc Colonial Film Unit
4 mins

The unrelenting struggle
(The history of the war told through speeches of Winston Churchill. Overseas only)
pc Crown *p* Basil Wright
15 mins IWM LC

West African church parade
pc Colonial Film Unit
6 mins

NEWSREEL TRAILERS

Advice bureau

Books, books, books
MoI & Min of Labour *pc* Concanen *d* Derrick de Marney

Coughs and sneezes
MoI & Min of Health *pc* Public Relationship *d* Richard Massingham
3 mins NFA

Cycle tyres
MoI & Min of Supply *pc* Nettlefold *d* Bladon Peake

Dangerous trophies
pc Brunner Lloyd *sp* War Office

Diphtheria VI
MoI & Min of Health *pc* Concanen *d* Derrick de Marney

Don't touch
MoI & Air Min *pc* Crown *d* Michael Gordon

Fruit picking
MoI & Dept of Ag for Scotland *d* Alan Harper

Gas about fuel
MoI & Min of Fuel and Power *pc* Crown *d* Michael Gordon

Golden glory
MoI & Dept of Ag for Scotland *pc* Film Traders *d* George Hollering

Hands off
sp War Office *pc* Film Traders *d* George Hollering

Help wanted
MoI & Min of Ag *pc* Film Traders *d* George Hollering

Kerb drill
MoI & Min of War Transport *pc* Merlin *d* Michael Hankinson

Land girls for Scotland
MoI & Dept of Ag for Scotland *pc* Crown

Leather must last
(See *Make do and mend* no 1)

A light to remember
MoI & Min of Fuel and Power *pc* Crown *d* Michael Gordon

Make-do-and-mend
Three cartoons. (1) Leather must last (care of shoes). (2) Mrs Sew-and-Sew (conversion of old clothes). (3) War in the wardrobe (destruction of moths)
Review MFB XV 149
MoI & Board of Trade *pc* Films of GB
5 mins

Ministry of Fuel's appeal
MoI & Min of Fuel and Power *pc* Pathé

More hanky panky
MoI & Min of Health *pc* Dufay Chromex

Mrs Sew and Sew
(See *Make do and mend* no 2)

Nightingales
Min of Labour *pc* Concanen *d* Derrick de Marney

No smoke without fire
sp Fire Officers Ctte *pc* Nettlefold *d* Bladon Peake

The old old story
MoI & Min of Supply *pc* Merton Park

Pandora's boxes
MoI & Min of Supply *pc* Merton Park

Paper possibilities
MoI & Min of Supply *pc* Film Traders *d* George Hollering

Post haste
GPO *pc* Public Relationship *d* Richard Massingham
2 mins

Post-war road safety
Min of War Transport *pc* Verity *d* Maxwell Munden

Potato turn up
MoI & Dept of Ag for Scotland *pc* Green Park *d* P Scott
2 mins NFA

Resettlement advice service
MoI & Min of Labour *pc* Verity *d* Maxwell Munden

Road sense
MoI & Min of War Transport *pc* Merlin *d* Michael Hankinson

Summer travelling
MoI & Min of War Transport *pc* Larkins *d* W Larkins

Take a letter please
MoI & Min of Supply *pc* Concanen *d* Derrick de Marney

Thereby hangs a tail
MoI & Min of Supply *pc* Brunner Lloyd *d* P Brunner

To be a farmer's girl
MoI & Min of Ag *pc* Verity *d* Charles de Lautour

Tombstone Canyon
MoI & Min of War Transport *pc* Dufay Chromex

War in the wardrobe
(See *Make do and mend* no 3)

1945
NEWSREEL TRAILERS

When winter comes
MoI & Min of Fuel and Power *pc* Crown

A woman's job
MoI & Min of Labour *pc* Concanen *d* Derrick de Marney

Writings worth while
War Office *pc* Dufay Chromex

1946

HOMEFRONT – General

And then Japan
The war in the Pacific and the social and industrial organisation that gave Japan its military strength
pc March of Time
18 mins

Children's charter
The Education Act, 1944, among other provisions, aims at giving every child a free secondary education from the age of 11 to 15 (and later 16) at the kind of secondary school suited to his or her abilities. Three kinds of schools, of which examples are shown, are to be established everywhere: Technical Schools (and in rural areas Agricultural Schools), Grammar Schools, and Modern Schools. The Act also lays down that all boys and girls not otherwise provided for will continue their general education from 16 to 18 on one day a week at Young People's Colleges
Reviews DNL V 83, MFB XIII 55
MoI & Min of Educ *pc* Crown *d* Gerald Bryant *ph* Jonah Jones, H E Fowle
18 mins

Coal mining today
Post-war jobs series *What's the next job?*
The film shows in considerable detail the course for mineworkers at the Mines Mechanisation Training Centre, Sheffield. This includes training in galleries constructed so as to reproduce underground conditions, as well as theoretical instruction. The key position of coal in our industry, and the importance of the miner's job to the country, are stressed
MoI & Mins of Fuel and Power, Labour
pc New Realm *p* Sylvia Cummins
18 mins NFA

A defeated people
(The government of the British-occupied zone of Germany and the problems of physical and moral rehabilitation)
pc Crown *sp* Allied Control Commission
p Basil Wright *d* Humphrey Jennings
22 mins IWM NFA

Diary for Timothy
An imaginative diary of the last phase of the war, set out for the later use of a child born during the period. Battles, working conditions of miners, bombs, plays, music and the sights and sounds of Nature are all seen as part of the child's inheritance
Reviews DNL VI 9, MFB XIII 13
MoI *pc* Crown *p* Basil Wright *d* Humphrey Jennings *comm w* E M Forster *comm s* Michael Redgrave
40 mins BFI IWM NFA (2 versions)

Farm work
Post-war jobs series. A discussion of the prospects of a man who goes to work on the land. A farming expert explains what risks must be faced if you take on a small holding, and how arduous is the life of a farm worker and his wife, but comes to the conclusion that if you are cut out for work on the land there is no life like it
Reviews DNL V 77, MFB XII 42, MFB XIII 178
MoI & Min of Ag & Min of Labour *pc* Crown *p* Basil Wright *d* Michael Gordon
21 mins IWM NFA

Food flashes
(Series of short message films with themes such as 'Eat potatoes not bread', etc)
MoI & Min of Food
2-5 mins each B&W and colour NFA

Heir to the throne
Princess Elizabeth at the age of 18. Both the public and the private aspects of her life are represented
Reviews MFB XIV 148, MFB XII 54
MoI *pc* British Movietonews *p* Gerald Sanger
11 mins NFA

Man – one family
An exposure by straight photography, diagrams, and cartoons, of the fallacy of race myths. Nazi and Japanese theories about 'pure blood' and 'master races' are contrasted with the scientific facts of the mixed origin of modern nations; the term 'Aryan' is shown to be applicable only to languages, not to race, and arguments are brought to prove that no nation or race can be considered 'inferior' or 'superior'
Reviews DNL VI 24, MFB XIII 119
MoI *pc* Ealing Studios *d & sc* Ivor Montagu *scientific advisers* Professor J B S Haldane & Dr Julian Huxley *p* Sidney Cole *comm s* Dr Julian Huxley
17 mins CFL IWM NFA

Mosquitoes in the making
Detailed record of the construction of a Mosquito aeroplane, the wings and fuselage of which consist almost entirely of wood
MoI & Min of Aircraft Production *pc* GB Screen Services
16 mins NFA

One man, two jobs
New jobs for the Home Guard which released men for the invasion of Europe
MoI & War Office *pc* British Movietonews *p* Gerald Sanger
11 mins IWM

Outworking
Organised part-time work outside factories
MoI & Min of Production *pc* Strand *p* Michael Hankinson *d* Gilbert Gunn
13 mins IWM LC

People to people
A record of the visit of four British war workers to American war factories, in which they discuss with American workers wartime achievements and post-war problems
US Office of War Information *pc* United Films
29 mins IWM

Seed of prosperity
Half of Scotland's crop of potatoes is

grown for seed, which is exported to the rest of Britain and overseas. The film surveys the history of the industry and its present condition under the close supervision of the Scottish Department of Agriculture, which awards certificates according to the disease-resisting qualities of the seed
Review MFB XIV 121
MoI & Dept of Ag for Scotland *pc* Campbell Harper *p* Edgar Anstey *d* Alan Harper *sc* Norman Wilson *ph* Henry Cooper, Ian Barrowman
19 mins NFA

Shaping the future
Post-war jobs series *What's the next job?* Commented by the Chief Industrial Officer, National Federation of Building Trade Employers, and the Secretary of the Amalgamated Union of Building Trade Workers, the film outlines the present position in the building trade. There is no unemployment. There is a wide variety of jobs, many of them highly skilled. New methods, including some mechanisation, have considerably changed the nature of the work. Government training centres have been set up in many large towns
Review MFB XIII 69
MoI & Mins of Works, Labour *pc* Gryphon *p & d* Donald Taylor
15 mins IWM

They live again
Principles of surgical treatment and rehabilitation methods as practised at a miners' hospital in the Midlands. (Shortened version of *Accident service*)
Reviews FoB 1944-5, MFB XII 125
British Council *pc* GB Instructional *d* A Dobson *ph* Frank North *sc* Mary Cathcart Borer *m* William Alwyn
18 mins NFA

Turn it out
Problems of the post-war production-drive; and the need for active cooperation by workers in industry. There are two big production-targets (i) for exports, so that we may pay our way, (ii) for the home market. Full production and full employment are complementary national aims
Review DNL VI 75
COI & Min of Labour *pc* Green Park *p & d* Kenneth Annakin *ph* Charles Marlborough *ed* Carmen Balaieff
11 mins

Women after the war
War Office *pc* Public Relationship *d* Richard Massingham *ph* Shaw Wildman

HOMEFRONT – Scotland

Birthday
Infant mortality in Scotland (as elsewhere) is still much too high. To ensure good health to all mothers during pregnancy is the first job. The film aims at convincing women of the importance of seeking medical advice during the very earliest stages, and taking full advantage of the existing maternity services. Diagrams showing the growth of the child in the womb, and the process of birth, are included
Review DNL VI 8
MoI for Dept of Health for Scotland *pc* Data *p* Donald Alexander *d* Budge Cooper *ph* Wolfgang Suschitzky
22 mins NFA

Good neighbours
How the inhabitants of a small town with few recreational facilities got together and, with the aid of a local clergyman, a local schoolmaster, a local Education Officer, and a little enterprise, established a community centre for all sorts of recreational and after-work activities. (Shortened version entitled *After six o'clock*)
Reviews DNL VI 74, MFB XV 148
COI & Scottish Office *pc* Green Park *p* Ralph Keene *d* Humphrey Swingler *ph* Raymond Elton *sc* Jack Common
20 mins

HOMEFRONT – Instructional

The big four
The four main elements of diet—calcium, protein, iron, vitamins—and the foods which contain them. Humorous cartoon treatment
Review MFB XIV 56
MoI & Min of Food *pc* Larkins *p* W Larkins
10 mins NFA

Frame concrete housing
Record of an experiment in quick construction
MoI & Min of Works *pc* Verity
22 mins

How to cook fish
MoI & Min of Food *pc* Films of GB *p* Andrew Buchanan *d* Henry Cooper *ph* Charles Francis
11 mins NFA

How to make cakes
MoI & Min of Food *pc* Films of GB *p* Andrew Buchanan *d* Henry Cooper *ph* Charles Francis
11 mins

How to make jam
MoI & Min of Food *pc* Films of GB *p* Andrew Buchanan *d* Henry Cooper *ph* Charles Francis
11 mins NFA

How to make salads
MoI & Min of Food *pc* Films of GB *p* Andrew Buchanan *d* Henry Cooper *ph* Charles Francis
11 mins

It might be you
Most road accidents are due to carelessness. Accident figures are excessively high. This film points the general moral, and illustrates the case by showing the circumstances of a typical accident between a private car, a cyclist, and a pedestrian
Reviews DNL VI 24, MFB XIII 11
MoI *pc* Crown *p* Basil Wright *d* Michael Gordon *ph* Fred Gamage *recording* Charles Poulton
14 mins NFA

Old wives' tales
Cartoon film on health, exploding three popular fallacies: (1) 'Ne'er cast a clout'; (2) 'A little dirt won't hurt you'; (3) 'Night air is dangerous'
Reviews DNL VI 59, MFB XIII 161
MoI & Min of Health & Central Council for Health Educ *pc* Halas & Batchelor *p* John Halas, Joy Batchelor *d* John Halas *m* Matyas Seiber
8 mins NFA

Outdoor tomato growing
How to select a site, prepare the ground, sow, transplant, acclimatise the plants, prune, water and 'stop' them, and protect them against disease
Review MFB XV 84
MoI & Min of Ag *pc* Films of GB *p* Andrew Buchanan *d* Henry Cooper *ph* Charles Francis
14 mins NFA

War on wheels
Care and conservation of tyres as a means to economy in rubber
MoI & Min of Supply *pc* World Wide *p* Ralph Bond *d* Ken Hughes
16 mins IWM

Your children and you
Practical suggestions to parents on care of young children from the first months to the age of four or five. The main stages of development are dealt with, from weaning, at about five months, onward. On the physical side, hints on training in sound and regular habits are included; on the psychological, hints on prevention of unnecessary fears, of boredom, of bad temper or maladjustment. Patience, firmness, and understanding are essential qualities in the parent

Review DNL VI 59
MoI & Min of Health & Central Council for Health Educ *pc* Crown *p* John Taylor, Alexander Shaw *d* Brian Smith *ph* A E Jeakins *m* William Alwyn
28 mins CFL MOMA NFA

Your children's ears
This film explains the structure of the ear by means of diagrams and shows the damage to hearing that may be caused by abscesses, insertion of small objects such as peas, internal inflammation due to colds, discharge from the ear, and adenoids. Methods of treatment by parents and doctors are shown
Reviews DNL V 102, MFB XIII 57
MoI & Depts of Health & Council for Health Educ *pc* Realist Film Unit *p* Margaret Thomson *d* Albert Pearl *ph* Alex Strasser *m* William Alwyn *comm s* Carlton Hobbs
17 mins CFL NFA PAC

Your children's teeth
This film shows the importance of antenatal care of mothers and of proper food in helping children to grow good teeth. Decay, which leads to loss of teeth and bad health, can be prevented or checked by proper diet, cleaning habits and regular inspection and treatment. The structure of teeth, the progress of tooth formation, and the process of decay are explained by means of diagrams
Reviews DNL V 102, MFB XIII 57
MoI & Depts of Health & Council for Health Educ *pc* Realist *p* Margaret Thomson *d* Jane Massy *ph* A E Jeakins *m* William Alwyn *comm s* Carlton Hobbs
15 mins NFA

HOMEFRONT – Specialised instructional

Accident service
An examination in detail of the service provided for injured miners at a combined Hospital and Rehabilitation Centre in the Midlands. (For medical and nursing audiences only. Short version for general use entitled *They live again*)
Review DNL V 30
British Council *pc* GB Instructional *d* A R Dobson *ph* Frank North
42 mins NFA

As others see us
Hints to Civil Servants on dealing with casual callers. For Government departments
MoI & HM Treasury
12 mins

Furnace practice
A fuel economy film, for furnacemen and plant managers, dealing with furnaces of all kinds–whether using coal, pitch, gas, oil or electricity. The aim is to get the maximum heat and transmit it with the minimum loss. The chief subjects touched are: firing methods; use of mechanical stokers; proper control of air supply; importance of cleanliness; repairs, maintenance and improvements; recovery of heat from chimneys; need for careful records as a check on running economy
MoI & Min of Fuel and Power *pc* CWS Film Unit *d & p* George Wynn
30 mins

How to erect the American prefabricated house
Demonstration, for building contractors, of how to erect the prefabricated house of which 30,000 have been sent from America
MoI & Min of Works
16 mins IWM

Killing farm rats
Ferrets and traps are not enough. Scientific study of the habits of rats has led to the pre-baiting poison and gassing methods in which Pest Officers have been trained to assist farmers. Farms cleared by these methods must be protected by denying all chances of food, water and shelter to rats coming in search of these
Reviews DNL V 64, MFB XIII 176

MoI & Dept of Ag *pc* Crown
16 mins NFA

Life saving at sea
Instructional film for seamen on use of life-saving appliances with which merchant-ship lifeboats and rafts are equipped. Equipment shown and demonstrated includes life-jackets and protective suits, the lifeboat motor, special food, Minimax KM Producer for distilling drinking water from sea-water, first-aid kit, flares, signalling mirror, radio receiver and transmitter, compass and charts
MoI & Min of War Transport *pc* Films of GB *p* Andrew Buchanan *d* Henry Cooper *ph* Charles Francis
38 mins IWM

Potato cultivation
(Correct way to plough potato fields)
Min of Ag *pc* Films of GB *p & d* Andrew Buchanan *assoc p* Edgar Anstey *ph* Charles Francis
18½ mins NFA

Put yourself in his shoes
For Ministry of Labour interviewers. How to plan and conduct an interview so as to give the maximum help to the man seeking a new job
MoI & Min of Labour *pc* Data *p* Arthur Elton *d* Jack Chambers
16 mins NFA

Stomach worms in sheep (parasitic gastritis)
Almost every sheep in the world at some time picks up from the pasturage stomach worms, which cause parasitic gastritis and may amount to 100,000 in a badly infected case. The film records, by means of photo-micrography, the life cycle of the parasite, and shows precautions which can be taken to reduce the danger of infection, and the methods of treatment of the disease
Review MFB XIV 70
MoI & Min of Ag *pc* Films of GB *assoc p* Edgar Anstey *p & d* Andrew Buchanan
19 mins NFA

Sugar beet. Part I: cultivation
Choice and preparation of soil, cleaning the soil, liming, dunging, ploughing, harrowing, dressing with artificials, scrubbing, rolling, drilling and sowing, hoeing, gapping, singling and hoeing the growing rows
Reviews DNL VI 25, MFB XIII 38
MoI for Dept of Ag *pc* Blackheath Film Unit *d* Ralph Cathles
24 mins NFA

Sugar beet. Part II: harvesting
Lifting by means of a beet-plough (side-lifter) or a two-pronged lifter, wilting, knocking, topping and piling. Use of mechanical harvesters. Carting and clamping. Methods of handling and treatment at the factory. By-product values of beet to the farmer
Reviews DNL VI 25, MFB XIII 38
MoI for Dept of Ag *pc* Blackheath Film Unit *d* Ralph Cathles
12 mins NFA

Tractor engine overhaul
Faulty running in a tractor may mean the engine needs an overhaul. The film shows in detail how to dismantle the engine completely, decarbonise, clean, oil and reassemble it; also how to check the steering
Review MFB XV 162
MoI for Dept of Ag *pc* Films of GB *p & d* Andrew Buchanan *ph* Charles Francis
25 mins NFA

Typing technique
Common typists' errors
MoI & HM Treasury *pc* Public Relationship *p* Richard Massingham *d* Michael Law *ph* Gerald Gibbs
23 mins

HOMEFRONT – Wartime social services

It began on the Clyde
On Clydeside in 1941 there began an experiment in medical treatment of war workers which has important possibilities for our peace-time system. Persons not ill enough to go to their own specialists, were taken into Emergency Medical Services hospitals to be thoroughly examined and treated before their condition should become serious. In four years over 10,000 workers of all ages were dealt with in this way
Reviews DNL VI 24, MFB XIV 30
MoI & Dept of Health for Scotland *pc* Green Park *p* Ralph Keene *d* Kenneth Annakin *ph* Charles Marlborough *sc* Brian Smith
15 mins NFA

Kitchen unit
MoI *pc* Basic *p* R K Neilson Baxter *d* Kay Mander

A start in life
A picture of the health services for children in Britain; pre-natal advice, maternity and children's clinics, day nurseries, and medical services and meals at junior and senior schools
MoI & Min & Board of Health *pc* Realist *p* John Taylor *d* Brian Smith *ph* Gerald Gibbs *sc* Albert Pearl *m* William Alwyn *comm s* Albert Pearl, Ophelia Segreda
22 mins NFA

FIGHTING SERVICES & CAMPAIGNS

Allied strategy in the southwest Pacific
(A history of the battles–fought predominantly by Australian troops–to stop and then reverse the Japanese advance in New Guinea)
MoI *pc* Merlin
30 mins IWM

Armament in action
sp Admiralty *pc* GB Instructional *p* Frank Cadman *d* Gaston Charpentier
33 mins

Attack! The battle for New Britain
A record, made from material shot on the spot, of the American attack on the Japanese at Arawe and Cape Gloucester in New Britain. The scenes are chiefly of attack from the sea, with the aid of landing-craft, and jungle warfare. Produced under the auspices of the Commanding General, South-West Pacific Area
Review MFB IX 142
sp US War Dept *pc* US Army Signal Corps & United Films
52 mins IWM NFA (German version entitled *Angriff!*)

From the Rhine to victory
(The war in Western Europe in 1945. Compilation film for release in liberated Europe)
MoI *pc* British Paramount News *compilation* A S Graham
50 mins IWM NFA

Journey together
(Documentary feature about a navigator in the RAF who wants to be a pilot)
MoI *pc* RAF Film Unit *p & d* John Boulting *cast* Richard Attenborough, Edward G Robinson, Jack Watling, John Justin, Sebastian Shaw, Rex Harrison, Bessie Love, Sheila Sim, David Tomlinson
80 mins IWM

Jungle mariners
Jungle warfare, as experienced by a small patrol of Marines in the SEAC area
Review MFB XIII 38
MoI & Royal Marines *pc* Crown *p* Basil Wright *d* Ralph Elton
16 mins IWM NFA

Naval technical training film
sp Admiralty *pc* Basic *p* R K Neilson Baxter *d* J B Napier-Bell

Personnel selection in the British Army – officers
The test course through which officer candidates pass and the selection board at work on the assessment of abilities
Reviews DNL VI 41, MFB XIII 30
MoI & War Office *pc* Shell *d* Geoffrey Bell *ph* Sidney Beadle *anim* Francis Rodker
40 mins CFL

Personnel selection in the British Army, 1944 – recruits
Two weeks at a Primary Training Centre are largely devoted to work of the Selection Department. A Matrix Test divides men into five classes called Selection Groups, and Army jobs are classified under seven headings called Training Recommendations. In addition to the Matrix Test for general intellectual ability, there are tests for concentration and coordination, two educational tests, Arithmetic and Message tests. Each man fills up a form giving details of his education, employment, experience, activities, and hobbies, and, after an interview, the Training Recommendation is made by the Personnel Selection Officer, who may ask for confirmation by a psychotherapist. The information now available is codified, the needs of each branch of the Army are considered, and the TR most likely to be of use is selected. Posting follows. (Short version entitled *Round pegs*)
Review DNL VI 9
MoI & War Office *pc* Shell *d* Geoffrey Bell
58 mins CFL IWM

The way from Germany
The Allies' problem of how to deal with 18 million prisoners of all nations, liberated on the fall of Germany, and mostly anxious to trek home at once
Reviews MFB XIV 171, MFB XIII 88
COI & Allied Control Commission & Army Film Unit *pc* Crown *p* Basil Wright *d* Terry Trench
11 mins IWM NFA

DOMINIONS & COLONIES – General

Dominion status
Using a meeting of the Dominion Prime Ministers as its starting-point, the film records the achievements of Canada, Australia, South Africa and New Zealand, both in peace and during the war. These achievements emphasise the autonomy of the free and equal nations making up the Commonwealth. Even the war-time neutrality of Eire underlines it
MoI *pc* British Paramount News *p* G T Cummins
19 mins LC

DOMINIONS & COLONIES – Africa

Achimota
Education and daily life at Achimota College, Gold Coast, a residential centre of higher education (secondary, teacher-training, and University up to intermediate standard) for Africans of both sexes from Nigeria and British West Africa. The teaching staff is European, Indian, and African, and the language of instruction is English
Reviews DNL VI 24, MFB XIII 159
MoI & Colonial Office *pc* Taurus *p & d* John Page *comm w & s* Dr Julian Huxley
19 mins NFA

Father and son
A simple parable contrasts the old and the new generations in East Africa, and indicates the gradualness of the processes of education
Reviews DNL VI 9, MFB XIII 143
MoI & Colonial Office *pc* Crown *d & ph* Leon Schauder
14 mins NFA

Southern Rhodesia
Using the point of view of an airman in training in Southern Rhodesia, the film reviews the means by which modern

ways of life are developed among the African population. The subjects touched are: technical training courses, physical training, and clinics; the use of modern methods in farming and industry; the production of asbestos, chromium, copper and tobacco; modern military training of Africans. (*Know the Commonwealth series* no 5)
Review MFB XIII 172
MoI & Govt of Southern Rhodesia *pc* Crown
9 mins

The story of Omolo
Omolo, a Kenya villager, goes to Bukura College and there learns scientific principles of agriculture which he takes back and applies in his native village
Review MFB XVI 149
MoI & Colonial Office *pc* Crown *p & d* Basil Wright
9 mins NFA

DOMINIONS & COLONIES – New Zealand

War and New Zealand
pc New Realm *p* Sylvia Cummins
18 mins

ALLIES – General

Town meeting of the world
A film based on a recording of parts of Mr Attlee's speech at the first session of the General Assembly of the United Nations in London (Jan 10, 1946); illustrated by shots of the session itself and of phases of the late war
Reviews DNL VI 30, MFB XIII 40, MFB XIV 18
MoI *pc* Crown *p* Basil Wright *d* Graham Wallace
12 mins IWM

ALLIES – China

This is China
An account of the rise of China to take her place among modern nations in recent years: showing the social and industrial advances brought about by Sun Yat-Sen after 1911; the impact of the Japanese war of aggression; and the outstanding problem of reconstruction for the future now that the war is over
Reviews MFB XIII 116, MFB XIV 43
MoI *pc* Verity *p* Julian Wintle
9 mins

ALLIES – Netherlands

The last shot
The immediate aftermath of war in Holland. Liberation brought not only peace but also enormous problems of reconstruction. Acres lay devastated, food and fuel were lacking, and starvation was widespread. These terrible problems, together with such others as those of displaced persons, returning prisoners of war, and anonymous war orphans, called not only for national but for international solution
Reviews DNL VI 24, MFB XII 158
MoI & Netherlands Govt *pc* Exploitation *d & p* John Ferno *comm w* Arthur Calder-Marshall *md* Muir Mathieson
16 mins NFA

ALLIES – Norway

All for Norway
Organising Norwegian resources outside Norway for the liberation of Norway
Review MFB IX 136
sp Norwegian Govt *pc* Strand *p* Donald Taylor
11 mins IWM

ALLIES – USA

People to people
A record of the visit of four British war workers to American war factories, in which they discuss with American workers wartime achievements and post-war problems
MoI & US Office of War Information *pc* United Films
29 mins IWM

Pipeline
This film replaces the film of the same title listed in the [CFL] 1944 Catalogue. It deals with the laying of an oil pipeline, 1,388 miles long, from Texas to New Jersey
Review MFB IX 139
US Office of War Information
10 mins

USA – The land and its people
This film aims at giving an overall impression of the country, which is sixty times as big as England and has almost as many varieties of climate as all Europe, of its people, deriving from almost every stock in the world, and their modes of life and work
MoI *pc* Rotha Productions
20 mins IWM

ALLIES – USSR

Supplies to the Soviets
An immense variety of supplies, both military and civil, went to Russia during the war from Britain and the Empire, via Murmansk and across Persia. The roots of future trade lie in these war arrangements
MoI *pc* Merlin *p & d* Michael Hankinson
9 mins IWM NFA

OVERSEAS DISTRIBUTION

Australians in London
Intended for overseas distribution only. (Special record of the Australian contingent's part in the Victory Parade)
pc Crown *p* Alexander Shaw *d* Colin Dean
9 mins IWM

Double thread
Good nursery schools and teachers are as important as good homes and parents to young children if they are to learn for themselves how to live and not be forced to live at adult pace
Reviews FoB 1946, MFB XI 35
sp Nursery School Assoc *pc* GB Instructional *d* Mary Field
33 mins NFA

From Italy to D-Day
(The war in Southern Europe from July 1943 to June 1944. Compilation film for release in liberated Europe)
MoI *pc* British Movietonews *compilation* Raymond Perrin
32 mins IWM NFA

From the Rhine to victory

General election
(Account of the 1945 general election in the Kettering constituency where John Profumo was a candidate)
Reviews FoB 1946, MFB XVI 33
sp British Council *pc* Technique *p & d* Ronald Riley *ph* Raymond Elton, Henry Hall *sc* Mary Benedetta
19 mins NFA

Heir to the throne

Land and water
MoI *pc* Colonial Film Unit
4 mins

Latin American raw materials
(Not shown in Britain. Spanish and

Brazilian versions)
MoI *pc* Merlin *p & d* Michael Hankinson
9 mins

Let's see
(The manufacture of optical glass and lenses)
Reviews DNL VI 8, FoB 1946, MFB XII 158
sp British Council *pc* Merton Park
17 mins colour NFA

The liberation of Rome
A conspectus of the Allied Italian campaign from the first landing on September 3rd, 1943, to the liberation of Rome on June 4th, 1944. (Compilation film for release in liberated Europe)
MoI *pc* US Army with British Service Film Units
21 mins CFL IWM MOMA NARS

Man – one family

Personnel selection in the British Army – officers

Personnel selection in the British Army – recruits

Victory march – East Africa
pc Colonial Film Unit

Victory march – Far East
pc Colonial Film Unit

Victory march – Middle East
pc Colonial Film Unit

Victory march – West Africa
pc Colonial Film Unit

Victory parade
(London's Victory Parade)
Review MFB XIII 145
pc Colonial Film Unit
19 mins colour NFA

Weaving in Togoland
Villagers in Togoland learn more modern methods of weaving and spinning from students trained at Achimota College, Ghana
pc Colonial Film Unit
22 mins NFA

West Africa was there
(Part played by West African troops in the war. Overseas only)
pc British Movietonews *p* Gerald Sanger
11 mins IWM

NEWSREEL TRAILERS

Agricultural holiday

Blood transfusions

Bricklayers

Bring 'em back alive

Briquette making

Deborah Kerr on behalf of the CTBF [Cinematograph Trades Benevolent Fund]

Diphtheria

Diphtheria VIII

Domestic workers

Employment of dis-abled persons

Export or die

Family allowances

Hospital car service

1946
NEWSREEL TRAILERS

Hot water

Increase the harvest
NFA

Influenza

Join the army

Join the navy

Land Army trailer

Olivier/Leigh on behalf of the CTBF [Cinematograph Trades Benevolent Fund]

Only good news

Paper publicity

Post haste

RAF trailer

Rags and bones

Safety first

Spare the hot water

Staggered holidays

Up the potato

Watch the fuel watcher

Who'll help the hospitals

Appendix 1

Films produced before 1939 and distributed by the Central Film Library during the period 1939-1945

Accra
12 mins silent

Across Canada in fifteen minutes
By rail and steamer up the St Lawrence to Quebec, Ottawa, Toronto, Hamilton, Lake Superior, Ontario, Winnipeg, Vancouver
15 mins silent

African explosives
Manufacture of dynamite
10 mins

African skyway
Depicting the British Overseas Airways Empire route through Africa from Cairo to Durban
Review DNL I Feb 12
pc Strand
30 mins NFA

After fifty years – Vancouver
In the short space of fifty years a small trading post has grown into the metropolis of Canada's far west
9 mins

Agriculture in Cyprus
10 mins silent

Air background
A description of the organisation behind the air-mail scheme. (Film made in 1937)
pc Strand
17 mins silent MOMA

Air enterprise
The fleets of flying boats used by Imperial Airways on their Empire routes
20 mins silent

Air road to gold
Air transport of stores and gold-dredging materials over the dense jungles of New Guinea. (Film made 1934)
Review MFB V 54
10 mins

Algonquin waters
Trout fishing in Algonquin Park
Review MFB I 98
10 mins

All aboard
A day in the life of a Canadian Pacific transcontinental train. (Film made in 1936)
Review MFB II 9
20 mins silent

All that is England
The relative merits of different parts of the English countryside
Review MFB IX 138
17 mins

Almost Arcady
The island and the life of the people of Cyprus. Farming is the chief industry, but women spin silk and make lace. (Film made in 1932)
Review MFB IX 9
10 mins NFA

Among the hardwoods
Lumbering in a forest of jarrah and karri, in Australia. (Film made in 1936)
Review MFB IV 21
pc Melbourne Dept of Commerce
10 mins NFA

Angling in the infinite
Scenery in Banff National Park, Rock Isle Lake, Mount Assiniboine and Marvel Park
10 mins silent

Animal life
(South Africa)
12 mins silent

Around the village green
Life in a typical English village. (Film made 1937)
Review S&S VI 203
sp Travel Association *d* Marion Grierson, Evelyn Spice
12 mins NFA

Ashanti
(Record of the visit of the crew of the destroyer *Ashanti* to the Ashanti tribe. Film made in 1939)
pc Tida
9 mins silent NFA

Atlantic
A diagrammatic film showing 500 years of Atlantic trade development
Review MFB VIII 21
pc GB Instructional *d* Mary Field
21 mins LC NFA

Australia calling
A 5,000-mile tour of the Commonwealth in fifteen minutes. From Perth to the great wheat belt and the famous West Australian gold mines; thence to Adelaide, Hobart, Melbourne and Brisbane
15 mins

Axes and elephants
Lumbering in New Zealand and Burma. Contrasts in methods of transport
6 mins silent

Bag net fishing
Catching salmon off the east coast of Scotland. (Film made 1932)
4 mins silent NFA

Banff
A tour of outstanding points of interest in and around Canada's great mountain playground, Banff, Alberta
10 mins silent

Barbados
15 mins silent

Battling the tuna
Sport with rod and line on the Atlantic seaboard
9 mins silent

Beef and cattle farming
(South Africa)
16 mins silent

Behind the headlines
A description of the production of a Canadian newspaper
10 mins

Big money
The machinery of Post Office finance and its relationship to that of the nation. (Film made in 1938. Silent version entitled *The budget*)
pc GPO *d* Harry Watt *p* Cavalcanti
15 mins NFA (sound version)

Big timber
Timber operations–from tree-felling to planks for export. (Film made in 1934)
10 mins

Bikaner – a Thar desert town
Daily life in Bikaner. Maps show how a town has grown up at a spot where there are many wells and therefore desert routes intersect. (Film made in 1934)
Review MFB I 35
pc GB Instructional
10 mins NFA

Birds and beasts of Canada
A comprehensive survey of wild life in Canada
12 mins silent

A bit of high life
Climbing near Lake Louise, depicting Bow Lake, and many adventurous climbs to the Columbia ice area and back to Laggan
6 mins silent

Blazing the trail – road-making and bridge-building
(British West Africa)
10 mins silent

The blue and silvery way
An aerial trip over the Union [of South Africa]. (Film made 1938)
pc African Film Productions
40 mins NFA

Book bargain
The printing and assembling by modern machinery of the London Telephone Directory. (Film made in 1937)
pc GPO *p* Cavalcanti
10 mins NFA

Border trails
A saddle-pony trip along the scenic trails of Waterton Lake National Park, Alberta
10 mins silent

Bournemouth
Night and day attractions at the beautiful south-coast tourist resort
6 mins silent

British Guiana
Demerara, depicting the sugar, rice and coconut industries. (Film made in 1933)
pc Empire Marketing Board
20 mins silent NFA

British made
How, as a result of technical developments in the last century, the old apprenticeship system, foundation of British craftsmanship, merged into an even closer application of skill to material
Reviews FoB 1940, MFB XV 148
sp British Council *pc* Tida *d* George Pearson *ph* Jonah Jones *ed* R Q McNaughton *sound* Ken Cameron *m* Ernst Meyer
9 mins NFA

British New Guinea
Life in Papua, showing houses on stilts, travel by water, coconuts, scenes of native life and costumes, and ending with a ritual dance
7 mins silent

The budget
The relation of the weekly account of the average housewife to the National Budget. The annual preparation and submission to the Treasury of Post Office estimates. The composition of the Budget. (This film is a silent version of much of the material in *Big money*)
15 mins silent

Burma
Life of the people. The Palace of Mandalay; the Shan Hills. (Film made 1936)
Review MFB IV 49
15 mins

Burma paddy cultivation
30 mins silent

Burning cheroots
The production of cheroots in Burma in contrast with English cigarette making
4 mins silent

By-ways of Jaspar
Views of Jaspar National Park
12 mins silent

Cable ship
A demonstration of the complex service attending the submarine telephone cables between England and overseas countries. (Film made 1933)
pc GPO *p* John Grierson *d* Stuart Legg
10 mins NFA

Cacao industry
(West Indies)
15 mins silent

Calendar of the year
Outline of a year's principal seasonal activities from January gales to Christmas sales, showing how the communication service is adapted to deal with them. Winter storms, Spring flowers, the ballet, the Derby, summer by the sea, Autumn lamb sales, Christmas toys, New Year's Eve. (Film made 1936)
Review MFB IV 46
pc GPO
16 mins MOMA NFA

Canada's cosy corner
A travelogue of Canada's smallest province, Prince Edward Island
10 mins

Canada's maple industry
(Film made 1936)
16 mins NFA

Canada's Pacific gateway
Vancouver and its waterside. Vancouver as a grain centre
8 mins silent

Canadian apples
An interesting record of the production and marketing of Canadian apples
15 mins silent

Canadian apples
Part I—Production: pollenisation, care of the young seedlings, pruning and grafting. The codling moth at work; spraying the trees. Irrigating the orchards, blossom time. Part II—Marketing: different methods of packing in Ontario and Eastern Canada. Grading and transport for overseas
23 mins each part, silent

Canadian mountain scenery
A journey by CPR from Calgary to Vancouver
13 mins silent

Canadian salmon
A full account of the Canadian salmon industry
13 mins

Canals
Why canals are necessary. How gradients are overcome by locks. The main canals of the British Isles shown diagrammatically. (Film made in 1932)
6 mins silent NFA

Candy from trees
Tapping maple syrup. Syrup dripping from trees into containers. Purification and bottling
4 mins silent

Canoe trails through mooseland
A scenic and nature film of a canoe trip through the wilds of north-eastern Canada, with glimpses of woodland and waterways, as well as many exceptional close-up 'action' views of moose, deer, bear, beaver and other wild life on land and water
12 mins silent

Captured sunshine
Study of the fruit industry of New Zea land
10 mins

Cargo from Jamaica
Large-scale banana operations in Jamaica. (Film made 1935)
Review MFB I 64
pc Empire Marketing Board *p* John Grierson *d* Basil Wright
7 mins silent NFA

Cathedrals of England
An instructional film showing some of the English cathedrals and explaining the basic principles of cathedral architecture. (Film made 1937)
pc Tida *d* Marion Grierson
10 mins NFA

Cementing the Union
Manufacturing of Portland cement. (Film made in 1936)
4 mins NFA

Ceylon – history and religion
(Extracts from *Song of Ceylon*)
20 mins

Ceylon – primitive life and the impact of the west
(Extracts from *Song of Ceylon*)
20 mins

Ceylon tea industry
30 mins silent

Children at school
A review of the system of public education in this country. (Film made 1937)
Reviews MFB X 34, S&S VI 145
pc Realist *p* John Grierson *d* Basil Wright
25 mins MOMA NFA

Children must laugh
(The story of a pre-war experiment in medical and social treatment of undernourished tubercular children from Warsaw)
re-ed Concanen
31 mins IWM

Children of the jungle
The various jungle tribes and the ceremonies at a Bhil wedding. (Film made 1939)
sp Times of India
21 mins NFA

Chiltern country
The beauty and historical associations of the Chilterns. (Film made in 1938)
pc GPO *d* Cavalcanti
13 mins silent NFA

Cities of the St Lawrence
Quebec, Montreal and places of historic and scenic interest in the province of Quebec
20 mins silent

City of Kano
(Nigeria)
10 mins silent

City of Madras
10 mins silent

City of ships
Everybody knows of the City of London, but do they also know that it is a great seaport and a city of ships? (Film made 1939)
pc British Films
30 mins NFA

City of the foothills
Life in Calgary, Alberta
8 mins silent

Climatic regions of the Empire
The film depicts typical scenes in the chief climatic areas–Polar, Continental, Mediterranean, Monsoon and in the Hot Dry and Hot Wet Regions
6 mins silent

Climbing Mount Tupper
Mountain climbing in Glacier National Park
12 mins silent

Clothes of the Empire
The evolution of clothing from the grass skirts of British Guinea and the skin garments of Eskimos to the clothing of modern Britain. (Film made in 1930)
pc Empire Marketing Board
12 mins silent

Clouds and rain
An experiment in the classroom showing the condensation of cold air and the formation of 'clouds'
Review MFB III 75
6 mins silent

The cocoa bean
Cultivation and harvesting of cacao in British West Africa. (Film made in 1933)
Review MFB IX 54
sp Cadbury *pc* Publicity
10 mins silent

Cocoa from the Gold Coast
Production of cocoa beans in British West Africa. (Film made in 1936)
Review MFB V 191
sp Cadbury
10 mins silent

Cocoa industry
(British West Africa)
10 mins silent

The coconut industry in Ceylon
30 mins silent

Coconuts and copra
(Malaya)
25 mins silent

Coconuts in Ceylon
From the picking of the nuts to the time the fibre is made into twine, the nut into desiccated coconut, and the shell into carbon for gas-masks
8 mins silent

Cold facts
The use of the diesel engine for transporting lumber
10 mins

The coming of the dial
Describes the conversion of London's telephone system from the old manual system to automatic working. (Film made 1933)
pc GPO *p* John Grierson *d* Basil Wright
20 mins NFA

Communication by wire
The history of telephone and telegraph development
sp GPO
12 mins

Conquering space
A revised sound version of *Methods of communication.* (Film made in 1934)
Review MFB X 117
pc GPO *p* Stuart Legg
10 mins NFA

The conquest of natural barriers
The developments of new lands with the opening up of communications. (Film made in 1932)
10 mins silent NFA

Conquest of the forest
Lumbering in Northern Ontario and Quebec
Review MFB IV 20
10 mins silent

The consoling weed
Tobacco industry. (Rhodesia)
6 mins

Cornwall calling
Cornish beauty spots and the glamour of life afloat
sp Austin Motor Co *pc* Publicity
16 mins

Cornwall: the western land
Relics of 4,000 years of Cornish history—its tin mines and important china clay workings; its fishing industry and the summertime amusements of visitors to this pleasant county of sunshine and wind-swept Atlantic shores
sp Great Western Railways *pc* Strand
15 mins

Cotton and wool
From raw material to finished article
12 mins silent

Country comes to town
Market gardening and the city's food supply. (Film made 1932)
26 mins NFA

Country currents
Electricity means power, heat and light, and brings comfort to the rural population. (Film made 1938)
sp British Electrical Development Assoc
14 mins NFA

Country fare
The Cotswold country, showing how farmers are producing fresh foods, such as milk, eggs and barley, for use in a modern food factory. (Film made 1937)
Review MFB IV 46
sp Cadbury *pc* Publicity
20 mins

Cradle of rivers
With pack horses to the glacial origin of the rivers Athabaska, Saskatchewan and Columbia
10 mins silent

Cups and saucers
Domestic pottery and how it is shaped on the potter's wheel
8 mins silent

Dairying
(South Africa)
22 mins silent

Dance of the harvest
Bullock-drawn ploughs preparing ground for rice cultivation. Sinhalese life. Harvest dance. Gathering and threshing. (Film made in 1935)
pc Empire Marketing Board
12 mins NFA

Darjeeling – a foothill town
The journey to Darjeeling by mountain railway. The various types of North Indian which form the population of the Himalayan foothills
pc G B Instructional
10 mins

Daylight and night
A novel account of what is happening in different parts of the Empire when it is midnight in Britain
10 mins silent

Drifting
Short classroom version of *Drifters*. (Film made 1932)
6 mins silent NFA

The drive is on
Lumbering
11 mins silent

Durbar at Zaria
(Nigeria)
12 mins silent

East Africa
Village life and customs in Tanganyika Territory, together with interesting scenes of wild life
5 mins silent

Eastern architecture
Portrays scenes of Indian architecture and fine views of the Taj Mahal
10 mins silent

Edinburgh
Old and new in the ancient capital city of Scotland. (Film made 1934)
Review MFB I 34
5 mins silent NFA

The English potter
A detailed illustration of the making of reproductions of the Portland vase and the methods used in its decoration. (Film made 1932)
Review S&S II 26
sp Empire Marketing Board
8 mins silent NFA

Enough to eat
Surveys inadequate food budgets among large numbers of people; suggests ways and means to good diet. (Film made 1936)
Review MFB II 187
sp Gas Light & Coke Co of London *d* Edgar Anstey, Frank Sainsbury
20 mins BFI MOMA NFA

Evergreen island
Scenic gems of Vancouver Island. (Film made 1936)
sp Canadian Pacific Railways
13 mins silent

Face of Scotland
(An account of the history, industry and countryside of Scotland. Film made in 1938)
sp Films of Scotland Ctte *pc* Realist *d* Basil Wright
14 mins MOMA NFA

Farm animals
Views of some of the animals to be found on a typical English farm. (Film made 1939)
Review MFB VIII 125
8 mins silent

Farmers of the prairies
The geological formation of the wheat belt and some of its agricultural problems
16 mins silent

The fens
An account of the agricultural industries of the Fen country. (Film made 1933)
Review MFB V 54
12 mins silent

First principles of lubrication
An introduction to the theory and practice of lubrication
Review MFB VII 142
pc Shell
6 mins NFA

First principles of the compression-ignition engine
(Film made 1939)
Review MFB VII 142
pc Shell
5 mins NFA

First principles of the petrol engine
The working principles of the internal combustion engine. (Film made 1939)
10 mins

Fish and fishing for everybody
Scenes showing the taking of eggs from fish and artificial hatching
10 mins silent

Fisherfolk of India
7 mins silent

Fishermen of the Caribbees
Arrival of the fishing fleet at Bathsheba, Barbados
5 mins silent

Fishin' the high seas
Canada's newest angling development. Fishing speckled trout in the Maligne-Medicine Lakes of Jasper National Park with Courtney Ryley Cooper and Irvin S Cobb
10 mins silent

Fishing banks of Skye
Great line fishing off the north-west of Scotland
10 mins

Five faces
(The people and industries of Malaya, key to the Indian and Pacific Oceans. Film made in 1938)
sp Federated Malay States *pc* Strand *p* Donald Taylor *d* Alexander Shaw
20 mins

For all eternity
A survey of England's cathedrals, which endeavours to show their significance in English history as well as their essential beauty in the English landscape. (Film made 1935)
pc Strand *d* Marion Grierson
20 mins MOMA NFA

Foretelling the weather
Post Office services in relation to the work of the Meteorological Office. (Film made pre-1940)
Review FoB 1940
sp GPO
10 mins silent

The four barriers
A sketch of Switzerland's economic history. (Film made in 1937)
Reviews MFB IV 137, MFB XV 151
sp GPO *pc* GPO & Pro Telephon *d* Cavalcanti
10 mins NFA

From acorn to oak
The evolution of a rubber tyre. (Film made 1938)
sp Dunlop Rubber Co *pc* Merton Park
5 mins NFA

From gold ore to bullion
Deals with the various methods of gold recovery from the ore and its refining into gold bars
27 mins

From seam to cellar
The various phases in the production, cleaning and distribution of Lancashire coal
10 mins silent

From the ground up
The development of the automobile industry of Canada
50 mins

Frontiers of the north
(Canada)
11 mins silent

Fruit canning
6 mins

Fruitlands
Fruit growing in Kent. (Film made in 1934)
Review MFB II 2
pc GB Instructional *d* Mary Field
12 mins NFA (under title *Fruitlands of Kent*)

The game is up
Mountaineering in Glacier National Park, British Columbia. (Film made in 1936)
10 mins

Gardens of the Orient
Scenery and life in a tea garden. Conveying the tea to the factory. Rolling, fermenting, firing and packing. (Film made in 1934)
Review MFB IV 260
pc GPO & GB Instructional
15 mins NFA

The gate of China
How British engineers have built Hong Kong on hilltops and land reclaimed from the sea
15 mins silent

Gateway to the East
Gibraltar ancient and modern
14 mins silent

Gem of the Rockies
The summer attractions of Jasper National Park in the Rocky Mountains and the largest of Canada's game reserves
20 mins silent

Gems of the lakes
Minaki Lodge and the summer attractions of this section of Ontario, named by the Indians 'Beautiful country'
10 mins silent

Gems of the Rockies
The lakes, mountain scenery and wild life in Jasper Park
10 mins

Glacier
The Southern Alps of New Zealand
Review MFB IX 81
10 mins silent

The glassmakers of England
A companion film to *The English potter* showing the craftsmanship of those who make the famous glassware. (Film made 1932)
sp Empire Marketing Board & Travel Assoc
7 mins silent NFA

Glimpses of the East
Views of native life and industries in India
16 mins silent

Glimpses of the Garden Route
(South Africa)
18 mins silent

Golden fleece
General life on a sheep station in New South Wales
10 mins

The golden fleece
The wool industry of New Zealand
8 mins

Golden harvest of the Witwatersrand
Gold mining in all its varied processes. (Film made 1935)
pc African Film Productions
90 mins NFA

Good-bye to all that
Trip by pack-train from Jasper National Park, Alberta to Mount Robson in Mount Robson Provincial Park, British Columbia
10 mins silent

Granton trawler
A short account of trawling in rough weather on the Viking Bank between the Shetlands and the Norwegian Coast. (Film made in 1934)
Review MFB VI 147
sp Empire Marketing Board *d* Edgar Anstey *ph* John Grierson
10 mins MOMA NFA

Grape fruit
(British Honduras. Film made 1938)
Review MFB VII 29
pc GB Instructional
8 mins NFA

Grey Owl's little brother
An excellent picture of Grey Owl and his

beaver filmed in the Riding Mountain National Park, Manitoba
10 mins

Grey Owl's strange guests
Grey Owl and his beaver in Prince Albert National Park
10 mins

Growing cotton
(Nigeria)
10 mins silent

Happy hunting ground
Photographic adventures with a long-distance lens in the big-game country of the Tobique River in New Brunswick
9 mins silent

Happy Uganda
68 mins silent

Harvests of the forest
Views of forest to dart club, saw-mill to violin craftsman, dockside to carpenter's shop
12 mins silent

Health and recreation
Canoeing, camping, tennis, swimming and diving at Lake Waskesiu in Prince Albert National Park
12 mins silent

Health from a heritage
Short story dealing with the growing of grapes and the making of grape juice
4 mins

Heart of an Empire
St James's Park and the interesting buildings that surround it. (Film made 1936)
Reviews MFB II 154, S&S IV 128
pc Strand
8 mins NFA

Here and there in New Zealand
Scenery from a rail-car in New Zealand
10 mins silent

Here and there with the birds of Canada
Various species of bird life in Canada. (Film made 1930)
9 mins silent

Heritage
An account of the fight to restore prairie lands to fertility. (French title *Notre héritage*)
sp Canadian Dept of Ag *pc* Union Films *p* Francis Coley *d* Arthur Bennett *ph* John W Warner
14 mins NFA

Highlands of Cape Breton
Scenic film with glimpses of home handicrafts, harbours and Margaree Valley
12 mins silent

Highways of the Empire
Illustrating the progress and quickening of communications, from the days of sailing ships up to the wireless and cable communications of to-day
5 mins silent

Home of the birds
The north shore of the Gulf of St Lawrence, where many varieties of Canadian sea fowl make their home and breed in protected areas
10 mins silent

Home of the buffalo
(Alberta buffalo reserve. Film made 1932)
pc Canadian National Parks Service
17 mins silent

Honey bees
The production and marketing of English honey on modern lines. (Film made 1939)
pc British Instructional
14 mins NFA

Hop gardens of Kent
Hop picking and drying in oast houses for the breweries. (Film made 1938)

Review MFB I 38
5 mins silent NFA

Horsey mail
Delivery of mails during the Norfolk floods. (Film made in 1938)
sp & pc GPO *d* Pat Jackson *ph* Fred Gamage
9 mins NFA

Hot ice
Ice hockey in Canada
28 mins

How stamps are made
The designer at work and the various processes of printing and manufacture. (Film made in 1936)
sp & pc GPO
10 mins NFA

How the dial works
A brief and simple diagrammatic film showing the essential principles of the automatic telephone system. (Film made in 1935)
Review MFB IX 107
sp & pc GPO
6 mins

How the Savings Bank works
A short description of the work and method of the Post Office Savings Bank showing the complex business organisation which deals with the accounts of ten million people
10 mins silent

How the telephone works
The principles of sound transmission. Silent version entitled *Inside the telephone.* (Film made in 1938)
Reviews FoB 1940, MFB IX 108
sp & pc GPO
9 mins NFA

Hunting without a gun
Camera shots of wild life in Canada—moose, elk, polar bear. (Film made 1930)
pc Canadian National Parks Service
12 mins silent

Hyderabad
An important State with its State railway and making its own money and postage stamps. Main industries are agriculture and handicrafts
14 mins

In the shadow of the Assiniboine
Mountain scenery showing climbers conquering Wedgwood
12 mins silent

Indian lac
Describing the production and manufacture of lac
25 mins silent

Indian rope trick
7 mins silent

Indian scrapbook
Sabu introduces us to a picture-book of Indian life showing the architecture, religious ceremonies, customs of the people and a spectacular picture of a round-up of wild elephants
10 mins

Indian tea
Production of tea in Assam
12 mins silent

Industrial Britain
The story of craftsmanship in British industry. (Film made 1931)
Review S&S II 26
sp Empire Marketing Board *p* John Grierson *d* Robert Flaherty
25 mins MOMA NFA

Industrial workers
Life in the cities, houses and factories of Ontario and Quebec
16 mins silent

Inside story
The processes involved in the production of Canadian canned salmon. (Film made in 1938)
pc Canadian Govt Motion Picture Bureau
10 mins NFA

Inside the telephone
Silent version of *How the telephone works*
Review MFB IX 108
12 mins silent

Iron and steel
The manufacturing processes of iron and steel
9 mins silent

Irrigation
(South Africa)
15 mins silent

Irrigation
Methods of irrigation in India, Australia, Canada and Egypt
pc Empire Marketing Board
9 mins silent

Jamaica harvest
Cultivation and harvesting of bananas. (Film made 1938)
Review MFB VII 100
pc GB Instructional
10 mins NFA

A June day on a Cotswold farm
Haymaking, including cutting, turning and lifting by mechanical means. Feeding cows and collecting and packing of eggs. (Film made 1939)
Review MFB VIII 126
6 mins silent

Jungle gods
A film that depicts the luxuriant tropical beauty of Ceylon
Review MFB V 269
sp Austin Motor Co *pc* Publicity
10 mins silent

Katmandu – a Himalayan town
The journey to Katmandu by mountain railway and rough road. The agricultural activities of the foothill region. The Chinese influence in racial types and buildings. The method of government of Nepal. (Sixth in the series *Secrets of India*. Film made in 1934)
Review MFB I 36
pc GB Instructional
10 mins

Kensal house
Life in a new housing estate in London. (Film made 1937)
sp Gas Council
14 mins MOMA

Kenya farm
12 mins silent

Kew Gardens
The 'behind the scenes' activities and research of the famous botanical station. (Film made 1937)
Review MFB IV 70
pc Short Film Productions *d* Philip Leacock
20 mins NFA

Key to Scotland
A vivid picture of Edinburgh in which the cameraman has caught inspiration alike from the high-perched castle–the Key to Scotland–and the superb beauty of the city, and endeavoured to link them with the romance of Scottish history. (Film made 1935)
Review MFB II 154
d Marion Grierson
20 mins MOMA NFA

The King's stamp
The designing and preparation of the King George V jubilee stamp. (Film made 1935)
pc GPO *d* William Coldstream
20 mins BFI NFA

The kinsmen
The story of the original (Marquis) hard

spring wheat of the Canadian prairies
sp Canadian Govt Wheat Board
45 mins

Lagos
12 mins silent

Lake of enchantment
A trail-riding trip from Jasper Park Lodge to the largest glacial lake in the Canadian Rockies, passing en route Maligne Canyon and Medicine Lake and returning via Shovel Pass
12 mins silent

Lancashire, home of industry
The development of industrial Lancashire from the days of water-power to modern days of electricity. (Film made 1935)
Review MFB III 206
sp Travel Assoc
10 mins silent NFA

Land of good hope
Rock climbing at the Cape and in Natal
7 mins silent

Land of Rhodes
Beautiful scenery through mountainous districts
20 mins silent

Land of splendour
Scenery showing the southern lake district of New Zealand
10 mins silent

Leaping rainbows
Rainbow trout and Dolly Vardens in Stuart, Tacla and Trembleur Lakes
12 mins silent

A lesson in geography
Diagrammatic film showing the area of Australia in relation to that of Europe
4 mins silent

Let's go ski-ing
Ski-ing among the vast mountain peaks that surround beautiful Skoki Valley in Banff National Park
10 mins

Letters to liners
A short film of a Mediterranean cruise, showing the special arrangements made for delivery and despatch of the ship's mail. (Film made 1937)
15 mins silent NFA

Life in ponds and streams
Making an aquarium at William Rhodes Modern School
12 mins silent

Life of a District Officer
(British West Africa)
10 mins silent

Lights o' London
Describing the making of electric light bulbs. (Film made 1938)
7 mins NFA

Line fishing
Fishing for hake and skate off the west coast of Scotland. Casting and hauling the nine miles of line
6 mins silent

Line to Tschierva hut
(Sound version of *Mountain telephone*. Connecting a climber's hut in the Alps with the world below. Film made in 1937)
Review MFB IV 138
pc GPO *d* Cavalcanti *m* Benjamin Britten
10 mins MOMA NFA

Lions and the others
Wild life in East Africa
14 mins silent

Locomotives
From the first primitive engine to the modern high-speed locomotive. (Film

made in 1938)
Review FoB 1941, MFB XI 51
d Humphrey Jennings *pc* GPO
10 mins NFA

London
(Film made 1933)
pc Tida
16 mins silent NFA

London on parade
Scenes of London, on the river, in the streets, the shops and markets. (Film made 1937)
Review S&S VI 203
d Marion Grierson
11 mins NFA

Lubrication of the petrol engine
Nature and effects of mechanical friction; how lubrication overcomes friction. (Film made 1937)
pc Shell
12 mins NFA

Lumbering in British Columbia
Felling the giant trees of the Pacific seaboard. (Film made 1930?)
9 mins silent NFA

Made in India
India has entered upon its industrial revolution. Large-scale industries such as iron, steel, cement, chemicals, shoes and paper are necessary to the economic development of the country and the raising of the standard of living. But the traditional village crafts such as spinning, weaving and tanning must also be fostered to contribute to India's future
10 mins

The magic carpet
Life in Chinese streets of Hong Kong
10 mins silent

Magic playgrounds of New Zealand
Rotorua natural hot water springs. Maoris fishing
7 mins

Maintaining Canada's salmon supply
Artificial methods of hatching salmon eggs
11 mins silent

Maize and wheat
(South Africa)
20 mins silent

Making a book
Silent version of *Book bargain*. (Film made 1937)
16 mins silent NFA

Making friends with wild life
Deer in the parks at Banff, Alberta and pictures of the Chickadee in a bird sanctuary at London, Ontario
10 mins silent

The man who knew too little
Revealing the importance of the use of gas by-products. (Film made 1936)
pc Publicity
6 mins

Manganese
Mining and Postmansburg; grading, sorting and transport of ore to Durban for shipment abroad or to Newcastle, Natal for conversion into ferromanganese for use in steel industry. (Film made 1939)
pc African Film Productions
10 mins NFA

Manufacture of gas
This film shows how gas is made, from the point, where the colliers come alongside the piers at Beckton, which lies on the north side of the Thames just below the Albert Docks. (Film made 1938)
10 mins NFA

Many harvests
Coastal natives beaching the primitive boats after a fishing expedition, cleaning and smoking the catch and repairing the nets. Inside a native kraal. The market in the interior. Soap-making, washing

clothes and native beauty culture. Collecting cocoa pods, extracting the beans and transport to England. (British West Africa)
12 mins

Market place
A short description of the work of the Post Office in relation to the life of a typical market town
10 mins silent

Maternity and child welfare centres (Darlington)
Hospital; clinics; Baby Day celebrations at Polam Hall; nursery school
8 mins silent

Meat we eat
From pasture to shop
12 mins silent

Men of Africa
The principles of British colonial administration are shown in the health, education and agricultural services in East Africa
Reviews DNL I June 7, FoB 1940, MFB XIII 72
sp Colonial Office *pc* Strand *p* Basil Wright *d* Alexander Shaw
20 mins IWM NFA

Men of the Alps
Survey of the principal features of Swiss national life. (Film made 1936-37)
Review MFB IV 137
pc GPO & Pro Telephon *d* Cavalcanti
10 mins NFA

Men who work
Work in a British automobile factory. (Film made 1935)
Reviews FoB 1940, MFB V 55
pc Tida
9 mins NFA

Methods of communication
An analysis of the primitive and modern, the simple and complex means of communication in Britain today. (Film made pre-1934. Revised version with sound entitled *Conquering space*)
sp GPO
20 mins silent

Mica industry
(India)
40 mins silent NFA

Miles from Malay
The manufacture of a motor car tyre. (Film made 1938)
pc Tida
11 mins NFA

The milky way
Dairying—pasture lands, prize herds, up-to-date milking sheds and factories, manufacture of butter. (Film made 1927)
10 mins silent NFA

Mineral wealth
(British West Africa)
10 mins silent

Miracle at Beauharnis
The weight of falling water has for centuries supplied inexpensive power for man's machinery
20 mins silent

Modderfontein dynamite factory
(South Africa)
20 mins silent

A modern Eden
Blossom time and harvest time in the great fruit belt of the Niagara Peninsula of Ontario
10 mins

Modern Post Office methods
The use of mechanical aids in the Post Office, including the PO Underground Railway with its driverless trains
10 mins silent

Modern voyageurs
Travelling by canoe through the extensive lake system of Prince Albert National Park, Saskatchewan
10 mins silent

Monsoon island
Elephants clearing jungle. Tea industry. Temples, fields and gardens of old and new Ceylon. (Film made in 1934)
Review MFB III 73
sp Empire Tea Board
10 mins NFA

Mother Ganges
Benares, sacred city of the Hindus on the banks of the mighty Ganges
Review MFB IV 2
10 mins silent

A mountain stairway
The relation of plants to altitudes. (Film made 1932)
sp Empire Marketing Board
5 mins silent

Mountain telephone
Connecting a climber's hut, high in the Alps, by telephone with the world below. (Made in 1937. Silent version of *Line to Tschierva hut*)
10 mins silent

Mountain waters
Scenery, waterfalls etc. (South Africa. Film made 1936)
pc African Film Productions
20 mins

Native animals of Australia
Porcupine, platypus, kangaroo, wallaby, opossum, wombat
Review MFB VII 105
12 mins silent

A native householder
The building of a native hut from grasses and branches. (British East Africa)
10 mins silent

Native wattle cultivation
Felling and stripping trees, bundles of bark carried on heads of natives to mill. Scenes of Nairobi
10 mins silent

Nature's bounty
Fruit growing, grading and packing. (New Zealand)
10 mins silent

The navy at work
Movements of British warships all over the world. (Film made 1939)
pc Tida
22 mins silent

Negombo coast
From Colombo's magnificent harbour the ships of all nations carry Ceylon's riches
12 mins

The new generation
Training the new generation for the work of the community. An account of Chesterfield's educational system
20 mins silent

The new operator
How a recruit learns the complexities of a modern telephone switchboard. (Film made 1934)
pc GPO *d* Stuart Legg
10 mins silent NFA

New worlds for old
Shows how gas has become a great heat and light producing industry. (Film made in 1938)
British Commercial Gas Assoc *pc* Realist
p Paul Rotha
28 mins MOMA NFA

New Zealand flax
The harvesting and preparation of New Zealand flax (phorium tenax)
7 mins silent

News by wire
The story of electricity in the world of today. (Film made 1939)
9 mins NFA

News for the navy
The delivery of mails to the Fleet in foreign waters. (Film made in 1938)
GPO *pc* GPO & Admiralty *d* Norman McLaren
10 mins NFA

Niagara the glorious
Summertime on the Canadian side of the falls
9 mins silent

Nickel tales
Mining and smelting
10 mins

Night mail

The Nipigon and north
New speckled trout waters. Whitesand and Wabibosh rivers–northern tributaries to the world-famous Nipigon
12 mins silent

Norfolk Island
The home of the descendants of the *Bounty* mutineers
15 mins silent

North of the border
A sketch of the Scottish postal system showing the communication problems created by scattered population, seasonal employment rushes and the difficult physical characteristics of the country
10 mins

North Sea
How the ship-to-shore radio service safeguards the lives of seamen. (Film made in 1938. Short silent version entitled *Distress call*)
Reviews FoB 1940, MFB XII 10
pc GPO *p* Cavalcanti *d* & *sc* Harry Watt *ph* Jonah Jones, H E Fowle *ed* S McAllister *m* Ernst Meyer
30 mins NFA

North-west frontier
North of the Mackenzie river lie 100,000 square miles of Canada inhabited by Eskimos and Indians, the mineral resources of which are now only being fully prospected. Exploration since 1920 has revealed oil, pitchblende for radium, lignite, lead, zinc and gold. The opening up of the territory presents social problems for the future of the native inhabitants; for them the Government must provide new means of livelihood and modern schools and hospitals
pc National Film Board of Canada
32 mins NFA

Northern provinces
(Nigeria)
10 mins silent

O'er hill and dale
Life of a Scottish shepherd in the border country. (Film made 1932)
sp Empire Marketing Board *d* Basil Wright
20 mins NFA

Oil from the earth
Formation of oil-bearing strata; various aspects of petroleum surveying (aerial and seismographic) followed by a very detailed treatment of drilling (boring, testing and casing). (Film made 1938)
Review MFB V 213
pc Shell
17 mins NFA

Oil palm industry
(Nigeria. Film made 1930)
pc New Era
9 mins silent NFA

On the road to Bethlehem
Scenes in and around Bethlehem associated with both Old and New Testament incidents

Review MFB IV 8
12 mins silent

On the Skeena River
Catching salmon for the canneries
8 mins silent

Open skyways in the Rockies
A motor trip through the central Rockies from Banff, Alberta to Golden, British Columbia along the Kicking Horse trail
10 mins silent

Ottawa
10 mins

Oudtshoorn
Depicting the beauties of the district and the Cango Caves
4 mins

Our daily bread
(New Zealand)
30 mins silent

Our daily bread
Wheat industry
11 mins

Our herring industry
Two-reel version of *Drifters*—the film epic of the North Sea herring fisheries
Review MFB I 65
pc GPO
18 mins silent

The outer isles
Life on the Hebrides from the rocky, almost barren east coast to the more fertile west. The crofters' life, sheep washing, highland cattle and fishing. (Film made 1932)
Review MFB III 75
10 mins silent

Paddy
Growing, reaping and preparation of rice. (Burma. Film made 1930)
12 mins silent

Pathways of the Rockies
The conquest of the Rockies barrier by road, rail and water
12 mins

People of the sea
Seals, octopods, lobsters, dogfish, beches-de-mer, crayfish, whales, tunas, salmon, herring
12 mins silent

People of Uganda: their life and industries
30 mins silent

Peoples of Canada
The story of the peoples of a dozen different nations who migrated to Canada, there to build new homes for themselves and a new nation
21 mins

Peoples of Tanganyika
(Documentary on the native tribes. Film made in 1936)
Review MFB IV 231
30 mins silent

Petroleum
(The drilling, transportation and refining of oil)
Review MFB VII 122
pc GB Instructional
10 mins

Pietermaritzburg
The beauty and buildings of the capital of Natal
10 mins

Pilgrims of the wild
A day in the life of Grey Owl in the woods of Prince Albert National Park, Saskatchewan
10 mins silent

Pineapples
(Australia)
10 mins

Pines and poles
The preparation of tree trunks for use as telegraph poles
GPO
8 mins silent

Pioneer trails
The development of Rhodesia
20 mins silent

Plantation people
A colour film of bananas, cocoa, sugar and grapefruit cultivation in Trinidad
Review MFB III 206
Cadbury
20 mins colour NFA

Playground of the prairies
Recreation facilities amid picturesque scenery in Riding Mountain National Park
12 mins silent

Pleasure trove
A holiday tour of New South Wales
10 mins

Plums that please
A description of the English plum harvest and the methods of marketing. Bottling in the home. (Film made 1934)
Review MFB I 54
Min of Ag
10 mins NFA

Post haste
History of 300 years of postal service, from the postboy of the seventeenth century, the stage coach and the first railway to the motor vans, high-speed locomotives and air mail of today. (Film made 1934)
pc GPO *d* Humphrey Jennings
10 mins NFA

Prairie gold
Canada's wheat industry. The preparation of the ground, research to produce the best wheat, harvesting, marketing and transport by grain boat via the Great Lakes to Montreal for shipping to Britain. (Re-edited two-reel version of *The kinsman.* Film made 1939)
Review MFB IX 108
Canadian Wheat Board & MoI
18 mins NFA

Prestea gold mine
(British West Africa)
10 mins silent

Pretoria
The public buildings, gardens and steel works of the Administrative Capital of the Union of South Africa
8 mins

The Punjab
Irrigation of the land—necessary because of seasonal rainfall. Life in the villages
15 mins

Quebec and the Maritimes
A journey by CPR from Montreal to Halifax
Review MFB X 59
12 mins silent

Regions of Africa
The grasslands north and south of the equator. The harvesting of cotton and maize
6 mins silent

Regions of Canada
A diagrammatic record of distances covered (miles and days sailed) on a voyage from England to Canada. Characteristic views and occupations in the principal areas of Canada
12 mins silent

Return of the buffalo
Fine views of the Government buffalo herd in Buffalo National Park, Wain-

wright, Alberta. (Film made 1932)
10 mins

Rice
(Malaya)
25 mins silent

Ride 'em cowboy
Calgary Festival Rodeo. Riding a wild steer, milking a wild cow etc. (Film made 1936)
8 mins silent NFA

Road transport
The development of road transport and improvement in the type of road vehicle during the present century
10 mins silent

Romance of a lump of coal
A day in the life of the housewife as told by the gas engineer's consumption graph, introducing the story of some of the byproducts. (Film made 1935)
Review MFB V 213
pc Pathé
8 mins

Romance of the grape
An outline of an important industry
20 mins silent

Romantic India
Temples; elephants and buffalo at work in the teak forests, workers in the rice fields and tea gardens; factory scenes; elephants bathing. (Film made 1935)
Review MFB IV 62
20 mins NFA

The Royal Canadian Mint
How gold bars are refined and transformed into pure gold bullion at the Royal Mint in Canada
10 mins

Rubber
(Malaya)
35 mins silent

Rubber for the road
The manufacture of a motor-car tyre. (Film made 1939)
pc Tida
16 mins silent

Saga of the silver horde
The various methods of salmon fishing in British Columbia. (Film made 1933-34)
Review MFB I 87
pc Canadian Govt Motion Picture Bureau
10 mins NFA

St James's Park
A description of one of England's most beautiful parks. (Film made 1934)
Review MFB I 37
pc Empire Marketing Board
10 mins silent NFA

The saving of Bill Blewitt
The value of thrift in a small village community. Scenes in a Cornish village with authentic characters, telling how two fishermen lost their boat in a storm, and by intensive saving were able to start again. (Film made 1936)
pc GPO *d* Harry Watt
23 mins BFI NFA

Savings bank
Sound version of *How the savings bank works.* (Film made 1936)
pc GPO
10 mins NFA

Seabirds of the Shetlands
Bird life on the rocky coasts of the Shetland Islands
11 mins silent

Seaports of the Empire
A diagrammatic and scenic illustration of the four main types of seaports—river, natural harbour, breakwater, surf-boat and lighter
7 mins silent

Seasons
Developments of animal life on English

farms throughout the different seasons
5 mins silent

Seasons of Canada
An account of Canada in the different seasons
10 mins silent

Shamba Ya Kahava
Coffee production in Tanganyika. (Film made in 1936)
Review MFB IV 231
12 mins

Shawinigan water power
A screen story of how water-made electricity serves the people of Quebec
pc National Film Board of Canada
60 mins silent

She climbs to conquer
A girl climber in Banff National Park
26 mins

Sheep and wool
Karroo scenes. (South Africa)
13 mins silent

Sheep shearing
Dipping and shearing sheep on the Welsh Hills. (Film made 1936)
Review MFB VI 227
pc Elder Dalrymple
5 mins silent NFA

Sheep's clothing
Shetland sheep are driven in for the 'shearing'. The wool is spun in the croft
10 mins silent

Shell Cine Magazine 1
The building of a reservoir; protection of fruit; oil tankers; development of the use of water power. (Film made 1938)
pc Shell
10 mins NFA

The shepherd
A description of the lambing season in Scotland. (Film made c.1939)
Empire Marketing Board
6 mins silent NFA

Ship for sale
(Silent version of *The saving of Bill Blewitt*)
15 mins silent

Shipshape
A day in the life of a liner
Canadian Pacific Railways
20 mins silent

Silver industry
Methods of refining, processes of mass-prodtiction, hand craftsmanship, hall-marking of silver articles
30 mins

Simple magnetism and electricity
An elementary explanation of some of the principles of magnetism and electricity utilised in the transmission of speech by telephone. (Film made 1936)
Review MFB IX 108
GPO *pc* GPO
15 mins NFA

Sisal and cattle
Natives harvesting sisal in Kenya. Transport to the factory. Separating, washing and drying the fibre. A sequence shows a Masai village and the natives herding their large, magnificent cattle and goats
10 mins silent

Sisal: its growth and development
(British East Africa)
20 mins silent

Ski-ing at Lake Louise
A ski-ing party in the Rockies
10 mins silent

Ski-ing in cloudland
A ski-ing holiday in Banff National Park
10 mins silent

Sky fishing
Scenic beauty and fishing possibilities of Maligne Lake, Jasper National Park. (Film made 1934)
10 mins

The smoke menace
The evil effects of the domestic and industrial misuse of coal. The up-to-date method of utilising coal in clean forms are discussed. (Film made 1937)
15 mins MOMA

Snakes and elephants
Snake charming. Elephants help with lumbering
6 mins silent

Snowtime in the Rockies
Canadian winter sports at Banff National Park
12 mins silent

So this is Lancashire
The effect of geological and climatic influence on the beginnings of Lancashire. It traces the progress of the country from the days of water-power to those of electrically driven machinery. (Film made 1933)
Review MFB II 6
pc Strand
24 mins silent NFA

So this is London
An attempt to focus the life of England's capital city, her salient features and arresting contrasts, her romantic past and bustling present. (Film made in 1933)
pc Strand *d* Marion Grierson
20 mins NFA

So this is Ontario
Toronto; a trip across the Great Lakes to the Niagara Falls, and a visit to Ottawa. (Film made in 1938)
Review MFB II 9
Canadian Pacific Railways
18 mins silent NFA

Solid sunshine
Butter—from New Zealand's dairy farms to Britain's consumers
10 mins silent

Song of Ceylon
A vivid picture, in four parts, of the life and customs of the people of Ceylon. (Film made in 1934)
Empire Tea Marketing Board *pc* GPO *p* John Grierson *d* Basil Wright
40 mins BFI MOMA NFA

Song of the reel
Sea fishing (around South Africa)
20 mins

Song the map sings
Manufacture of motor cars in Canada
Ford Motor Co, Canada
30 mins NFA

Sons of the surf
Swimming, surf-boarding and life-saving along the Australian coast
8 mins silent

Sorting office
The work of the Western District Office in London
10 mins silent

South African fruit harvest
Typical scenes of the South African fruit industry
10 mins silent

South African orchards
Deciduous fruits
10 mins silent

A southern April
A sound version of *South African fruit harvest*
11 mins

Southern provinces
(Nigeria)

pc New Era
10 mins silent NFA

Southward ho
A tour of the South Island of New Zealand
16 mins silent

Sponges
(Bahamas)
pc GB Instructional
9 mins

Springs
A simple explanation of how motor car springs are made and how they work. (Film made in 1938)
pc Shell
10 mins NFA

Stake net fishing
This film depicts another method of salmon fishing off the east coast of Scotland
4 mins silent

Stalking big game
Scenes in National Parks of Rocky Mountain sheep and goats. Black-tailed or 'jumping' deer, moose, caribou and black bear
10 mins silent

Steel highway
A railway journey showing the scenery typical of England
pc Selwyn
16 mins silent NFA

Steel, wire and nails
The making of steel and subsequent processes of reducing the billets to wire gauge, and finally the making of nails
12 mins silent

Stirling
A film of historical interest and scenic beauty
10 mins silent

Story of a disturbance
Explains the conditions represented by isobars, 'fronts', and other symbols on a weather map
pc GB Instructional
19 mins silent

The story of Kenya coffee
28 mins silent

The story of nickel
Uses of nickel in industry
10 mins

Story of South African steel
From ore to the finished product
60 mins

The story of stamps
The evolution of stamps. In the earliest days of postal service the addressee paid the postage. With the introduction of the present day system of prepayment of postage of the sender, came stamps. Scenes of early postage stamps
10 mins silent

Story of stone
Quarrying in Ontario. Using the finished stone in building
12 mins silent

The story of the Canadian pine
From forests to export of finished products
30 mins

Story of the wheel
The evolution of the wheel from prehistoric times up to the innovation of the locomotive. (Film made 1934-35)
Review MFB X 108
pc GPO
10 mins NFA

Sugar and coffee
Harvesting sugar-cane and coffee berries in British East Africa
pc British Instructional
10 mins silent NFA

Sugar cane industry
A detailed description of the cultivation and harvesting of sugar-cane
30 mins

Sugar factory, Trinidad
20 mins silent

Summer days at Waskesiu
A typical day around Lake Waskesiu in Prince Albert National Park
12 mins silent

Tea is served
This was adapted from *Rose of the Orient*. (1938. The tea industry of Ceylon)
Min of Food *pc* Verity *p* Jay Gardner Lewis
7 mins

Tea-time topics
An entertaining film showing some of the tea customs of the world
15 mins silent

Telephone workers
The story of the coming of the telephone to a newly built suburb and of the telephone workers who make the new service possible. (Film made 1933)
pc GPO *p* John Grierson *d* Stuart Legg
10 mins NFA

This changing world
Old and new methods of nickel production
10 mins

This was England
A record of the continuous agricultural tradition existing in Suffolk from the Stone Age to the present day
Review MFB II 163
pc GB Instructional
22 mins NFA

Through the Norway of America
Cruising between Puget Sound and Alaska
10 mins silent

The tides
Classroom demonstrations of the relation between moon and tides. Observations on the sea's shore. William Rhodes Modern School
10 mins silent

Timber front
Modern methods in the Canadian lumber industry. Wasteful cutting has been stopped, and tree-replacement begun on a large scale. From lofty watch-towers outbreaks of fire in the forests can be seen and dealt with
pc National Film Board of Canada
20 mins

The tocher
A tocher is the Scottish term for a marriage portion or dowry. A fairy story in silhouette of the good fortune which befell the possessor of a Post Office Savings Bank book. (Film made 1938)
pc GPO *d* Lotte Reiniger *m* Rossini *arranged by* Benjamin Britten
5 mins NFA

Toilers of the Grand Banks
The fishing industry of the East Coast of Canada
16 mins silent

Tonquin trails
Trail-riding and rainbow-trout fishing in the Amethyst Lake section of Jasper National Park
12 mins silent

Top of the world
Scenery of Banff in the Rocky Mountains. (Film made 1939)
10 mins NFA.

Trails to the wilderness
Patrolling the lakes of Jasper National Park
10 mins silent

Transport
The development of transport in South Africa
10 mins

Transport
World-wide methods of moving men and merchandise
10 mins silent

Travel in Kenya and Uganda
64 mins silent

Treasures of Katoomba
Blue Mountains scenery
12 mins

Tropical lumbering
(Lumbering in British Honduras. Film made in 1938)
pc GB Instructional
11 mins

Udaipur – a central Indian town
The position of the town shown by maps and views. Work in the streets. The Rajah's three palaces and his procession to his summer palace on the lake
pc GB Instructional
10 mins

Under the city
Beneath the City's streets there is a whole world of communication: gas, electricity, water, the underground railway and the Post Office cables. (Film made 1934)
Reviews MFB I 73, MFB XII 42
pc GPO *d* Alexander Shaw
12 mins NFA

Unlocking Canada's treasure trove
Every phase of the gold industry
65 mins

Upstream
The story of the salmon fishers and the migration of the salmon up a Highland river. (Film made 1932)
Review MFB I 38
Empire Marketing Board *d* Arthur Elton
20 mins NFA

Veterinary services
(South Africa)
24 mins silent

Victoria
A visit to the capital of British Columbia
10 mins

Victoria: 100 years of progress
Early exploration and foundation of the state. Its activities and scenic attractions. Melbourne today
11 mins

Villages of Lanka
Scenes in villages, homes, streets and workshops. Native life and industries. (Film made 1935)
12 mins NFA

Vineyard of the empire
The complete story of the South Australian wine industry. (Film made in 1938)
Review MFB I 38
pc Australian Govt
12 mins NFA

Voyageur trails
Fishing in Canadian rivers. How to shoot rapids in canoes
10 mins

The war without end
A screen record of some of the wonderful achievements of medical science and of the work of our hospitals today
17 mins

Warriors of the deep
Fishing for the broad-bill swordfish around the coast of Cape Breton
12 mins silent

Water power
This film illustrates modern methods of utilising water power to generate electricity
pc GB Instructional
11 mins

Water power
The energy of rushing water transformed into electrical power. The turbine in action and the uses in which the resulting power is employed
5 mins silent

Waterton
An excellent picture depicting the scenery and recreational opportunities in Waterton Lakes National Park
10 mins silent

Waterways of Canada
The importance of the rivers and lakes of Canada in her trade and development. (Film made in 1941)
Review MFB IX 109
pc National Film Board of Canada
16 mins silent

Wattle
Cultivation of wattle bark and manufacture of wattle extract for tanning purposes
20 mins silent

We live in two worlds
One—the world of separate states and national frontiers: the other, that of international trade and communications. (Film made 1937-38)
Review MFB IV 138
pc GPO & Pro Telephon *p* John Grierson *d* Cavalcanti
15 mins NFA

We visit tea estates of Kenya
22 mins silent

Wealth of Australia
The development of Australia since the landing of the first settlers in the early nineteenth century. The wool industry. Mining of gold, silver, lead and zinc. Wheat growing. Views of Sydney
10 mins

We'll all have tea
Tea plucking at Darjeeling
12 mins silent

West coast mountains
How men live and work in the Rocky Mountains which divide Canada
14 mins silent

West Indian cattle
A round-up of Indian and mixed herds for dipping, from the north-west pastures of Jamaica
6 mins silent

Wheatlands
Wheat growing in East Anglia
pc GB Instructional
20 mins

When spring is in the air
Present-day methods of tapping trees, gathering sap and the fabrication of maple syrup in comparison with the methods of the pioneer days. (Film made 1936)
10 mins NFA

When the day is done
The various aspects of the activities of the Miners' Welfare Fund
17 mins

Where fighting beauties rise
Fishing for Kamloops trout in Lake Knouff, British Columbia
10 mins silent

Wild life trails
Fine shots of wild life in New Brunswick
10 mins silent

Wine romance
(South Africa)
7 mins silent

Winter witcheries of Niagara
Fantastic designs made by snow and ice
9 mins silent

The wires go underground
Short silent film on the same theme as *Copper web*
sp GPO
8 mins

With cargo to Cannibal Islands
The trip of the island steamer which does the journey only once in 6 weeks, from Sydney to the islands with cargo. (New Hebrides)
11 mins silent

Wizard in the wall
The history of the development of electrical industry
10 mins

Workaday
How cocoa, Bourn-vita and chocolate are made at Bournville
30 mins

World exchange
The international telephone exchange in London
Review FoB 1940
sp GPO
11 mins silent

Yoho
Yoho, the Indian name for surprise and wonder, is given as a name to a little valley in the Canadian Rockies
10 mins silent

A Zambesi holiday
Brief story of Livingstone and its environments as a holiday resort
4 mins

Zanzibar
20 mins

Appendix 2

Films produced during the war and subsequently distributed by the Central Office of Information

According to our records
A War Office film on the vital importance of strict accuracy in record-keeping. Shows what serious results can come of apparently trivial errors
War Office *pc* Army Kinematograph Services
30 mins IWM

After work
Groups of Canadian factory workers, in various towns, pool their energies and resources to provide themselves with recreational (and educational) facilities. Recreational associations are formed, community halls built, and many spare-time activities organised
pc National Film Board of Canada
10 mins

Australia is like this
First impressions of two US soldiers, who find Australian city life surprisingly like that of America in many ways. The scenes are chiefly in Sydney but there are glimpses of Melbourne and the hinterland
Review MFB XIII 78
pc Australian Dept of Information & US Army, SW Pacific Area
19 mins IWM

Australian army at war
The fighting story of the Australian Army on both sides of the world; in North Africa, Greece, Crete and Syria; in Malaya and Singapore; and in New Guinea, the second largest island in the world, where the Australians stopped the Japanese advance at Eoribaiwa Ridge, the turning-point of the Pacific war. They then played a large part in the Allied drive which threw the invaders back over the Owen Stanley Range. The film ends at the capture of Shaggy Ridge
sp War Office *pc* Army Kinematograph Services
28 mins IWM

The battle for the Marianas
Close battle-pictures showing the reconquest by US forces of the Mariana Islands, Saipan, Tinian and Guam (the first piece of American territory the Japanese conquered)
Review MFB XII 79
sp US Office of War Information *pc* US Marine Corps & Warners
21 mins IWM NFA

A better tomorrow
New York City's school system includes 1,000 schools providing free education for nearly a million pupils. This film summarises the facilities provided, from the nursery classes to the senior high schools, some of which latter are technical or specialised but most of which offer courses that prepare students for the Universities
Review MFB XIII 73
pc US Office of War Information
23 mins

Bharata Natyam
The technique of the Bharata Natyam dance, showing mudras (or hand gestures), Natanam Adinar, a dance story in praise of Lord Nataraj, Lord of the Dance, and Tillana, an example of pure rhythmic dancing without story
pc Information Films of India
10 mins

Birds of the village
English resident birds and summer visitors, and how farmers and gardeners benefit by the activities of many of them. Birds included are: (residents) rooks, tree-creepers, coal tits, blue tits, missel-thrushes; (visitors) sand-martins, house-martins, chiff-chaffs, willow-warblers, cuckoos, chaffinches, linnets, turtle-doves
Review MFB XIV 105
MoI & Min of Ag *pc* Films of GB *p* Andrew Buchanan *assoc p* Edgar Anstey *d* Eric Hosking *ph* Charles Francis
18 mins NFA (incomplete)

The bridge
Post-war reconstruction in Yugoslavia. One of the most pressing needs is the restoration of communications, so that food and other supplies can be brought to places where they are needed. The film concentrates largely on the reconstruction of a typical village, and of an important bridge, with the miles of railway track leading up to it. Voluntary aid is enlisted from the local communities so that the work may be finished in time
Review DNL VI 47
sp COI *pc* Data *p* Donald Alexander *d* Jack Chambers *ph* Wolfgang Suschitsky *sc* Arthur Calder-Marshall
39 mins NFA

Britain can make it, no 1
(1) Prefabricated dry docks. (2) Motion study in factories. (3) A war artists' exhibition
Reviews DNL VI 24, MFB XIII 11
MoI & Min of Supply & Board of Trade *pc* Films of Fact *p* J B Holmes
11 mins NFA

Britain can make it, no 2
(1) Prefabricating kitchen and bathroom units. (2) Mannequin parade at a factory. (3) Works 'uncles'—a welfare experiment
Review DNL IV 24
MoI & Min of Supply & Board of Trade *pc* Films of Fact *p* Paul Rotha
11 mins

Britain can make it, no 3
(1) Change-over from airplane building to prefabricating houses. (2) Designing a new wireless set. (3) Canadian cattle round-up
MoI & Min of Supply & Board of Trade *pc* Films of Fact *p* J B Holmes
10 mins NFA

Britain can make it, no 4
(1) Germans, under Allied direction, clear up the wreckage of their country. (2) Youth Hostel holidays in Britain. (3) Women's shoes made from plastics
MoI & Min of Supply & Board of Trade

pc Films of Fact *p* J B Holmes
10 mins

Britain can make it, no 5
(1) Ways of using scrap from air-raid shelters. (2) Radar registers effects of sunspots. (3) A child visits a toy factory
MoI & Min of Supply & Board of Trade
pc Films of Fact *p* J B Holmes
10 mins

Britain can make it, no 6
(1) Converting airfield buildings to farm dwellings. (2) Making cricket bats from English willow. (3) Navigation by means of radar
MoI & Min of Supply & Board of Trade
pc Films of Fact *p* J B Holmes
11 mins

Britain can make it, no 7
(1) Mablethorpe plans a new type of sea-front. (2) Use of plastic models in aero-engine design. (3) Swindon Public Library's wide range of services
MoI & Min of Supply & Board of Trade
pc Films of Fact *p* J B Holmes
11 mins

Britain can make it, no 8
(1) Varied jobs of a harbour tug at Southampton. (2) Scientific methods of packing eggs. (3) A Cornish derelict mining area now produces mine-drilling equipment
MoI & Min of Supply & Board of Trade
pc Films of Fact *p* J B Holmes
11 mins

Britain can make it, no 9
(1) British production of agricultural machinery. (2) Machines for testing accuracy to one-millionth of an inch. (3) Designing new electrical equipment for domestic use
MoI & Min of Supply & Board of Trade
pc Films of Fact *p* J B Holmes
11 mins

Britain can make it, no 10
(1) A new type of folding boat, the peace-time venture of a famous aircraft factory. (2) Post-war British clock-production. (3) Setting up an undersea repeater station to improve cable communication with the Continent. (4) Making porous glass-filters
MoI & Min of Supply & Board of Trade
pc Films of Fact *p* J B Holmes
11 mins

Britain can make it, no 11
(1) Making a new ordnance survey map: including some experiments in a new technique, that of aerial survey. (2) Brick-making for the rebuilding of Britain
MoI & Min of Supply & Board of Trade
pc Films of Fact
11 mins

Britain can make it, no 12
The 'Britain can make it' exhibition of post-war goods at the Victoria and Albert Museum, London, in autumn 1946
MoI & Min of Supply & Board of Trade
pc Films of Fact
11 mins NFA

Canadian wheat story
Canadian work and wealth series. The story of the harvesting and milling of Canada's wheat, beginning on the farms and proceeding through all the stages until the grain issues finally in the form of loaves, which are turned out in thousands by the bakeries in the cities
Review MFB XIV 165
pc National Film Board of Canada
6 mins

Cattle country
Canadian work and wealth series. The care and raising of cattle in the Canadian West, for the markets of the world. Modern methods of protection and breeding are shown, and the vast herds are seen in seasonal migration. Finally

comes the time of marketing in the autumn
Review MFB XIV 165
pc National Film Board of Canada
8 mins

Civil Pioneers
The Civil Pioneers are a force drawn mainly from the landless labouring classes of remote villages. They undertake work anywhere in India, clearing forests and building roads, bridges and airfields. They have learnt new ways of living and working and new ideas about India
Review MFB XIV 133
pc Information Films of India
8 mins

Conquest of the forest
Lumbering in Northern Ontario and Quebec
Review MFB IV 20
10 mins silent

Corvette, Port Arthur
The story of a Canadian corvette escorting an Atlantic Convoy
pc National Film Board of Canada
22 mins IWM

Cyprus is an island
Changes brought about by modern methods to rural Cyprus under British administration
Reviews DNL VI 30, MFB XIV 165
MoI & Colonial Office *pc* Green Park *p & d* Ralph Keene *ph* George Still *sc* Laurie Lee *ed* Peter Graham Scott
34 mins NFA

Democracy at work
Supplementary film to *Partners in production* showing the work of Joint-Production and Labour-Management Committees in British factories to increase production during the war. Committees of this kind embody representatives of both management and workers, and normally operate also through specialised sub-committees, such as Absentee Committees and Accident Prevention Committees
pc National Film Board of Canada
20 mins

The development of the rabbit
Biology series. The film shows the simple cell division of the embryo sea urchin, describes the simplest species of egg-laying mammals, and proceeds to the embryology of the rabbit. Development of the rabbit embryo is shown by dissections and animated diagrams
Reviews FoB 1942-3, MFB XIV 13
sp British Council *pc* GB Instructional *p* C C Hentschel *d* Mary Field *ph* Frank Goodliffe
35 mins NFA

A factory in the Urals
The setting up, in record time, of a wartime automobile factory in the Urals, and an indication of its work of mass-production, not only for war but for the more lasting purposes of peace
sp Soviet Film Agency *pc* Central Documentary Film Studios
10 mins

Fight for life
The difficulties of native farming on the Gold Coast, through barren or misused soil, unhealthy conditions, and backwards methods, are being tackled and lessened by the local Department of Agriculture. Tsetse and other pests are being driven out, cattle immunised and their breeding and employment improved, wells dug, demonstration farms set up, and so on. The principle is that of indirect rule, through the native chiefs, and of partnership between white men and black
Review MFB XIV 165
MoI for Colonial Office *pc* Crown *d* John Page
17 mins NFA

Fighting sea fleas
MTBs of the Royal Canadian Navy in

action. (*Canada carries on* series)
pc National Film Board of Canada *p* Sidney Newman *d* Nicholas Read
11 mins IWM

From silkworm to parachute
The story of the breeding of silkworms, spinning of silk from the cocoons and processing of silk threads in the villages and factories of India
pc Information Films of India
12 mins

Garden of Eden
Life on the Euphrates, as seen from a cinema show-boat which served the riverside towns and villages during the war
Review MFB XIV 71
pc MoI (Middle East)
11 mins

Gold Coast builders
As a result of Achimota experiments, the government has introduced the manufacture of bricks, made from local clay. A demonstration shows how brick houses can replace the old mud huts
Review MFB XIV 134
MoI & Colonial Office *pc* Exploitation
11 mins

Golden coast
Old and new methods of gold production
pc New Zealand Govt
10 mins

The great game
Association Football, how it is played, what crowds it draws, and what it means to the players and spectators. The game is traced in its various forms from School Soccer to first-class professional play, and passages from the 1944 Cup Final games, showing at the end Bolton beating Chelsea, are included
Reviews FoB 1946, MFB XIV 167
sp British Council *pc* Verity *p & d* Reg Groves
29 mins NFA

Greetings to our English friends
Children at the Pravda Home for War Orphans send us a film of their activities, at work and play, as a greeting
sp Anglo-Soviet Youth Alliance *pc* Central Documentary Film Studios *ph & ed* P Atasheva, R Chalushakov, A Ovanessova
10 mins NFA

Handle with care
The inside story of a Canadian explosives factory. The nature and chemical composition of TNT is explained in moving diagrams. Work is done under special safety conditions and with deliberate slowness to avoid risks of disastrous explosions. (*Canada carries on* series)
pc National Film Board of Canada *p* Graham McInnes *d* George L George
18 mins IWM

Hands for the harvest
Half a million people left Canadian farms in war time for the Forces. The film describes how farming manpower was organised and shifted both within the industry and from outside—High School students and city workers—to meet successive harvest peaks across the varied farmlands of Canada
Review MFB XV 161
pc National Film Board of Canada *d* Stanley Jackson
22 mins

Hillmen go to war
Wool, timber, charcoal, resin, silk, starch from chestnuts, tea and potatoes from the villages of the Kulu Valley in the Himalayas in war time
pc Information Films of India *p* Ezra Mir *d* Kenneth Villiers *ph* Jinraj Bodhye *ed* S G Desai *m* Walter Kaufman
11 mins NFA

In rural Maharasthra
Daily life in the country of the soldier-farmers, the Mahrattas. The place of both men and women in the rural

economy is shown and the film includes a harvest celebration, a wedding ceremony, a religious festival, and a fair
Reviews DNL V 103, MFB XIII 144
pc Information Films of India
12 mins NFA

Indian handicrafts, no 1
Examples taken from Kashmir and the United Provinces in North India: Pashmina cloth, papier mâché work, wood carving, tapestry and rugs, brass-ware, modelling in clay and marble
Review MFB XII 159
pc Information Films of India *d* Krishna Gopal
11 mins

Indian handicrafts, no 2
Handicrafts of Travancore in South India: handbags and mats plaited from fibrous leaves; use of coloured sands and shells of Cape Comerin for ornamenting boxes; carving of buffalo horns into figures of birds and animals; hand-made lace of elaborate design
Review MFB XIV 122
pc Information Films of India
11 mins

Indian rubber
Natural rubber production in Travancore. The film shows preparation of the soil for plantations, grafting methods used to increase yield, collection of latex, and conversion first into sheet rubber and then into tyres
pc Information Films of India
11 mins NFA

Indian timber
Blue pine, walnut, fir, deodar and chini are among the more valuable timber-bearing trees in the forests of India. The film shows felling, sawing, transport to the mills and some of the war-time uses of the timber
Review MFB XIV 166
pc Information Films of India *d* M Bhavnani
10 mins NFA

Island target
A story of the Royal Australian Air Force typical of its work in the Pacific islands air war
pc Australian News & Information Bureau
d Ralph Stuart *nar* Wilfrid Thomas
19 mins IWM

A journey
Pictures of four communities solving local problems in war time: at Norfolk (Virginia), Detroit (Michigan), Mobile (Alabama), and Cache Valley (Illinois)
pc US Office of War Information
16 mins

Jungle patrol
An Australian infantry patrol takes a Jap post in New Guinea
Review DNL V 53
pc Australian News & Information Bureau
d Tom Gurr *ed* Frank Coffey
19 mins IWM

Kathak
Kathak is the classical dance of North India. The film gives a short 'dictionary' of the most common hand gestures and shows two dances, one of them accompanying a song in Sanskrit
Review DNL V 72
pc Information Films of India *p* Ezra Mir *d* Modhu Bhose *ed* Pratap Parmar
12 mins NFA

Kathakali
The gestures and pantomime of Kathakali, the dance drama of Malabar, one of the schools of classical Indian dancing, including scenes from Mahabharata
pc Information Films of India
10 mins NFA

Lessons in living
How the life of Lantzville, a small town in British Columbia, was transformed by a project which gave the children a creative part in the community life. They made furniture, curtains etc., for the schoolhouse. A derelict barn was reno-

vated, and served as community hall, gymnasium and workshop. Dramatics, folk-dancing, a farm radio forum, music appreciation classes, a school library and a school wireless set, were the result
pc National Film Board of Canada
22 mins

Library of Congress
An account of the scope and methods of operation of the Library of Congress at Washington. The Library's contents include valuable historical material, newsreel records of outstanding events and personalities, and Braille and talking-books (on discs) for the blind. (*American scene* series)
Review DNL VI 25
pc US Office of War Information
20 mins

Life on the western marshes
The measures taken by 'Ducks Unlimited' to protect North America's wild ducks and geese from the dangers which threaten them in their breeding grounds among the Western Marshes of Canada. The film also deals with the preservation of moose, beaver, musquash, the Canadian goose and cedar waxwing
pc National Film Board of Canada
13 mins colour

Manganese
Mining at Postmasburg: grading and sorting. Production of hard manganese steel
pc African Film Productions
10 mins NFA

Maori movielogue
1. Thermal regions; 2. A Maori village; 3. Holiday making on Stewart Island; 4. Moeraki rock formations; 5. A flight over the New Zealand Southern Alps
pc New Zealand Govt
10 mins

Melody of Hindustani
A description in picture and sound of some of India's musical instruments: Bansari (a flute), Mridanga (a drum), Sarangi (a fiddle) and Jaltarang (bowls filled with water)
pc Information Films of India
12 mins NFA

Mosquito squadron
Canadian-built Mosquitos of British design flown by Canadian and British airmen trained in Canada. (*Canada carries on* series)
pc National Film Board of Canada
11 mins IWM

Music in the wind
The craft of pipe-organ building, as practised at a factory in Quebec which has been in existence for a hundred years. Organ music accompanies the film throughout
pc National Film Board of Canada
10 mins

Musical instruments of India
India has more than 500 different instruments. This film shows the Saraswati Veena (string), the Senai (wind), the Sursagar and Sitar (string), and the Tabla and Baya (percussion)
pc Information Films of India
10 mins NFA

Niagara frontier
Full of orchards and fishing grounds and by tradition a tourist country, the Niagara peninsula is also an arsenal of hydro-electric power and a shipping and railway centre
Review MFB XIII 117
pc National Film Board of Canada
11 mins

Our northern cousins
Life and customs in a village of the Punjab, 'Land of the five rivers'
Review MFB XIV 90
pc Information Films of India *p* Ezra Mir
d Roop K Shorey
11 mins

Palmyrah
From the roots, the leaf, the trunk and the fruit of the Palmyrah tree a remarkable range of products is derived: sugar, alcohol, baskets, mats, temple fittings, fans, brushes, water channels, and much else
Reviews MFB XIII 38, MFB XIV 31
pc Information Films of India *p* Ezra Mir *d* K Busrahmanyam
9 mins

Papworth village settlement
The Papworth settlement for tubercular patients is a self-contained village community with full facilities both for the medical treatment of tuberculosis and for the living and working needs of the patients. Recovered patients can stay on at Papworth, living in hostels or in cottages with their families, and earning a normal livelihood, despite any remaining disability, in one of the settlement's own industries. (Film made in 1945)
Reviews DNL VI 8, FoB 1946, MFB XII 158, MFB XV 21
British Council *pc* World Wide *d* James Carr
20 mins NFA

Partners in production
The story of the Joint Production Committees in British war-time industry, with comments on their usefulness by Sir Stafford Cripps, then Minister of Aircraft Production, Mr Oliver Lyttelton (Minister of Production), and Major Gwilym Lloyd George (Minister of Fuel and Power). The kernel of the film is an incident at a north-country coal mine, when a pit committee's recommendation on a problem of reorganisation is referred to a branch meeting of the Miners' Union for acceptance. (Supplementary film issued in 1944 entitled *Democracy at work*)
pc National Film Board of Canada
28 mins

Passage to freedom
The story of how the Norwegian merchant navy was mobilised to serve the common cause
Review MFB XI 62
pc Norwegian Govt & Strand *d* Ivan Moffat *comm s* Valentine Dyall
20 mins IWM

Patterns of American rural art
Characteristic examples of rural arts and crafts in the US, including hand-weaving, tapestry, wood-carving, clay-modelling, metal work and pottery, figurines, and the beautiful cotton fabrics of Indian art
Review MFB XII 142
US Office of War Information *pc* US Dept of Ag
10 mins colour

The peacebuilders
Recapitulation of the international conferences which led to the formation of UNO. The Atlantic Charter meeting; the Washington meeting of 1942; Casablanca; the two Quebec Conferences; the Moscow Pact meeting; Teheran; Bretton Woods; the UNRRA meeting. Montreal (1944); Dumbarton Oaks; the World Trade Union Conference, London; Yalta; San Francisco
Review MFB XIV 90, MFB XIV 180
pc National Film Board of Canada
10 mins

People's bank
Spreading westwards from Quebec and the Maritimes to Ontario and the Prairie Provinces, Credit Unions have been formed in fishing, farming, mining and industrial communities, and put the practice of co-operative finance to the test of half a century. The film explains the structure of a typical Credit Union and shows how new branches and unions are organised
pc National Film Board of Canada
21 mins

Potato growing
Potato production on a fairly extensive

scale, using modern machinery. The operations shown are: ploughing and preparation of the soil, choosing seed, ridging, application of fertiliser, planting, covering, rolling, harrowing, cultivation (including hand-hoeing), earthing-up, spraying or dusting, lifting, picking, riddling and bagging
Review MFB XIII 176
MoI *pc* Films of GB
19 mins NFA

Potteries
Making crockery for daily use in a large mass-production factory in Gwalior State, where, as in Travancore and Bengal, pottery industries have recently grown up around the rich clay deposits of the region
pc Information Films of India
10 mins

Pottery in the Gold Coast
Achimota College brings to Africans, who have ancient pottery traditions, some of the skill of other countries
Review MFB XIV 30
MoI & Colonial Office *pc* Exploitation *p* James Mellor
10 mins NFA

Prescription for rubber
Synthetic rubber manufacture at the Polymer plant, Sarnia, Ontario. Out of the necessity of war-time needs has grown an important native industry, fulfilling peace-time as well as war-time purposes
Canadian Dept of Munitions and Supply *pc* National Film Board of Canada
8 mins

Proudly she marches
Women in the Canadian Services. (*Canada carries on* series)
pc National Film Board of Canada
18 mins IWM

RAAF over Europe
A view of the Royal Australian Air Force's work in Europe from 1939 onwards, as seen through the eyes of a member of an all-Australian bomber squadron based on Britain
Royal Australian Air Force *pc* RAF Film Unit
18 mins IWM

Radar
Newsreel account of the war-time uses of Radar in enemy plane spotting, ack-ack defence, naval operations, and rescue work. The uses of Radar in peace are hinted at
Review MFB XIV 133
pc Universal News
8 mins

School for farmers
An experimental school where classroom lessons are related to tasks and problems of farming, and practical farming is part of school work
Review MFB XIII 89
pc Information Films of India
10 mins NFA

Ship-busters
Planning and execution of a Mosquito attack on a German convoy in a Norwegian fjord
MoI & Air Min *pc* RAF Film Unit
15 mins CFL IWM

Soil erosion
A picture of the causes and effects of soil erosion in India and of the work of the Forest Department in showing villagers how to win back richness and health for their land
Reviews DNL V 93, MFB XIII 176
pc Information Films of India *p* Esra Mir *d* Kenneth Villiers
11 mins NFA

Steel town
Steel-making in Youngstown, Ohio—scenes from the foundries and mills, and

from the homes and private lives of the workers and their families
pc US Office of War Information
16 mins

Student nurse
Post-war jobs series *What's the next job?* This film was originally produced by the British Council for showing overseas, and has been adopted for this series. It reviews the three-year training from probationer to fully qualified State Registered Nurse, giving a picture of the trainee's daily life both on and off duty. Emphasis is laid on the thoroughness of the training and the seriousness of the nurse's responsibilities, and the film ends by indicating the opportunity open to a qualified nurse
Reviews DNL V 64, FoB 1944-5, MFB XIII 90
British Council *pc* GB Screen Services *d* Francis Searle *ph* Brendan Stafford
34 mins NFA

Substitution and conversion
The story of the turn-over to war production and of success achieved by American industry and the US Army in reducing the use of materials in short supply by using substitute materials and by redesigning equipment
US War Dept *pc* US Army Signal Corps
23 mins IWM

Sunshine province
Principal crops of New Zealand
Review MFB XV 36
pc New Zealand Govt
10 mins

Teheran
Teheran, the capital of Iran (Persia), looks both to the past and the future. The film shows the modern-style Parliament, characteristic palaces, mosques and shrines, and examples of Persian art
Review MFB XIV 171
pc MoI (Middle East) *p* Charles Martin *d & ph* Frank Hurley *comm s* Freddie Grisewood
9 mins NFA

This is colour
The meaning and many uses of colour. The development of modern synthetic dyes
Review DNL III 71
ICI *pc* Strand *p* Basil Wright *assoc d* Jack Ellitt *ph* Jack Cardiff *comm s* Dylan Thomas, Marjorie Fielding, Joseph Macleod, Valentine Dyall *m* Richard Addinsell
15 mins colour NFA

This is our Canada
A survey of Canadian life and of the development of the country's tremendous natural resources from the time of the pioneers to the present day. The film covers the depression of the 1930s and shows how war brought a great impetus to production and employment. (*Canada carries on* series)
pc National Film Board of Canada
19 mins

To the shores of Iwo Jima
The storming and capture, by American land, sea and air forces, of this key island in the Pacific, heavily fortified by the Japanese
Review MFB XII 113
US Office of War Information *pc* US Service Cameramen
20 mins NFA

Toscanini, hymn of the nations
Toscanini, seen both as musician and anti-Fascist, conducts the NBC Orchestra playing the overture to Verdi's *La Forza del Destino* and (with Jan Peerce and the Westminster Choir) Verdi's *Hymn of the Nations*, which includes Manueli's *Song to Italy, God Save the King*, and the *Marseillaise,* and to which he adds *The International* and *The Star-Spangled Banner* in his own orchestration

Review MFB XI 109
pc US Office of War Information *d* Alexander Hackenschmeid
28 mins

The town
Life in a typical American small town, Madison (Indiana). (*American scene* no 4)
Review MFB XI 35
pc US Office of War Information *p* Philip Dunne *d* Josef von Sternberg *sc* Joseph Krumgold *ph* Larry Madison
12 mins NFA

Trans-Canada express
In the building of Canada the railways have brought together the communities of the Atlantic and Pacific coasts, across the mountain ranges and the vast prairies, winding round the Great Lakes and reaching up to the sub-Arctic north. In the war they have played an essential part in the transport of men and arms to the fronts. (*Canada carries on* series)
pc National Film Board of Canada *d* Sidney Newman
18 mins

Trappers of the sea
Lobster fishing in Nova Scotia, which ships 28 to 30 million cans of lobster to all parts of the world every year. Since 1932 co-operative methods have been developing
pc National Film Board of Canada
12 mins

The tree of wealth
Wealth from the coconut palms of Travancore. The oil is used for soap, cooking and light, the fibre for yarn and matting, the flowers for making toddy and vinegar, the leaves for roofing, and the shells for fuel
Review MFB XIII 144
pc Information Films of India *d* Bhaskar Rao
11 mins NFA

Trees that reach the sky
Canadian work and wealth series. The story of a Sitka spruce from the forests covering the Pacific coast of Canada and how it was cut down, transported by road and water, and finally turned into a Mosquito bomber
pc National Film Board of Canada
8 mins

Tube wells
A new method of irrigation in the plain of the Ganges. Tube wells are drilled 50 to 200 feet deep. The water is brought to the surface by electrically driven pumps and is piped through cement pipes laid beneath the surface to the fields
pc Information Films of India
10 mins NFA

Universities at war
Canada's scientists and technicians help to win the war and plan the peace. (*Canada carries on* series)
pc National Film Board of Canada
20 mins IWM

Valley of the Tennessee
Soil erosion reduced to homelessness or poverty many of the inhabitants of the Valley of the Tennessee, which covers an area of 40,000 square miles. In 1933, under the inspiration of President Roosevelt, the Tennessee Valley Authority was created by Congress. A plan was made to build a series of great dams, to check floods and open the river to navigation from mouth to head waters; to help farmers restore the fertility of the soil; to re-forest millions of acres; to rehabilitate and develop industry in the cities; to electrify the farms. 'Test demonstration farmers' were persuaded to try out new methods of farming–contour-ploughing, use of new fertilisers, new cropping methods. Cooperative use of machinery was developed. A gigantic piece of national planning has become an unquestioned success in practice

Reviews MFB XII 41, MFB XIII 40
pc US Office of War Information *d* Alexander Hammid *nar* Frederick March
28 mins CFL

War birds
Carrier pigeons with the Royal Canadian Air Force. (*World in action* series)
pc National Film Board of Canada
16 mins IWM

Appendix 3

Why We Fight

The *Why we fight* series was produced by the War Department of the government of the United States. The films were designed to be an integral part of the training of American soldiers. They were vigorous, lavishly produced compilation films, related in concept and style to both the *March of time* series and to Nazi films such as *Feldzug in Polen*.

British views were divided over the films' usefulness as propaganda for Britain. Churchill liked them and wanted to have them promoted in Britain with a filmed introduction by himself. The Films Division, on the whole, opposed the approach represented by them. Hence, the films were not distributed by the Central Film Library until September 1944, and then only in limited numbers of copies. However, the Ministry of Information did not actively discourage individual cinemas from showing them when they appeared, and in the case of some, assisted in their theatrical distribution.

1. **Prelude to war**
   By recapitulating and illustrating the story of the rise of Fascism in Italy, Germany and Japan, and the history of Japanese and Italian territorial aggression before 1939, this film traces the basic reasons for America's participation in the war back beyond Pearl Harbour days, and describes the conflict as a war between two worlds—the world of the free peoples and the world of those who would put them back into slavery

sp US War Dept *pc* US Army Signal Corps *d* Major Frank Capra *sc* Major Eric Knight, Capt Anthony Veiller *nar* Walter Huston *m* Dmitri Tiomkin *ed* Capt William Hornbeck
52 mins CFL IWM

2. **The Nazis strike**
This film traces the story of German aggression from the rise of Hitler to the fall of Poland. The salient points are: German mania for conquest reaches a hysterical climax in Hitler; Haushofer and his 'geopolitics': Hitler's technique of aggression; militarisation of the Rhineland; seizure of Austria and Czechoslovakia; the Russo-German treaty; invasion of Poland; Russian occupation east of the Bug; declaration of war by Britain and France
Review MFB X 125
sp US War Dept *pc* US Army Signal Corps *d* Lt-Col Frank Capra, Major Anatole Litvak *sc* Major Eric Knight, Capt Anthony Veiller, Robert Heller *nar* Walter Huston, Capt Anthony Veiller *m* Dmitri Tiomkin *ed* Capt William Hornbeck
41 mins CFL IWM

3. **Divide and conquer**
The Germans halt in the east and turn west, invading and over-running Denmark and Norway, Holland, Belgium, Luxembourg and France. The evacuation of British and French troops from Dunkirk and the emergence of General de Gaulle as the leader of the French resistance outside France conclude this film
Review MFB X 123
sp US War Dept *pc* US Army Signal Corps *d* Lt-Col Frank Capra, Major Anatole Litvak *sc* Capt Anthony Veiller, Corp Robert Heller *nar* Walter Huston, Capt Anthony Veiller *m* Dmitri Tiomkin *ed* Capt William Hornbeck
56 mins CFL IWM NFA

4. **The Battle of Britain**
The defeat of the German plan to knock out the RAF and invade Britain in 1940 . . . The resistance of the RAF, the Londoners and the entire British people. (Loan limited to adult audiences)
Reviews DNL IV 227, MFB X 112
sp US War Dept *pc* US Army Signal Corps *sc* Capt Anthony Veiller *nar* Walter Huston, Capt Anthony Veiller *ed* Major William Hornbeck *m* Dmitri Tiomkin
53 mins CFL IWM NFA

5. **The battle of Russia**
This film covers the German campaigns in Russia up to the decisive turning of the tide of invasion at Stalingrad. The Nazis turn east again, attracted by the vast raw material supplies of Russia. The Balkans reduced to vassalage or conquered. Russia invaded, June 22nd, 1941. The Russian defence in depth; use of cities as fortresses; scorched earth policy; guerilla tactics; united resistance of the entire people. The first Russian Winter Offensive, 1941-42. The seige of Leningrad. Renewed German attack, 1942, directed on the Caucasus and the oilfields. Second Russian Winter Offensive and the German capitulation at Stalingrad, February 2nd, 1943
Reviews MFB XI 54

sp US War Dept *pc* US Army Signal Corps *d* Lt-Col Anatole Litvak *sc* Lt-Col Anatole Litvak, Capt Anthony Veiller, Corp Robert Heller *nar* Walter Huston, Capt Anthony Veiller *m* Dmitri Tiomkin *ed* Major William Hornbeck
83 mins CFL IWM NFA

Appendix 4

War Pictorial News

Special newsreels called *War pictorial news* were issued for distribution in the Mediterranean theatre of war; they were substantially compiled from items used by the newsreel companies in England but with a different commentary. The Imperial War Museum has an almost complete holding of this newsreel, but information concerning the date of issue has not been found for all of the surviving issues.

However, a reasonably full record has survived of the way events – at the front, at home and in the world at large – were presented to those serving in what was, for most of the war, the largest of Britain's armies.

1. Sept 1940?
The Fleet sinks an Italian warship in the Mediterranean–the warships *Ajax* and *Arethusa*: Egypt gives her loyal help to Britain–mobilization in Egypt: RAF raids Libya: India helps guard Britain's gateway to the East–Indian troops in Egypt: Captured Italian material: The Commander-in-Chief, General Sir Archibald Wavell issues his order of the day to the armies of the Middle East

2. Oct 1940?
In the Middle East–attack on a frontier fort in Libya: Prisoners of war–Italian: Kumangetit–the delivery of supplies to men in the outposts: The Polish legion: British Cavalry in Transjordan: A rich prize–merchant ship with £150,000 of goods: Egypt's coastal defences

3. Oct 1940?
In the Middle East—war in the Sudan: RAF in Western Desert: The Royal Navy bombards Capuzzo and Bardia

4. Nov 1940?

5. Nov 1940? Special edition
News from England—honours for the brave—King George VI awards decorations to members of the RAF: The Queen visits a hospital: General Ironside inspects home defences—inspection of troops: Women take over—women undertake war work: Aeroplane factories work day and night: Australian and Canadian troops reach England

6. 2 Dec 1940
Anthony Eden in the Middle East: Polish troops in England: Inspection of Free French Forces by HM the King and General de Gaulle: Greece on the warpath—funeral of the first British airman killed in Greece: Further RAF re-inforcements land in Greece: War views of third-time President Roosevelt

7. 16 Dec 1940
London can take it: 3026 planes brought down over England: Britain prepares to strike—the mechanisation of the Army since Dunkirk: Don't let's waste anything: Republic day in Turkey: The Greeks advance—Koritza falls: Off to the front—Greeks force their way into Albania on all fronts: Albania—Greek mountain troops capture Koritza road

8-12. (Not yet catalogued)

13. 10 March 1941
Britain mightier yet—British tank units on manoeuvres: New Governor of Cyrenaica—General Sir Harry Wilson: Mr Anthony Eden visits Turkey: Eritrea—Allied troops maintain forward drive against Italians: Wendell Wilkie visits England

14. (Not yet catalogued)

15. 7 April 1941
Britain is ready—Churchill visits Britain's defence forces: General de Gaulle in Cairo: Giarabub surrenders: Capture of Keren

16. 21 April 1941
General de Gaulle entertained at British Embassy in Cairo: Malta's air defence—people go about normal work: Battle of the Matapan: Re-inforcements for Greece: Fall of Asmara: Adi Ugri—a prison camp of Indian and British soldiers is liberated

17-24. (Not yet catalogued)

25. 25 Aug 1941
Syria–British military authorities arrange for the repatriation of Vichy troops: Abyssinia–the story of Mussolini's last Abyssinian stronghold: News from England–parachute troops in England undergo training

26-28. (Not yet catalogued)

29. 20 Oct 1941
RAF Shark Fighter Squadron: Russian and British troops in Iran: Dramatic pictures of the war in Russia–spirit and morale of Russian people very high

30. (Not yet catalogued)

31. 17 Nov 1941
Turkey–18th anniversary of Foundation of the Republic: Russia–Odessa: All eyes on Singapore

32. 1 Dec 1941
Shells from South Africa: New Hurricane on warpath–the 4 cannon gun Hurricane: Latest news from Russia–struggle for Russia continues: Western desert–General Cunningham and Admiral Cunningham meet before the main advance

33. (Not yet catalogued)

34. 22 Dec 1941
South Africa's total effort: Gondar falls–Italy loses her last remaining stronghold in Abyssinia: News from England–King George VI and Queen Elizabeth visit an RAF Personnel Reception Centre: Russia hits back–Russia on the offensive–Nazis retreat

35-38. (Not yet catalogued)

39. 26 Jan 1942
News from England–American manufactured lend-lease planes to be assembled into complete machines in Britain: South America–Brazil's modernized submarine fleet, and her sympathies with America and the Allies: Canada–the production of tanks at Montreal: New Zealand–parade of troops and women, and war materials produced by New Zealand

40-41. (Not yet catalogued)

42. 16 Feb 1942
Soviet offensive–including the arrival in Moscow of General Sikorsky

43. (Not yet catalogued)

44. 2 March 1942
To-gether to Victory—Churchill receives a huge welcome in Ottawa and at the White House

45. 9 March 1942
The day will come—special issue about Japan

46. 16 March 1942
America's new Flying Wing: Indian heroes honoured: The Yanks arrive: Polish troops in Russia: Abyssinia—agreement ratified between Britain and Ethiopia

47. (Not yet catalogued)

48. 30 March 1942
South Africa—a Transvaal military camp: Personalities in the Middle East—King George of Greece and Sir Stafford Cripps visit Egypt: Russia—Sevastopol

49. 6 April 1942
The rape of Russia—a small Russian town, captured by Germans

50. (Not yet catalogued)

51. 20 April 1942
India—special issue about the contribution of India

52. 27 April 1942
Russia—entertainment is part of the war effort: Exchange of prisoners of war—Italian POWs, officers and men who are sick and wounded exchanged for British POWs—British POWs arrive back in Alexandria and are welcomed by the dockers there: Where next?—practice manoeuvres for the invasion of Bruneval in Northern France: Lofoten—a similar raid here: Spitzbergen: Vaagso—the commandos strike again

53. 4 May 1942
Bomber Command strikes again: Two nations unite—China and India: Russian offensive—Marshal Timoshenko in conference with his staff

54-56. (Not yet catalogued)

57. 1 June 1942
Duke of Gloucester visits Iran: Greece fights on—Greeks celebrate National Day of Greece in Egypt: Personalities in the Middle East—Field Marshal Smuts: With the Free French in the Chad

58. 8 June 1942
Commandos raid on Boulogne: Russia will avenge—Sassino village burns after German attack: New tank triumphs—American tanks for the Libyan Campaign

59-61. (Not yet catalogued)

62. 13 July 1942
'Well done'—British destroyers enter Courier Bay on expedition to Madagascar

63. (Not yet catalogued)

64. 27 July 1942
On Three Fronts! British help to Russia—RAF raid on Cologne—Action at Alamein

65. 3 Aug 1942
News from America: News from England—General Sir Alan Brooke sees US troops in Northern Ireland: 20th May 1942—Russian bomber bearing Mr Molotov arrives in England for signing Anglo-Soviet Treaty: Western Desert

66-68. (Not yet catalogued)

69. 31 Aug 1942
News from England—speed-up of tank output: Fighting France—Bastille Day 1942—Free France celebrates in London: Britain delivers the planes

70. (Not yet catalogued)

71. 14 Sept 1942
15th September 1940—This day saved the world—the Battle of Britain

72-73. (Not yet catalogued)

74. 5 Oct 1942
News from England—Norwegians in Britain: Lancashire—the provision of a creche for working mothers: More and more tanks: Malta gets George Cross

75-76. (Not yet catalogued)

77. 26 Oct 1942
News from England—American armies cross the Atlantic as in 1917: Brazil enters the war: Another convoy reaches Malta

78. 2 Nov 1942
News from England—Mr Churchill inspects the Civil Guard: Dieppe Operation:

The 8th Army attacks–General Alexander decorates French heroes of Bir Hakeim: Friday October 23rd 1942–8th Army's attack on Rommel's line begins

79. (Not yet catalogued)

80. 16 Nov 1942
China today–Wendell Wilkie visits Chiang Kai-Shek

81. 23 Nov 1942
News from England–American Squadrons of Flying Fortresses: The Axis runs west–the capture of General von Thoma

82. 30 Nov 1942
Promises fulfilled–convoy of ships bearing arms and tanks for Russia: American Eagle Squadrons transfer to the US Air Force: Port Moresby, Papua–Australians supplied by Papuan people

83. (Not yet catalogued)

84. 14 Dec 1942
Commando spirit spreads–Colonial troops: Russian offensive

85. 21 Dec 1942
Where next, Mussolini?–The Middle East fighting front

86-87. (Not yet catalogued)

88. 11 Jan 1943
New British battleships–HMS *Hove* and HMS *Anson*: Fighting French commandos: Genoa bombed–keynote, vengeance

89-95. (Not yet catalogued)

96. 8 March 1943
Raid on Naples: Russia–President Kalinin addresses the people of Russia at Christmas time

97. 15 March 1943
India–homeless victims of Bengal cyclone are fed from relief kitchens: New Zealand–United Nations Day in New Zealand: Russia 'The struggle against the Hun invader goes on relentlessly'

98. 22 March 1943
Canada–trainees of Commonwealth Air Training Plan: Greek Navy: ATS sewing school: Russia–counter offensive on Northern front

99. 29 March 1943
Stalingrad—last few hours of the siege

100. 5 April 1943
100th Edition: Introduction by Rt Hon Mr R G Casey, British Minister of State for the Middle East, who speaks of how *War Pictorial News* tries to give the true reflection of the pattern of events. The events leading up to the present stage of the war are shown retrospectively

101. 12 April 1943
Rough riders—military police training depot in the Middle East with training courses for Americans and British: China: Proof positive—close-ups, before and after, of precise bombings of specific targets of RAF

102-111. (Not yet catalogued)

112. 28 June 1943
Allies' Week opens in Cairo: Clothing the army—a laundry and repair depot in the Middle East: US bombers raid Taranto

113. 5 July 1943
Churchill's tour of the Middle East: North African rest camp: Russia—Black Sea navy: Thanksgiving for Victory in Tunisia

114. 12 July 1943
News from England—holidays—what to do in them now that travelling is discouraged: Paratroops in Middle East: Supplement—tribute to a great leader—General Sikorsky

115-119. (Not yet catalogued)

120. 23 Aug 1943
News from England—the Allies' swimming event is won by Home Guardsman Grey: New Zealand—a NZ sheep station: Sicily—the Sicilian campaign is over

121-126. (Not yet catalogued)

127. 11 Oct 1943
King of Yugoslavia arrives in Middle East: Burma—Indian soldiers take enemy-occupied ridge and village: Persia—travelling dispensaries provided by British and Indian Army Medical Services: Dogs of the Army: News from England—how British workers spend their well-earned leave

128. (Not yet catalogued)

129. 25 Oct 1943
Mission to Moscow—Mr Eden en route for Moscow, visits Cairo: Alamein

1943—now a peaceful wayside station: The Italian battlefront—the Allies liberate Southern Italy

130. 1 Nov 1943
Strong Arm of the RAF—Germany bombed: Egypt digs for Victory: In New Guinea Jungle—General Sir Thomas Blaney inspects difficult terrain: With the Black Sea Fleet

131. (Not yet catalogued)

132. 15 Nov 1943
Egypt—King Peter of Jugoslavia is presented with 4 bombers by Major General Royce: Training pilots, Australia: Raids on Burma: Moscow Conference

133. 22 Nov 1943
Blitzing German airfields: Italy day by day: News from England—the King and Queen inspect a contingent of 4th Indian Division in Britain: Russia—ceremony in Stalingrad

134. 28 Nov 1943
England—ATS Birthday parade: Russia—War in the Kuban: Middle East—armour on parade—parade on anniversary of Alamein Battle

135. 16 Dec 1943
The Mahmal leaves for Mecca: Cotton goes to war: Rewards for gallantry: Smashing German war targets: Russia—the battle for the guns

136. 13 Dec 1943
The Grand Alliance: Official Record of the Pacific Conference and the Teheran Conference

137. 20 Dec 1943
Women who serve the guns: Christmas cheer for home—Troops stationed in the Middle East go Christmas shopping in the bazaars of Cairo: Elephants push for the war effort—Burma: Around the clock in Stalingrad—rebuilding the city

138. 27 Dec 1943
Middle East Field Marshal Smuts visits Cairo: Russia—action along the Black Sea front

139-140. (Not yet catalogued)

141. 17 Jan 1944
Gunners of Hindustan: Hospital toy makers—convalescent troops, recovering at a military hospital near Cairo: Demon pilots of Australia: Russia—the southern section

142-145. (Not yet catalogued)

146. 21 Feb 1944
Aviation news–the new helicopter: Middle East News: War news–Malta–sinking of the *Scharnhorst*

147. 28 Feb 1944
News from England–Winston Churchill, home again: Middle East News–service men and women visit ancient pyramid: Russia–the Russian offensive up and down the entire front, Stalin makes speech

148-149. (Not yet catalogued)

150. 20 March 1944
Burma–on Arakan front: Middle East News–football match–Wanderers versus Egyptians: Russia–Russians cross the Dnieper

151-153. (Not yet catalogued)

154. Britain today

155. 24 April 1944
The 'Eyes' of war–the process by which lenses are made

156-157. (Not yet catalogued)

158. 15 May 1944
India–Lord Wavell visits Bombay Province: Middle East News–a bicycle race in Cairo, organised by British forces: Australia–Chinese refugees: Bombing of the *Tirpitz*

159-161. (Not yet catalogued)

162. 50 Years of cinematography: special issue

163. 6 June 1944
Special–invasion!–Allied invasion of Northern France: Middle East News–on the birthday of George VI: Pacific–the Ramu valley in New Guinea: News from England–the problems of the maintenance of supplies to the Anzio beach-head: Russia–Stalingrad being rebuilt

164. 26 June 1944
The Fall of Rome: The invasion of France

165. 3 July 1944
Invasion battlefront–France

166-173. (Not yet catalogued)

174. 1944
France–retreating Nazis–US troops liberate Rennes–Red Army enters Rumania

175-176. (Not yet catalogued)

177. 25 Sept 1944
Paris–the inside story of the French Resistance

178-180. (Not yet catalogued)

181. 23 Oct 1944
Italy–advance on Tuscany: Burma–general scenes of jungle fighting

182. (Not yet catalogued)

183. 6 Nov 1944
Western Front–bombing by RAF of enemy ships at Brest: Airgraphs–process of transferring letters to microfilm: Greece–Allied paratroopers embark for assault on Greece

184. (Not yet catalogued)

185. 13 Nov 1944
Liberation of Greece–special issue

186. (Not yet catalogued)

187. 3 Dec 1944
Holland (Allied campaign to clear Scheldt Estuary): Poland–Marshal Rokossovsky watches his men cross the River Bug: Churchill in Russia

188. 11 Dec 1944
Western Front–the battle of the Scheldt Estuary: Women railway workers–women seen doing all jobs necessary to keep the railways running: Italy–the 4th Indian Division smash through the Gothic line

189. 18 Dec 1944
Burma–the 14th Army in Arakan: Sinking of the *Tirpitz*: Churchill in Paris

190. 25 Dec 1944
Pacific–General MacArthur moves his forces from Port Moresby: News from England–King George VI visits the Centre for Islamic Culture in London: Nazi atrocities in Poland

191. 1 Jan 1945
Albania–in Tirana, the people celebrate independence day: Tribute to a cameraman: A story of wood–how plywood is processed and made into Mosquito planes

192-194. (Not yet catalogued)

195. 29 Jan 1945
Greece–Athens welcomes British troops: Russian advance–the eve of the final assault on Warsaw

196-198. (Not yet catalogued)

199. MacArthur returns to Philippines–Leyte Island: Greece–supplies arrive for the Greek people: An historic meeting–Mr Churchill sets out for an important meeting in Cairo

200. 5 March 1945
News from RN–HMS *Indefatigable* is inspected by King George VI: The 'Big Three' meeting–the Yalta Conference: Egypt mourns a great leader–the funeral of Ahmed Maha Pasha

201. (Not yet catalogued)

202. 19 March 1945
King Farouk visits British Navy: Burma–on the road to Mandalay

203. (Not yet catalogued)

204. 2 April 1945
Australia–members of the WAAF service, a Spitfire, and the guns: Alexander meets Tito: Nylon goes to war: Britain's post-war homes: Churchill on Siegfried Line

205. 9 April 1945
Into Germany

206. 16 April 1945
Queen Wilhelmina in Holland: Victory at Mandalay

207. (Not yet catalogued)

208. 30 April 1945
News from England—the King and Queen visit Lancashire: British Fleet in the in the Pacific: Western Front

208A. Victory in Europe—special issue reviewing the history of the war

209. 7 May 1945
In Memory of President Roosevelt: With the medical services: Cleaning up the Ruhr

210. (Not yet catalogued)

211. 21 May 1945
East meets West—advance units of American and Soviet Armies meet on the banks of the Elbe river: Germans capitulate—8th Army enters Bologna: Mass German surrender in Italy: This is the moment—Montgomery receives surrender of German Forces

212. 28 May 1945
Holland freed: On the Burma front—14th Army goes into action

213. 4 June 1945
Food to Holland: Germany 1945—unconditional surrender: London—victory celebrations

214. 11 June 1945
Prisoners fly home: Liberation of Denmark: War in the Pacific

215. 18 June 1945
Ethiopia—Haile Selassie discusses the modernisation of the Ethiopian Army with British advice: U-Boats surrender—British Navy rounds up U-Boats: Germany today—German leaders arrested—concentration camps film compulsorily shown

216. 25 June 1945
Inside Germany: Czechoslovakia—President Benes returns amid rejoicing crowds: Rangoon freed

217. (Not yet catalogued)

218. 9 July 1945
Liberation of the Channel Islands: Bridge-carrying tanks: Pacific landings on Borneo: London welcomes Eisenhower

219-220. (Not yet catalogued)

221. 30 July 1945
Special–Potsdam Conference: Draining flooded Holland: The war against Japan: Berlin–Berlin in full Allied occupation

222-223. (Not yet catalogued)

224. 20 Aug 1945
Victory over Japan–special issue reviewing story of Japan's wars

225. (Not yet catalogued)

226. 3 Sept 1945
First hours of Peace–opening of Parliament: Labour Government: Thanksgiving: Lights go on

227. (Not yet catalogued)

228. 17 Sept 1945
King and Queen with the Princesses lead the nation in a day of thanksgiving for victory over Japan: Japs surrender in Burma: The Atomic Bomb–test explosion

229. 24 Sept 1945
Middle East News–Alexandria–high ranking British and Egyptian officers hold commemoration of the Battle of Britain: The Far East–on the Battleship *Missouri* American and British celebrate victory: News from England–a factory goes back to peace time manufacture–from Spitfires to cars: *Beaverbell* the first ship to be launched on Clydeside since the war

World Pictorial News

From issue 230 *War pictorial news* became *World pictorial news*, which was distributed in occupied territories until August 1946.

230. 1 Oct 1945
News from England–racing in peace time, the St Leger: Harvest time–harvesting the grain, fruit and vegetables in Britain–German prisoners of war help with root harvest: Dances–old and new in Burma

231. 8 Oct 1945
Singapore–official surrender of the Japanese: Five Power Conference–Lancaster House, St James–a council of the foreign ministers of Britain, America, Russia, China and France: Middle East News–the SS *Marawi* comes into Suez with 40,000 ex-POWs from the Far East: Allied Fleet in Tokio Bay

232. 15 Oct 1945
Britain's finest hour—a gathering in London for the 5th Anniversary of the Battle of Britain: Belsen trials: Surrender signed—Japan

233. 22 Oct 1945
Royal visit to Scotland—Princess Elizabeth attends a Girl Guide rally in Edinburgh—a victory parade and march past: Frog men—the part played in D-Day: The Far East—armoured columns move into Tokio

234. (Not yet catalogued)

235. 5 Nov 1945
The Far East—the aftermath: Hainan—British POW camp visited: Singapore—Japanese guards remove the prison barricades—the skeleton-like prisoners scramble for cigarettes: Southampton—ex-POWs return: Liverpool—ex-POWs return: Singapore—parade welcoming the Allies

236. 12 Nov 1945
The Far East—suspected war criminals: V2 rocket—the rocket, fired by British engineers over the North Sea: Germany—refugees and new education for German children

237-238. (Not yet catalogued)

239. 3 Dec 1945
Personality parade—the Middle East: Domestic use of plastics: Germany—conditions in Berlin: Air-speed record—the British Meteor

240. 10 Dec 1945
Europe—German children evacuated from Berlin: German prisoners enlarge the courtroom for the trials of Nazi war criminals: Anniversary of liberated Dutch town: The Far East—Royal Navy arrives in Korea: New Delhi—celebrations and decorations: Attlee visits America

241. 17 Dec 1945
Trial begins—Nuremberg

242. 24 Dec 1945
Europe—Churchill visits Belgium, fuel-problems in Germany, refugee camps, etc

243. (Not yet catalogued)

244. 7 Jan 1946
Fashions of today: Last of the U-Boats—Navy destroys the last U-boats: Midget car race: We must remember—return of Australian POWs, film of Changi POW camp

245. (Not yet catalogued)

246. 21 Jan 1946
India–the Kashmir Valley: England–aircraft carriers and jet fighters: Empire Pool, Wembley, gymnastic display: Japan: Vienna today

247-249. (Not yet catalogued)

250. 18 Feb 1946
Civil aviation: Rugger–Kiwis versus Wales: Japs evacuate Korea: Germany–health in Hamburg: Farewell to US troops

251-252. (Not yet catalogued)

253. UNO elects Secretary General: The latest in British hairstyles: UNRRA Supplies to Europe

254. More goods on the way–British industry's peace time work: Nobel Peace Prizes: Flax industry–Australia: Rough riders at Rodeo–Australia

255. (Not yet catalogued)

256. News from England: India–shark fishing: Britain's food problem: Russians and Japs at the polls

257-265. (Not yet catalogued)

266. Repair work is in progress: News from Germany–repairing bombed towns: News from England

267-270. (Not yet catalogued)

271. News from England–De Haviland Dove airliner: Italy votes: Arab Legion presents Colours: News from Germany–a fair in Berlin

272. News from Italy: Sports news–Ascot and Wimbledon: The wonders of Science–National Physical Laboratory, Kew: Paris–Big Four talks

273. Munich museum–rare musical instruments

274. (Not yet catalogued)

275. 12 Aug 1946
News from England–Mountbatten receives freedom of City of London: Tragedy in Jerusalem–bomb at King David Hotel: The Atomic Bomb–Bikini

276. (Not yet catalogued)

277. 26 Aug 1946
Paris, Peace Conference: Jubilee of motoring–fifty years of motoring in Great Britain: Sports news

Warwork News & Worker and Warfront

From the summer of 1942 two special newsmagazines were prepared for showing in factories and places of social recreation to people working in the war industries–*Warwork news* and *Worker and warfront.*

The following two lists are based on viewing the issues.

Warwork News

Each part of *Warwork news* was issued fortnightly. Some stories were reissued in commercial newsreels such as British Paramount News.

The Imperial War Museum has complete holdings of these newsreels, including the first two which were pilot issues made in the Spring of 1942.

A. Grand alliance–Molotov greets Eden in Russia: Halfava stormed by RAF: Cripps on Russia: Mines in millions

B. How your work delivers the goods–Patrick Ashley Cooper, Minister of Finance: Army lifts veil over latest gun–new 'Viza' in action: Commandos of the air–the Parachute Squad

1942

1. Sir Andrew Duncan, Minister of Supply, explains aims of *Warwick News*: Weapons of war–the Ministry of Supply

2. Factory beats bomber: Biggest convoy reaches India

3. British enter France

4. Workers fire guns they make: Lumberjills save timber exports–the Women's Timber Corps at work: Moscow meeting–Churchill flies to Moscow

5. Warworkers meet Dieppe raiders

6. Former gaol—new factory: Red flows the Don

7. Band adds fuel to miners effort—a Yorkshire colliery: Big flax harvest aids war effort—Aberdeenshire

8. Exchange plan ends tool bottle-neck: New nursery scheme for working mothers

9. The offensive phase: Eisenhower and the American Campaign from Casablanca to Algiers

10. The road of Tunis

11. From dump to front line—waste nothing in the Army: Tripoli: Special—Italy blitzed

12. From slag heaps to dream cities—speeding war production by machine: With RAF over Holland

1943

13. Ministry of Supply receives 8th Army's thanks: The promise of 1942—stirring events shown: The promise of victory

14. Italy 'gets it' from North Africa: New men-o-war swell US Navy—a new battleship *New Jersey*: How 8th Army spent Christmas: British mission sees China at war

15. Warrior of the week—Major Albrook: The other man's job—making copper cables: They planned victory—the Anglo-American meeting in Casablanca

16. The other man's job—bombs from sea water: The victory you made possible—8th Army attack Tripoli

17. Warrior of the week—Major Ling of Royal Tank Regiment: The other man's job—making the guns: Stalingrad—the end

18. There's not much women can't do: You are sending them the tools

19. Warrior of the week—Captain Harris, 8th Army: The other man's job—locomotives for 2nd front: New supplies aid Tunis offensive

20. The other man's job—the manufacture of jerry-cans: Tunis—all set for victory

21. Allies mass on Tunisian front: Warrior of the week: King honours war workers: Bomb cases for 1,000 pounders

22. Royal Academy portrait of the girl–Miss Ruby Loftus, a factory worker: On the Soviet industrial front–factory life in the USSR: Warrior of the week–Sergeant Miller: Allies on move East of Suez: Breakthrough in Tunisia

23. Warrior of the week–Squadron Leader Hall: The other man's job: Air power–the means of victory: First victory parade in Tunis

24. ATS train dogs of war: Mr Churchill in Congress in Washington: Mediterranean now *our* lake: Boy-labour runs key war-plant: The other man's job–ship repairers beat U-boats

25. The other man's job–new lamps for victory: Warrior of the week–Flying Officer McCann: Pantellaria surrenders–first pictures

26. The other man's job–reclaimed timber: Warrior of the week–Gunner Wright: London honours premier

27. The other man's job–making tank landing craft: Warrior of the week–Master Sergeant Watkins: Mubo wrested from Japanese–New Guinea: Arms pour into Sicily

28. Weapons display draws London: Warrior of the week–Sergeant Cowan of the Royal Marine Artillery: The other man's job–making tank transporters: Italy going out

29. The other man's job–steel tubes for victory: Warrior of the week–Captain Lal Kapur of the 4th Indian Division: Last hours in Sicily

30. More and more from less and less–super-salvage exhibition in London: Warrior of the week–Engineer Sub Lieut W J Scarlett: Churchill in Quebec: Battle of Berlin: Allies enter Messina

31. The other man's job–medals to the brave: Warrior of the week–Major Ashford-Russell of the Commandoes: Italy opens way to Nazi Germany: Canada honours President Roosevelt

32. China aids growing Far East offensive: Churchill in US: Thunderbolts speed Flying Forts over Europe: The other man's job–the sword of Stalingrad

33. Cotton goes to war–the other man's job: Allies enter Naples

34. Alamein–a year after: Allies prepare drive on Rome: The other man's job–manufacture of ball bearings

35. The other man's job–making stings for Mosquitos: AMGOT brings Naples bread: Personalities in the news–the Marquess of Linlithgow, Viceroy of India: Red Army and Moscow talks shorten war

36. How to make do and mend: News in flashes: The other man's job–equipment for airborne troops

37. Food for thought–factory canteens: Allies resume the offensive: Surrender or else–Malta

1944

38. Duce rescued from captivity–captured German film: 8th in Ortona, 5th go forward: In 1944 your health is the first front–Air Chief Marshall Harris advises war workers to keep fit

39. New pipeline serves Allies in Italy: Ulster at arms–the war effort

40. The other man's job–making copper and brass tubes: Mines and detectors: 8th Army hits out as landing goes well: Allies turn on heat in Pacific

41. RAF stave off day attack on French targets: King and Queen tour Yorks coalfields: The other man's job–runways for attack

42. Monastery bombed, Monte Cassino: The other man's job–the 'eyes' of the warrior–manufacture of lenses

43. The battle of Germany–the increasing use of very heavy bombs by the RAF: Monty on the factory front–General Montgomery visits factory workers

44. The other man's job–carbide in war: Cassino bombing–first pictures

45. The other man's job–new boots from old: Workers man improved night defences

46. Heiress to the throne–Princess Elizabeth: Tito partisans train in Malta: News in flashes: The other man's job–jute output meets myriad war-time needs

47. War leaders see best war Academy: PM's wife visits 'Churchill House': The miracle of penicillin–the practical results of war-time research

48. King sees Navy on invasion eve: The other man's job–plastics give eyes to the forces

49. Nazis jittery say returned prisoners: Rome in sight–General Alexander sends a large force to Anzio: The other man's job–felt goes to war on all fronts

50. Churchill visits war front—the battle of Normandy

51. Cherbourg captured (first pictures): Holidays at home will speed peace: The other man's job—the Bailey bridge to victory

52. Battle in Normandy—'the great campaign for which we have toiled since Dunkirk': The other man's job—plywood invades Europe

53. How Nazis left Rome—first pictures: Deep shelters make alert—underground shelters for Londoners: The other man's job—Bren carriers fall out for victory

54. The crucial phase—Northern France: The other man's job—puncture proof tyres

55. Medical supplies make Army fittest ever—the other man's job: To victory through France

56. The other man's job—springs for victory: Flying bombs defeated—full story

57. Send troops your books: The other man's job—rockets give fighter planes a new punch: Greatest airborne operations—Arnhem

58. Bases of victory—control of the Channel reverts to Britain: The other man's job—British flame thrower is master weapon

59. The other man's job—how Army packs its punch: These men are heroes: Allies prepare new offensive

60. Cologne a dying city—Bomber Command: Allies win both banks of Scheldt: The other man's job—mica the vital insulator

61. China suffers local set-back: The other man's job—panniers for airborne: RAF sink *Tirpitz*

62. Pressure mounts in Saar battle: Shells, shells, more shells—Eisenhower explains to workers: The other man's job—the Earthquake bomb—12,000 pounder bombs

1945

63. Soviet Army frees Lublin: News in flashes: The other man's job—demand soars for TLC engines

64. The other man's job—women speed primer output: News in flashes

65. Awards to the heroes of filling factories: Allies stop the rot—Montgomery and the Battle of the Bulge

66. Millboard means good munitions: The capital of mercy—Geneva carries on: British land at Akyab—SW of Mandalay: All snowbound on the Western front

67. Paint preserves vital weapons: How Allies repaired the bridges: Accent on carriers

68. Stormboats for War in Pacific: RAF fly to aid Chinese: Eve of assault in West: Rockets for the Japanese

69. The other man's job—glass to stop bullets: Cologne captured

70. The other man's job—filling Ten-Ton Tess: Remagen bridge collapses: British storm island off Burma: Balloons warn Germans

71. Tokio under fire: The other man's job—feeding the Five-point-fives: Monty sweeps through Reich

72. Industry looks ahead—new scheme for training: Advance discloses German horrors

73. Germany in the dust—death of a nation

74. 'Our dear Channel Islands': Clothing for war and peace—the other man's job: Denmark and Norway hail the British

75. The other man's job—the Bridgelayer tank: Lancaster back from Polar flight: Fido secret released: Aftermath in Germany

76. The other man's job—tanks to beat Japan: London honours General Eisenhower

77. Moscow salutes victory: Army print newspaper in 5 languages: War factory in Guy Fawkes cellars: Flame against the Hun invasion—secret revealed

78. King and Queen visit Isle of Man: The other man's job—close shave for Tommy: Desert Rats in Berlin—the utter defeat in Germany

79. Pétain faces trial: Packing speeds end of Japs—the other man's job: Desert Rats in Berlin—a victory march

80. The other man's job—gears for everything: World War over—Japan surrenders

81. The other man's job–it's cooler inside–manufacture of refrigerators: Scientist praises Atomic Bomb–at a Foyle's luncheon: Berlin still 'going down': Borneo–the last phase

Worker and Warfront

These newsreels were produced by Paul Rotha Productions and Films of Fact, and each has a running time of ten minutes.

All issues are held by the Imperial War Museum, except for numbers 11 and 17.

1. May 1942
Priority cards for essential war workers: Sand filters for tanks in the desert: American tug *Narcissus*, used in *Tugboat Annie* now at work in Britain as the *Sabine*: Spiders' webs used in optical gunsights: Workers brass band

2. July 1942
1942 wartime agricultural show contrasted with the Royal Agricultural Show in 1939: National Union of Seamen use country house as HQ after being bombed out of London: Extending part-time employment of housewives: USSR factory, entertainment and work

3. Nov 1942
British dockers repair ships in record time: Removal of park railings: Cartoonist Low on Soviet war cartoons: 'Hi Gang' cast item for war workers

4. Jan 1943
Building an airfield in Britain for US bombers: How recipes are selected for Freddie Grisewood's radio programme *Kitchen front*: Making camouflage netting: Queensbury Club services membership

5. May 1943
Wartime work in the Northumberland coalmines: New production methods and uses of charcoal: Sortie by Bristol Beaufighters in North Africa

6. July 1943
Women workers make barrage balloons and rubber dinghies: 'Airgraph' communications explained: Rhondda Valley choir sings translated Russian anthem as tribute

7. Sept 1943
Secrecy at work as workmen find out that they are to clean statues moved out of London for safety: National Production Contest for British factories: Agricultural workers cooperate to solve shortages

8. Nov 1943
Manufacture of the De Havilland Mosquito: Cartoon warning about blood-poisoning: Blitzed cinema now makes mine detectors

9. Jan 1944
London taxi drivers form mobile Home Guard column: Making diamond dies: Men and women at timber camp: West Indian messages for home at BBC studio

10. Feb 1944
Ballet Rambert visits Midlands factory: Photographs for *British Ally* published in Moscow: Mechanics spend holiday at agricultural volunteer camp: Manufacture from paper of jettisonable fuel tanks for fighter aircraft

11. April 1944
Portable wire mesh track for landing grounds for aircraft: Children's Clothing Exchange: 'The grenade', a cartoon by Giles

12. Sept 1944
LCC exhibition of rebuilding of Bermondsey: Scots postwoman in the Highlands wears trousers: Cameras for aerial reconnaissance

13. Nov 1944
National Fire Service girl dispatch riders: Plans to reclaim cement works as youth centre: Making nylon and its wartime uses: Tour of Ministry of Works prefabricated house

14. The Hawker Typhoon: South Wales miners' accident service: Tommy Handley and the ITMA team at a factory

15. March 1945
Three-woman crew of canal boat carrying coal: Making and using fibre glass: Stage Door Canteen opens in London with Fred Astaire and Bing Crosby

16. June 1945
Scots bagpipe school: Farmers' inventions: Barracudas for Pacific aircraft carriers

17. [late 1945] (This issue was not released)
Packing supplies for the Far East: Operation Pluto: DDT, new insecticide

18. Jan 1946
Hackney uses bomb-damage rubble to stop flooding: Reclaiming magnesia from seawater: Wedgwood factory moves to new garden-city site

Appendix 5

Central Film Library Index

The following index is from a wartime catalogue of the Central Film Library (CFL). It is reproduced to show the subject categories used by the CFL and to demonstrate the basis for the authors' choice of subject divisions used within each year in this descriptive MOI catalogue.

ABYSSINIA

AFRICA

AGRICULTURE:

UK 221 Spring Offensive
UK 266 The Turn of the Furrow
UK 273 Salute to Farmers
UK 274 Fighting Fields
UK 290 Kill that Rat
UK 291 The Rabbit Pest
UK 325 New Acres
UK 326 How to Thatch
UK 327 Ditching
UK 328 Hedging
UK 329 Harness Your Horsepower
UK 330 Welsh Plant Breeding Station
UK 331 Food from Straw
UK 332 A Way to Plough
UK 336 Clamping Potatoes
UK 337 Growing Good Potatoes
UK 339 Fruit Spraying
UK 345 Land Girl
UK 365 Twelve Days
UK 383 The Harvest Shall Come
UK 384 Winter on the Farm
UK 385 Spring on the Farm
UK 386 Summer on the Farm
UK 387 The Crown of the Year
UK 388 Young Farmers
UK 405 The Great Harvest
UK 406 Clean Milk
UK 428 Fuel and the Tractor
UK 429 Welding Helps the Farmer
UK 430 Cereal Seed Disinfection
UK 431 Seeds and Science
UK 446 Vegetable Seed Growing
UK 447 Stooking and Stacking
UK 512 Making Good Hay

UK 513 Reseeding for Better Grass
UK 514 Making Grass Silage
UK 528 Potato Blight
UK 529 Grass and Clover Seed Production
UK 530 Flax
UK 1041 Mediaeval Village
UK 1042 Protection of Fruit
C 210 Prairie Gold
SU 202 Soviet Harvest
US 208 Henry Browne, Farmer
US 209 Home on the Range
US 211 Democracy in Action
US 212 Crops for Combat
US 216 Cowboy
US 302 Power and the Land
US 306 Harvests for Tomorrow

AIR FORCES:
UK 203 Into the Blue
UK 220 Airscrew
UK 263 Fighter Pilot
UK 302 Britain's RAF
UK 312 Airwoman
UK 369 Venture Adventure
UK 370 Air Operations
UK 371 The Pilot is Safe
UK 375 Royal Observer Corps
UK 422 Speed-up on Stirlings
UK 423 Sky Giant
UK 424 In the Drink
UK 426 Towards the Offensive
UK 504 Workers' Week End
BE 203 RAF Action
C 205 Wings of Youth
NZ 200 New Zealand Has Wings
SA 200 Fighters of the Veld
P 103 Diary of a Polish Airman
SU 209 The Other RAF

AIRCRAFT RECOGNITION

ANTI-GOSSIP:
UK 248 Now You're Talking
UK 249 All Hands
UK 250 Dangerous Comment
UK 282 You're Telling Me

ARMIES:
UK 201 Raising Soldiers
UK 205 Sea Fort
UK 265 Ack Ack
UK 270 Northern Outpost
UK 277 Lofoten
UK 304 Citizens' Army
UK 308 Winged Messengers
UK 309 ATS
UK 314 Home Guard
UK 374 Special Despatch
UK 438 The Right Man
UK 439 Troopship
UK 440 The Siege of Tobruk
UK 441 The Army Lays the Rails
UK 442 Paratroops
UK 443 Kill or Be Killed
UK 444 Street Fighting
UK 505 ABCA
UK 521 Of One Blood
UK 523 Prelude to Service
UK 531 Man Wounded
BE 201 The Empire's New Armies
C 206 Guards of the North
C 208 A Visit from Canada
C 211 Wood for War
C 212 Motor Cycle Training
C 213 Battle Is Our Business
SA 200 Fighers of the Veld
IN 200 India Marches
IN 201 Defenders of India
IN 202 The Handymen
CE 202 War Came to Kenya
P 104 Poland's New Front
SU 204 Odessa Besieged
SU 205 Strong Point 42
V 211 Lift Your Head, Comrade
ET 200 The Lion of Judah

AUSTRALIA

BRITISH EMPIRE

BRITISH WEST INDIES

CANADA

CHINA

CIVIL DEFENCE:
UK 207 War and Order
UK 209 The Front Line
UK 264 Neighbours under Fire
UK 278 Canteen on Wheels
UK 279 Mr Proudfoot Shows a Light

UK 284 Living with Strangers
UK 297 Knights of St John
UK 303 War Front
UK 311 Ask CAB
UK 315 Post 23
UK 317 Shunter Black's Night Off
UK 341 WVS
UK 356 Queen's Messengers
UK 357 Emergency Cooking Stove
UK 375 Royal Observer Corps
UK 381 Newspaper Train
UK 382 All Those in Favour
UK 415 Control Room
UK 416 A New Fire Bomb
CD 50 Decontamination of Streets
CD 51 First-Aid Post
CD 52 Civil Defence Ambulance
CD 53 Debris Tunnelling
CD 54 Factory Fire Guard
CD 55 First Aid on the Spot
CD 56 Fire Guard Plan
CD 57 Debris Clearance
CD 58 Butterfly Bomb
CD 59 A Fighter Has Crashed

CZECHS

EDUCATION AND YOUTH:
UK 235 Village School
UK 241 Tomorrow is Theirs
UK 242 Britain's Youth
UK 275 Our School
UK 285 Cally House
UK 287 Youth Takes a Hand
UK 288 Out and About
UK 289 Action
UK 299 They Speak for Themselves
UK 313 Sea Cadets
UK 362 Dinner at School
UK 367 For This Our Heritage
UK 368 Men of Tomorrow
UK 369 Venture Adventure
UK 378 CEMA
UK 380 Battle of the Books
UK 388 Young Farmers
UK 407 Paving the Way
UK 448 Double Thread
UK 507 A Ride With Uncle Joe
UK 523 Prelude to Service
SU 208 Soviet School Child
US 305 Adventure in the Bronx
US 307 A Child Went Forth

FIGHTING FRENCH

FOOD, DIET AND COOKING:
UK 211 Food Convoy
UK 222 Miss T
UK 223 When the Pie was Opened
UK 224 Green Food for Health
UK 225 Two Cooks and a Cabbage
UK 226 Crust and Crumb
UK 251 Oatmeal Porridge
UK 252 Herrings
UK 253 Potatoes
UK 254 Steaming
UK 256 Wisdom of the Wild
UK 272 Bampton Shows the Way
UK 354 Simple Soups
UK 355 All about Carrots
UK 356 Queen's Messengers
UK 357 Emergency Cooking Stove
UK 358 Hot on the Spot
UK 359 He Went to the Cupboard
UK 360 Eating at Work
UK 361 ABCD of Health
UK 362 Dinner at School
UK 363 For Children Only
UK 364 Rat Destruction
UK 365 Twelve Days
UK 508 Catering
UK 526 Oven Bottling
UK 527 Egg and Milk
V 230 World of Plenty

GARDENING, DOMESTIC POULTRY AND RABBITS:
UK 319 Dig for Victory
UK 320 How to Dig *and* Compost Heap
UK 321 Sowing and Planting
UK 322 Cultivation
UK 323 Storing Vegetables Indoors
UK 324 Storing Vegetables Outdoors
UK 333 More Eggs from Your Hens
UK 334 Keeping Rabbits for Extra Meat
UK 335 Filling the Gap
UK 338 Feeding Your Hens in Wartime
UK 351 Garden Tools
UK 352 Garden Friends and Foes
UK 353 Saving Your Own Seeds
UK 511 Winter Work in the Garden

UK 525 Simple Fruit Pruning

GOVERNMENT AND CITIZENSHIP:

UK 230 Health in War
UK 238 Britain at Bay
UK 240 The Londoners
UK 268 Dawn Guard
UK 269 The Heart of Britain
UK 283 Words for Battle
UK 295 Dangers in the Dark
UK 296 A Good Landfall
UK 299 They Speak for Themselves
UK 311 Ask CAB
UK 315 Post 23
UK 318 The Team
UK 340 The Countrywomen
UK 341 WVS
UK 350 Atlantic Charter
UK 365 Twelve Days
UK 376 Breathing Space
UK 378 CEMA
UK 379 Wales—Green Mountain, Black Mountain
UK 380 Battle of the Books
UK 382 All Those in Favour
UK 383 The Harvest Shall Come
UK 394 Builders
UK 414 New Towns for Old
UK 419 When We Build Again
UK 420 Listen to Britain
UK 432 Power for the Highlands
UK 434 Good Health to Scotland
UK 505 ABCA
UK 518 Manpower
UK 519 Tyneside Story
UK 520 Words and Actions
UK 1041 Mediaeval Village
BE 200 From the Four Corners
C 207 Peoples of Canada
IN 205 The Changing Face of India
CE 200 Men of Africa
US 200 America Speaks her Mind
US 206 New England's 8 Million Yankees
US 215 Swedes in America
US 300 The City
US 304 What So Proudly We Hail
V 200 They Met in London
V 203 A House in London
V 208 Common Cause
V 215 New Earth
V 217 The Silent Village
V 230 World of Plenty

HEALTH, HYGIENE AND MEDICINE:

UK 224 Green Food for Health
UK 228 White Battle Front
UK 229 Nurse!
UK 230 Health in War
UK 232 Mother and Child
UK 242 Britain's Youth
UK 267 Fitness for Service
UK 276 Red Cross in Action
UK 280 Oh, Whiskers!
UK 286 Carry On, Children
UK 288 Out and About
UK 289 Action
UK 292 Defeat Diphtheria
UK 293 Breath of Danger
UK 297 Knights of St John
UK 298 Victory over Darkness
UK 343 Hospital Nurse
UK 349 Believe It or Not
UK 361 ABCD of Health
UK 362 Dinner at School
UK 363 For Children Only
UK 396 No Accidents
UK 408 Defeat Tuberculosis
UK 409 The Nose Has It
UK 410 Blood Transfusion
UK 411 Plastic Surgery in Wartime
UK 412 In Enemy Hands
UK 413 Life Begins Again
UK 419 When We Build Again
UK 433 Highland Doctor
UK 434 Good Health to Scotland
UK 435 Neuro-psychiatry
UK 436 Subject for Discussion
UK 437 Scabies
UK 437X Scabies Mite
UK 448 Double Thread
UK 507 A Ride With Uncle Joe
UK 517 Mass Radiography
UK 521 Of One Blood
UK 524 Lifting
UK 531 Man Wounded

INDIA

KENYA

LABOUR AND INDUSTRY:

UK 100 Buried Treasure
UK 210 Shipbuilders
UK 214 Transfer of Skill
UK 217 Furnaces of Industry
UK 218 Behind the Guns

UK 219 Big City
UK 220 Airscrew
UK 233 Wartime Factory
UK 260 It Comes from Coal
UK 303 War Front
UK 305 Ulster
UK 306 Scotland Speaks
UK 307 Steel Goes to Sea
UK 342 Jane Brown Changes Her Job
UK 347 Women Away from Home
UK 360 Eating at Work
UK 377 HM Motor-Launches
UK 379 Wales–Green Mountain, Black Mountain
UK 390 They Keep the Wheels Turning
UK 391 Machines and Men
UK 392 Night Shift
UK 393 Mobil Engineers
UK 394 Builders
UK 395 The Birth of a Tank
UK 396 No Accidents
UK 397 Essential Jobs
UK 417 Radio in Battle
UK 422 Speed-up on Stirlings
UK 423 Sky Giant
UK 445 Boiler House Practice
UK 449 Our Film
UK 450 Worker & War Front No. 1
UK 451 Worker & War Front No. 2
UK 452 Worker & War Front No. 3
UK 453 Worker & War Front No. 4
UK 454 Worker & War Front No. 5
UK 455 Worker & War Front No. 6
UK 456 Worker & War Front No. 7
UK 457 Worker & War Front No. 8
UK 458 Worker & War Front No. 9
UK 459 Worker & War Front No. 10
UK 501 Coalmine
UK 502 Clydebuilt
UK 503 Danger Area
UK 504 Workers' Week End
UK 510 Wartime Shipment of Packed Petroleum
UK 518 Manpower
UK 519 Tyneside Story
UK 522 Cameramen at War
UK 524 Lifting
UK 530 Flax
BE 204 Building for Victory
C 209 The Strategy of Metals
C 211 Wood for War
A 242 Australia Marches with Britain
SA 201 Sinews of War
IN 203 Arms from India
IN 204 Made in India
IN 206 Men of India
CE 210 The Modern Spirit
US 205 Lake Carrier
US 210 Pipeline
US 213 Autobiography of a Jeep
V 209 Fighting Allies
V 220 The Battle for Oil

MALTA

NATIONAL FIRE SERVICE

NAVIES:
UK 54 Sailors without Uniform
UK 56 SOS
UK 202 Raising Sailors
UK 210 Shipbuilders
UK 211 Food Convoy
UK 301 Merchant Seamen
UK 307 Steel Goes to Sea
UK 313 Sea Cadets
UK 344 WRNS
UK 372 Corvettes
UK 373 HM Minelayer
UK 377 HM Motor-Launches
UK 421 HMS King George V
UK 425 Malta Convoy
UK 502 Clydebuilt
UK 506 Up Periscope!
UK 509 Men from the Sea
UK 510 Wartime Shipment of Packed Petroleum
UK 519 Tyneside Story
BE 202 HM Navies Go to Sea
BE 205 Heroes of the Atlantic
BE 207 Battle of Supplies
C 202 Atlantic Patrol
A 241 It's the Navy
A 243 Keeping the Fleet at Sea
SA 200 Fighters of the Veld
P 102 The Poles Weigh Anchor
V 202 Free French Navy

NETHERLANDS:
V 215 New Earth
V 216 The Dutch Tradition

NEW ZEALAND

NORWAY

POLAND

SALVAGE AND THRIFT:
UK 245 Feed the Furnaces
UK 246 Salvage with a Smile
UK 389 Arms from Scrap
UK 398 A Few Ounces a Day
UK 399 It All Depends on You
UK 400 Handicraft Happiness
UK 401 Rugmaking
UK 402 Quilting
UK 403 Thrift
UK 404 Dustbin Parade
UK 445 Boiler House Practice
UK 515 In Which We Live
UK 516 Pots and Pans

SOUTH AFRICA

STRATEGY, CAMPAIGNS AND TACTICS:
UK 205 Sea Fort
UK 265 Ack Ack
UK 270 Northern Outpost
UK 277 Lofoten
UK 370 Air Operations
UK 417 Radio in Battle
UK 425 Malta Convoy
UK 426 Towards the Offensive
UK 440 The Siege of Tobruk
UK 443 Kill or Be Killed
UK 444 Street Fighting
BE 206 Battle for Freedom
BE 207 Battle of Supplies
C 206 Guards of the North
C 213 Battle is Our Business
CE 203 Malta GC
SU 205 Strong Point 42
P 100 This is Poland
V 204 Via Persia
V 206 China
V 207 Men of Norway
V 210 100 for 1
V 212 War in the Pacific
V 220 The Battle for Oil
ET 200 The Lion of Judah

UNITED NATIONS

USA

US SHIPBUILDING FILMS

USSR

WOMEN IN INDUSTRY AND CIVIL LIFE:
UK 229 Nurse!
UK 232 Mother and Child
UK 235 Village School
UK 236 They Also Serve
UK 340 The Countrywomen
UK 341 WVS
UK 342 Jane Brown Changes Her Job
UK 343 Hospital Nurse
UK 345 Land Girl
UK 347 Women Away from Home
UK 390 They Keep the Wheels Turning
UK 392 Night Shift
UK 397 Essential Jobs
IN 207 Women of India
SU 207 100 Million Women

WOMEN IN THE SERVICES:
UK 309 ATS
UK 312 Airwoman
UK 344 WRNS
BE 208 She Serves Abroad
SU 206 Three in a Shell Hole
SU 207 100 Million Women

Index of titles

The page number for the main entry of each title is indicated by Roman type; additional entries are designated by page numbers in italics.

Index of credits